Treasures of
British Columbia

By: William Faubion

Part of the Morgan & Chase "Treasures" Series
www.mcpbooks.com

Morgan&Chase
Publishing inc.

Published by:
Morgan & Chase Publishing, Inc.
531 Parsons Drive
Medford, Oregon 97501
888-557-9328
www.mcpbooks.com

Printed by:
C & C Offset Printing Co., Ltd. - China

First edition 2005

ISBN: 0-9754162-4-3

I gratefully acknowledge the contributions of the many people involved in the writing and production of this book. Their tireless dedication to this endeavor is inspirational.
        Damon Neal - Publisher

Editors: Cindy Tilley Faubion
              Brenda Rosch

Contributing Writers:
        Mark Allen
        Joanne Bowyer
        Diane Dickinson
        Leslie Fazio
        Dave Fox
        Jonathan Heerema
        Kelly Kenyon
        Joy Kieras
        Jan Maddron
        Mickie McCormic
        Rick Owen
        Yvonne Rains
        Kathy Stolz
        Stephani Tansky
        Susan Vaughn

Graphic Design:
        Jesse Gifford
        C.S. Rowan
        Craig Tansley

Story Coordinators:
        Tamara J. Cornett, Wendy Gay and Devona Hamilton.

Website:
        Jessica Guaderrama and Rebecca Woodruff.

Cover Photo of Empress at night by:
        Cliff MacArthur, cliff0108@gmail.com

Special Recognition to:
Janna Sample, Anita Fronek, Genevieve Hartin, Ernest Li, Nicolas Deruiter and Michael Couture.

Dedication

This book is dedicated to the unusually pristine landscape of British Columbia and her best resource, the people who live there.

Announcing
Golden Opportunities to Travel

Receive your FREE gold Treasure Coins

Treasures listed inside this book can also be found on our popular and interactive website: **mcpbooks.com**. For your convenience, this book's treasures are easily located by clicking the corresponding area on the map on our home page. This will lead you to a list of cities covered by this book. Within each city, treasures are listed under the same headings as in the book: Accommodations, Attractions, etc.

Look for treasures that have a **treasure chest** next to their name. This means they have made a special offer, redeemable by presenting one of our Gold Treasure Coins. **The offer may be substantial; anything from a free night's stay to a free meal or gift. Many offers can be worth over $100.00 or more!**

To get **3 free Gold Treasure Coins**, just send us the receipt for the purchase of this book.

Please send the receipt to:
Morgan & Chase Publishing
Gold Coin Division
PO Box 1148
Medford, OR 97501-0232

Please include your name and address and we will send the coins to you.

Table of Contents

Forward..**6**

How To Use This Book..**7**

British Columbia Region Maps.....................................**9**

Accommodations and RV Resorts................................**18**

    Vancouver Island **20**

    Greater Vancouver **34**

    Fort Langley Area **40**

    Thompson-Nicola..**41**

    Okanagan **44**

    Kootenays-Rockies **46**

    Northern BC..**48**

Attractions **50**

    Vancouver Island **52**

    Greater Vancouver **62**

    Fort Langley Area **66**

    Whistler **67**

    Thompson-Nicola..**68**

    Okanagan **70**

    Kootenays-Rockies **74**

    Northern BC..**77**

Candy, Ice Cream, Bakeries and Coffee 78

Greater Vancouver 80

Fort Langley Area 81

Thompson-Nicola 84

Okanagan 85

Kootenays-Rockies 86

Northern BC 87

Galleries 88

Vancouver Island 90

Greater Vancouver 92

Fort Langley Area 104

Whistler 106

Thompson-Nicola 108

Okanagan 110

Kootenays-Rockies 112

Northern BC 113

Gifts 114

Vancouver Island 116

Greater Vancouver 120

Fort Langley Area 129

Whistler 131

Thompson-Nicola. 132

Okanagan 135

Kootenays-Rockies 137

Northern BC. 138

Health & Beauty. 140

Vancouver Island 142

Greater Vancouver 143

Fort Langley Area 144

Thompson-Nicola. 145

Okanagan. 146

Kootenays-Rockies 148

Northern BC. 150

Home Décor, Gardens, Flowers and Markets. 152

Vancouver Island 154

Greater Vancouver 156

Fort Langley Area 162

Thompson-Nicola. 166

Okanagan. 168

Kootenays-Rockies 171

Museums 172

   Vancouver Island 174

   Greater Vancouver 176

   Kootenays-Rockies 177

Restaurants 178

   Vancouver Island 180

   Greater Vancouver 196

   Fort Langley Area 218

   Whistler 224

   Thompson-Nicola. 230

   Okanagan 234

   Kootenays-Rockies 240

   Northern BC. 244

Wineries...............248

Vancouver Island 250

Fort Langley Area 252

Okanagan 254

Index...............258

About the Author . . . . Inside Back Dust Cover

Forward

Welcome to the Treasures of British Columbia. This book represents a magical place where heaven truly meets earth. The most amazing aspect of British Columbia is definitely its people. They are warm, friendly, giving and fun-loving. During the production of this book we met only the most hospitable personalities. Add to that the raw beauty and vast expanse of British Columbia itself, with miles of evergreens, coastal areas and breathtaking vistas awaiting travelers.

Canada is home to Whistler, one of the best ski resorts in the world, and future site for the 2010 Winter Olympics. Then there is Vancouver, the most metropolitan city on the west coast of the North American Continent. It's a city so diverse that it's exciting no matter which direction you choose to explore. The Okanagan Valley is famous for its unbelievably rich farmlands and the incredible produce it yields annually.

What is felt here is also worth mentioning. The influence of the indigenous people of British Columbia is widespread and highly revered. Historical influence, artisanship and a basic love of nature is evidenced in nearly everything produced in this land of multiple wonders. One can't help but be humbled by the spirit of cooperation and the mutual respect that's so freely shared in British Columbia.

Several places in British Columbia are well-known to the rest of the world, but we've found there are far more hidden Treasures than not. Many Canadians choose to holiday in British Columbia because of its outstanding recreational and cultural choices. This book aims to shed light on some of those wonderful attractions, opportunities and people. The Treasures in this book were personally selected by secret shoppers, writers and the publisher's representatives. We're certain that any place you choose to visit from within these pages will make your visit here memorable.

Cindy Tilley Faubion

How to use this book

This book is divided by geographic areas and type of business. The primary divisions are; Vancouver Island, Greater Vancouver, Fort Langley, Whistler, Thompson-Nicola, Okanagan, Kootenays-Rockies and Northern British Columbia.

The types of businesses include; accommodations, attractions, coffee and candy shops, galleries, gardens and markets, gifts, health and beauty, museums, restaurants and wineries.

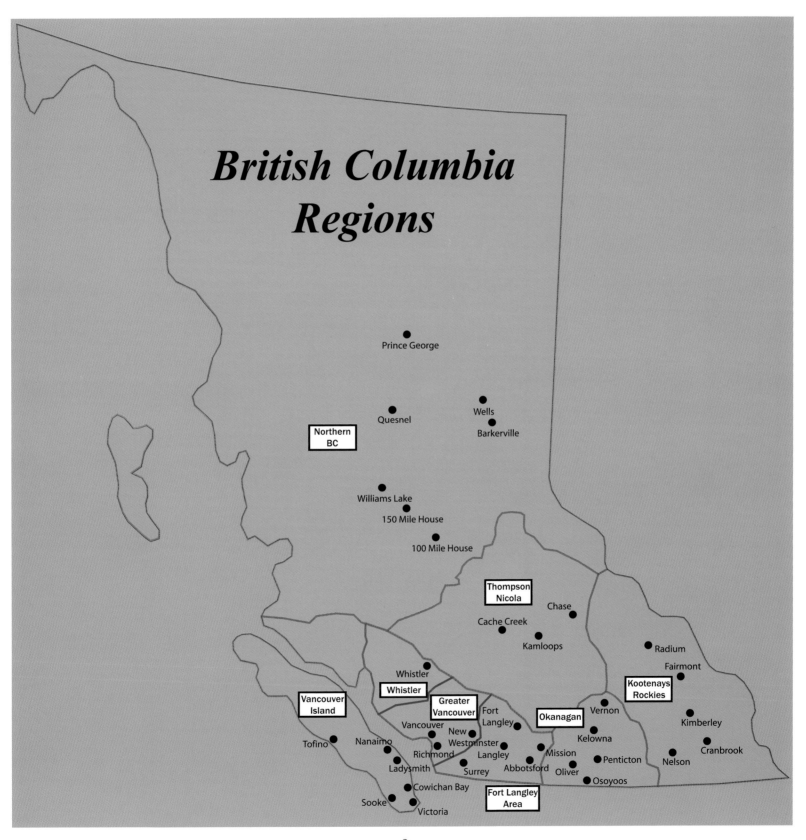

British Columbia
Regions

Prince George

Wells
Quesnel
Barkerville

Northern
BC

Williams Lake
150 Mile House

100 Mile House

Thompson
Nicola
Chase
Cache Creek

Kamloops
Radium

Fairmont
Whistler

Whistler
Kootenays
Rockies
Vancouver
Island
Greater
Vancouver
Fort
Langley
Vernon
Okanagan
Vancouver
New
Kimberley
Kelowna
Tofino
Nanaimo
Westminster
Richmond
Langley
Mission
Cranbrook
Ladysmith
Surrey
Abbotsford
Penticton
Nelson
Cowichan Bay
Oliver
Osoyoos
Sooke
Fort Langley
Area
Victoria

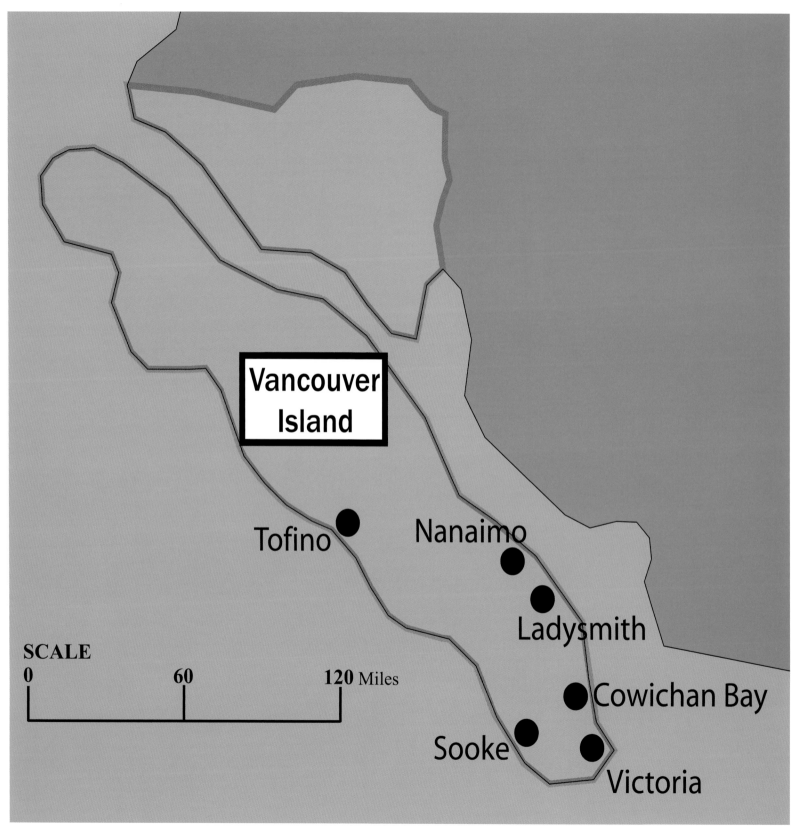

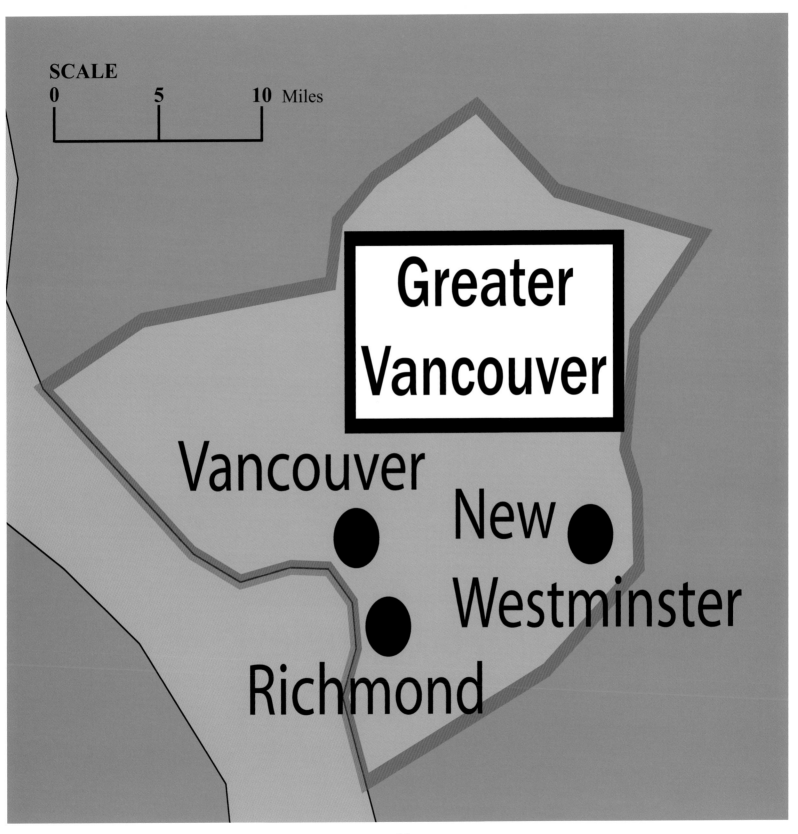

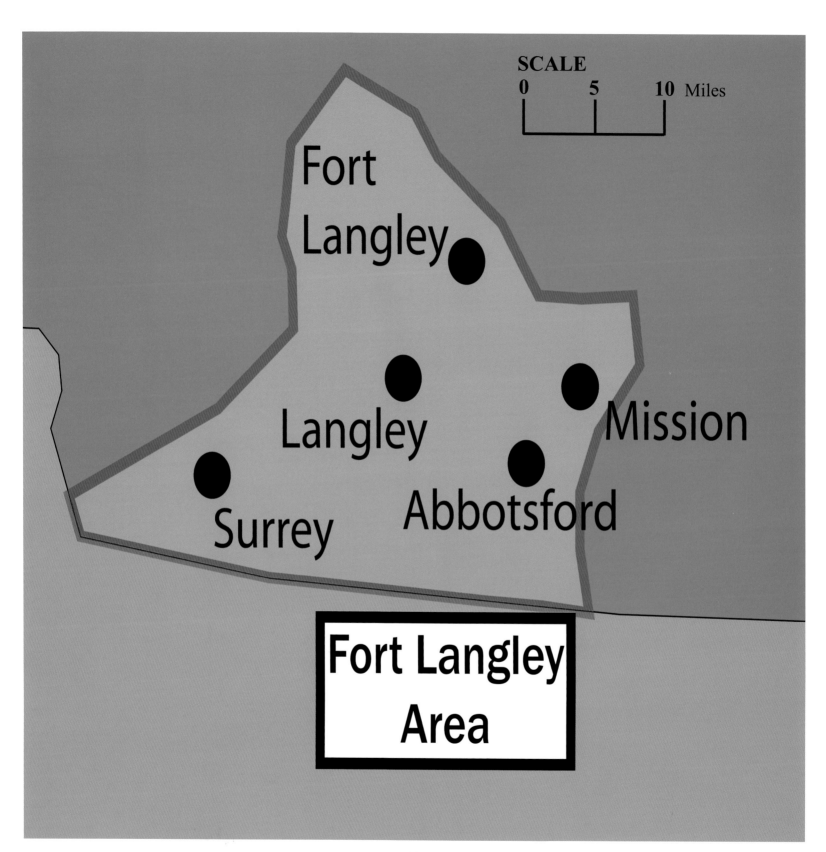

SCALE
0   5   10 Miles

Fort
Langley

Langley

Mission

Surrey

Abbotsford

**Fort Langley
Area**

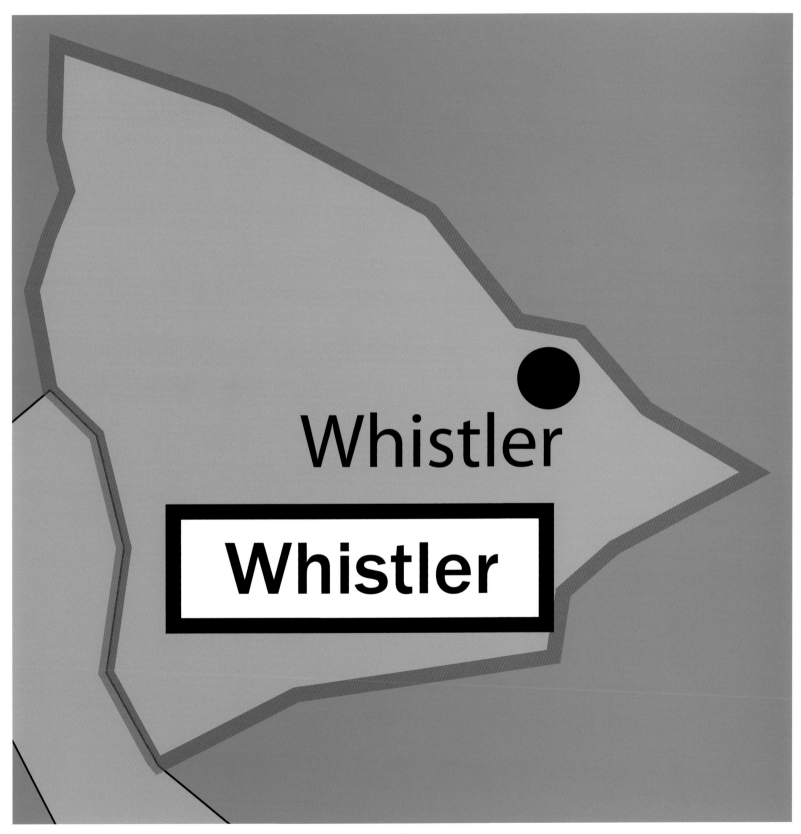

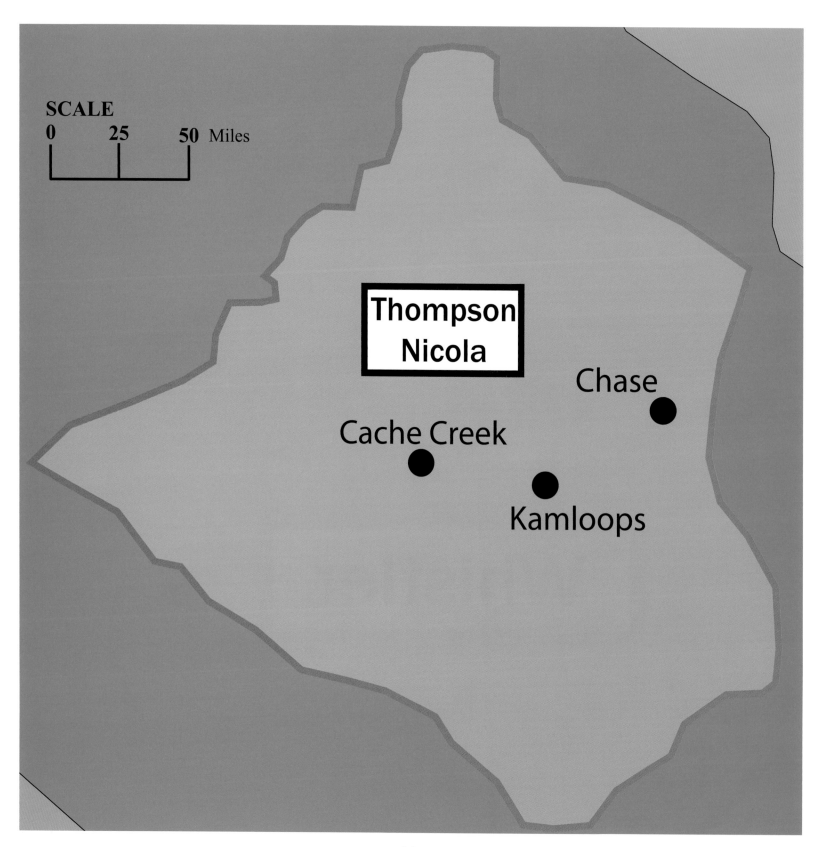

SCALE

0   25   50 Miles

Thompson
Nicola

Chase

Cache Creek

Kamloops

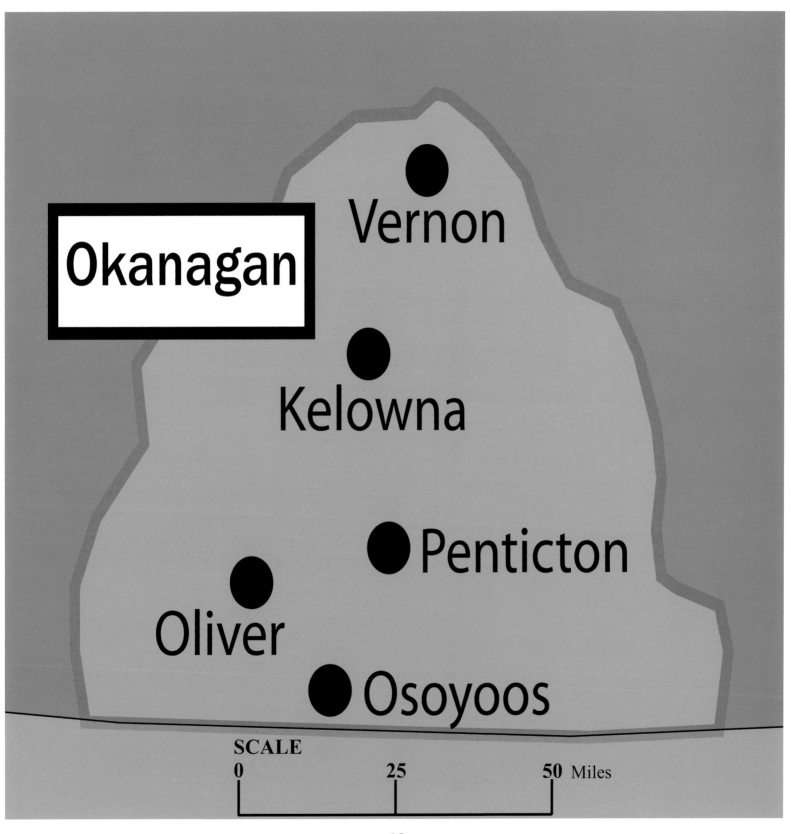

Okanagan

Vernon

Kelowna

Penticton

Oliver

Osoyoos

SCALE

0   25   50 Miles

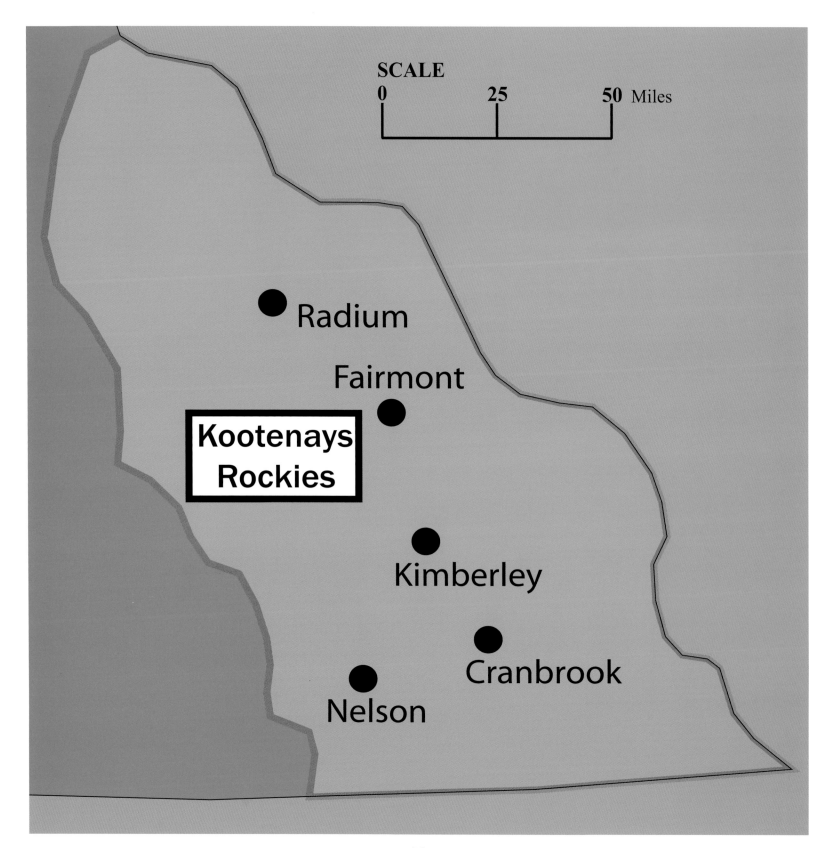

SCALE

0   25   50 Miles

Radium

Fairmont

Kootenays Rockies

Kimberley

Cranbrook

Nelson

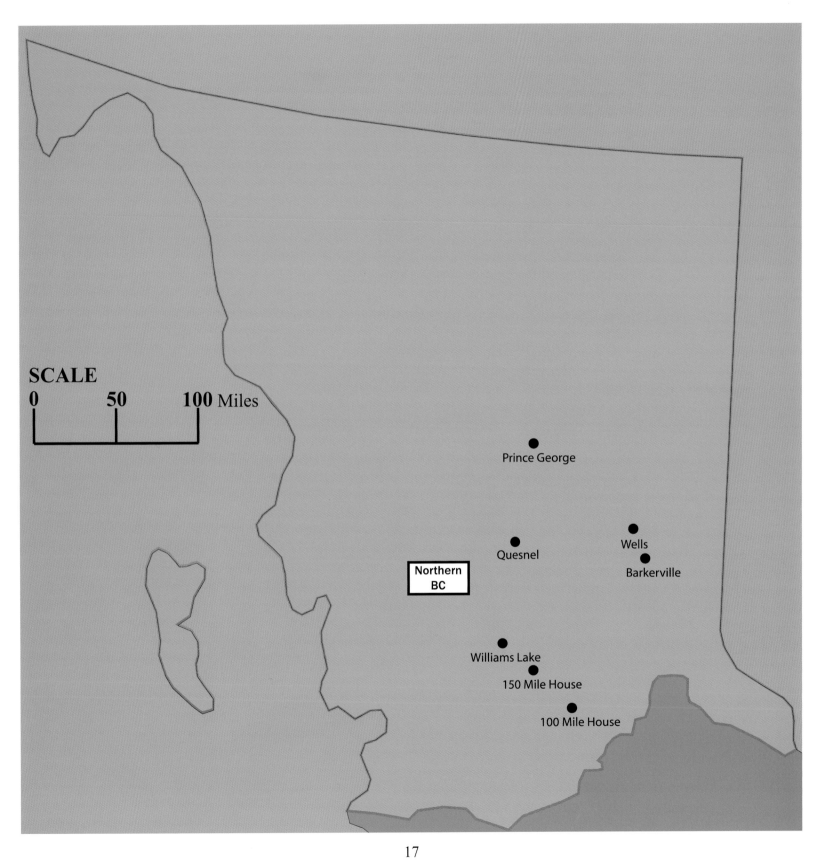

SCALE

0   50   100 Miles

Prince George

Wells

Quesnel

Barkerville

Northern
BC

Williams Lake

150 Mile House

100 Mile House

Accommodations
and
RV Resorts

Long Beach Lodge Resort

Tim Hackett fell in love with the Pacific coast of Vancouver Island when he first visited it in the 1960s, camping out on the beaches at night. He has come to believe that Cox Bay is one of the most beautiful beaches in the world. When he decided to crown thirty years of experience as a builder and developer with the creation of his own coastal resort and lodge, Cox Bay was the location he chose. Working with his brother Tony, Tim oversaw every aspect and detail of the resort's design and construction. Since opening in April 2002, the 41-room lodge and twenty luxurious cottages have attracted much attention and praise, from a feature in *Architectural Digest* to the honor of membership in the Distinguished Inns of North America Select Registry. Whether you choose to stay in the lodge or a cottage, you'll be impressed by the comfort and service. There's a wide choice of recreational activities to enjoy during your stay, from whale watching excursions to surfing, golfing, or visiting the local museums and art galleries. Or you may choose to simply relax in the Great Room of Long Beach Lodge Resort, enjoying the warmth of the massive granite fireplace and watching the sunset over the ocean.

1441 Pacific Rim Highway, Tofino BC
(250) 725 - 2442 or (877) 844 - 7873
www.longbeachlodgeresort.com

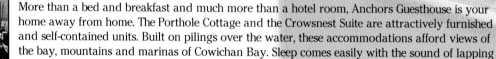

Anchors Guesthouse

More than a bed and breakfast and much more than a hotel room, Anchors Guesthouse is your home away from home. The Porthole Cottage and the Crowsnest Suite are attractively furnished and self-contained units. Built on pilings over the water, these accommodations afford views of the bay, mountains and marinas of Cowichan Bay. Sleep comes easily with the sound of lapping water and scents of cedar and pine. You are likely to see working timber ships, occasional regattas and canoe races, and an abundance of boats of all descriptions. Guests are welcome to enjoy the deck or have a barbecue. A dinghy and crab traps are also available. Anchors Guesthouse is central to many activities. Golf courses, tennis courts, riding stables and restaurants are nearby, as are wilderness walks, hiking trails, and tours of wineries and farms. Crabbing and fishing are right outside the door. Cowichan Bay is treasured for its eagles, herons, and amazing variety of other birds and marine life. Plan on beauty, plan on tranquility, and plan on welcoming hospitality when you visit Anchors Guesthouse for your next vacation.

1793 Cowichan Bay Road, Cowichan Bay BC
www.anchorsguesthouse.com

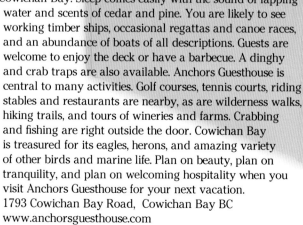

The Wickaninnish Inn & Pointe Restaurant

"Rustic elegance on nature's edge" is the hallmark of the Wickaninnish Inn & Pointe Restaurant, the McDiarmid family's unique lodging destination on the rugged west coast of Vancouver Island, just a few minutes outside Tofino. The Wickaninnish Inn integrates the natural setting outside with the spaces inside: each room offers breathtaking views of the open Pacific and Chesterman Beach. They are further enhanced by artworks contributed by a variety of artisans, including the renowned local woodcarver Henry Nolla. Managing Director Charles McDiarmid learned to love nature from his father, Dr. Howard McDiarmid, who was instrumental in establishing the Pacific Rim National Park in 1971. Amenities at the Wickaninnish Inn include the Ancient Cedars Spa, nestled under the edge of the old growth rainforest next to the Inn. Featuring the Aveda skincare line, Ancient Cedars offers natural treatments to rejuvenate body and spirit. Skilled professionals practice their healing arts in this serene and tranquil setting. The Inn also offers world class dining at the award winning Pointe Restaurant. Diners can enjoy the spectacular 240-degree view of the ocean while savoring fresh coastal cuisine, locally grown organic produce and the best British Columbia wines. The cozy On-the-Rocks Lounge has an excellent selection of scotches, ports and sherries to relax with. The McDiarmid family's accomplishment in creating the Inn was recently recognized when the Inn was chosen to host the Relais & Châteaux North American Congress. Membership in this group is only by invitation, and the McDiarmid family is justly proud of the honor.
Box 250, Tofino BC (250) 725 - 3100 or (800) 333 - 4604 www.wickinn.com

Birds of a Feather Oceanfront Bed & Breakfast

Birds of a Feather Oceanfront Bed & Breakfast is exquisitely situated on the edge of the Esquimalt Lagoon Migratory Bird Sanctuary. You will be treated to views of Victoria Harbour, the Strait of Juan de Fuca, and the Olympic Mountains from the B & B's private dock. From the front step, you can see Fisgard Lighthouse and Hatley Castle and Gardens. The area abounds with wildlife and is a haven for birdwatchers. There are more than 70 species of birds including eagles, heron, osprey and swans. Sea lions, otters and seasonal visits from pods of orcas are also favorite attractions. The setting is one of extraordinary natural beauty and Annette Moen and Dieter Gerhard are pleased to share it with travellers from all over the world. The guest rooms are charmingly decorated with birding and lighthouse motifs. A hearty breakfast is served every morning and guests are welcome to use the canoe, kayaks and bicycles onsite. There are miles and miles of pristine beaches, biking and hiking trails, and easy access to all of the area's attractions. Annette and Dieter can tell you anything you want to know about their environs and they always make good on their promise "to create an experience for our guests, not just an accommodation."
206 Portsmouth Drive, Victoria BC (250) 391 - 8889 or (800) 730 - 4790 www.VictoriaLodging.com

Constable Matheson's Artisan Cottage

Sheila Beech is a felt maker with an exceptional eye for potential. When Sooke's historic provincial courthouse and jail became available in 1993, Sheila bought it and converted it into a gallery for her fibreworks business. In 1996, she converted the gallery into a bed and breakfast and named it Constable Matheson's Bed & Breakfast after the second constable to serve at this site. She took over the garage to serve as her Exhibit Room III Gallery Shoppe. Sheila practices the ancient craft of felt-making and her work has earned an international reputation. Fashion designer Donna Karan commissioned Sheila's work and New York's Metropolitan Opera also commissioned twenty square yards of her hand-felted material for a production. The gallery features her delightful GnomeKnockers slippers (no two can match!), wearable art clothing, and designer wools for fashion and interiors. The Bed & Breakfast is a four-room whimsy of deluxe amenities, warmth and comfort. This very private place has a fully stocked kitchen, fireside Jacuzzi, and a sitting room decorated with works by local artists. The delightful bedroom is the former jail cell. The cell bars can be found in the fencing of the beautiful surrounding garden. One comment noted in the guestbook read, "If this is jail, I hope to get life." Sheila has created a serene retreat just 45 minutes from Victoria and central to beaches, rain forest, hiking trails, and the people, arts and history of this beautiful part of the world.
2050 Drennan Street, Sooke BC (250) 642 - 7176 or (866) 642 - 7176 www.constablematheson.com

Yellow Point Lodge

In the 1890s when Gerry Hill was a little boy, his uncle Claude showed him a wild and beautiful point of land overlooking the Gulf Islands of British Columbia. The place took root in his heart. As he grew, survived service in the First World War, and weathered the Great Depression, the vision of Yellow Point grew with him. Gerry imagined a big country house "where everybody was welcome and nobody went hungry." He worked as a logger, a rum-runner, a dam builder, and eventually won a contract to head up a team of backpackers. They climbed mountains carrying construction materials for transmission lines from the new dams. The proceeds from all this work allowed him to purchase the 185 acres that encompass Yellow Point. His retreat opened in 1939 with seven little cabins and a cookhouse. A massive log lodge was added later. Destroyed by fire in 1985, it was rebuilt and continues the tradition of warm hospitality on the edge of an old-growth temperate rainforest. With all your meals included, you may choose to stay in a room in the lodge, a private cottage, or go really rustic in the beach or field cabins. The preservation of this site allows guests the opportunity to view deer, otter, herons, seals, sea lions and even orcas on occasion. You may hike through stands of giant Douglas Fir and Western Red Cedar or wander the pristine coastline where bald eagles fish for salmon. There are no room phones, no televisions, just quiet and beauty all around. If you long for renewal in nature's embrace, you will find it at Yellow Point Lodge. 3700 Yellow Point Road, Ladysmith BC (250) 245 - 7422 www.yellowpointlodge.com

Strathcona Hotel

Originally designed for business offices, the building that now houses the Strathcona Hotel had only been open for a year when it abruptly became part of global events. It was requisitioned by the Canadian Army to serve as officers' barracks during the First World War. When the war ended, the owners decided to take advantage of the temporary conversion of offices to living quarters by repurposing the building. The Strathcona Hotel was born. In 1946, the "Strath" was acquired by H. G. "Barney" Olson, and it has been owned and operated by the Olson family ever since. Among its landmark accomplishments was receiving the first liquor license ever granted in British Columbia in 1954. It became one of the most popular nightspots in the city almost overnight. Today Victoria's nightlife is still centered on the hotel, which is home to the largest nightclub in the city, Legends. Founded in 1967, it has been host to literally millions of visitors since then. Other attractions (in addition to the fine rooms) include Strath Ale, Wine, and Spirits Merchants, which offers Victoria's best selection of single malt scotches; the Sticky Wicket Pub; the Clubhouse Lounge; and Big Bad John's, a "hillbilly" bar that's coming up on its fiftieth anniversary. The history of Victoria is alive and well at the Strathcona Hotel. 919 Douglas Street, Victoria BC (250) 383 - 7137 or (800) 663 - 7476 www.strathconahotel.com

Whispering Waters Executive Suite Inn

Whispering Waters Executive Suite Inn is a very private home away from home in the hub of Vancouver Island. Perched over Long Lake, it is available for short or long-term stays and amenable to personal and business requirements. With high-speed Internet access, TV, DVD, CD and cassette players, you won't miss a thing during your stay. There is a dining room and living room, a well-equipped kitchen, and a separate bedroom. An artistic eye was engaged in designing and decorating this lovely retreat. Furnishings are unusual and attractive and incorporate every amenity you could want or need. Snuggle down in front of the fireplace or linger on the spacious covered deck. You can enjoy a soak in the private hot tub and watch a flotilla of Canadian geese emerge from the mists of the lake. From the sunny wrap-around walkway, you are likely to see eagles, kingfishers and all manner of birds, as well as otters, beavers and water weasels. Surrounded by natural beauty, this is a secluded and quiet place. As the day draws to a close, you can look forward to nestling into a king-size feather bed for the most peaceful sleep of your life. Make time for a restful and rejuvenating stay at Whispering Waters Executive Suite Inn.
500 Woodhaven Drive, Nanaimo BC (250) 751 - 2808 or (866) 751 - 2809 www.whisperingwatersexecutivesuiteinn.com

Prancing Horse Retreat

High above Finlayson Arm, you'll find the enchanting and utterly romantic Prancing Horse Retreat. This turreted villa is the stuff of fantasy, affording luxurious accommodations in a setting of natural wonder. Perched above a bird sanctuary, each suite of the retreat enjoys an eagle's view toward the Olympic Mountains. The garden, terraced rockery and gazebo are perfect places for viewing deer, rabbits, quail and doves that roam the property. Just twenty minutes from Victoria and ten minutes to Butchart Gardens, this serene retreat provides all the amenities. Elaine and Alan Dillabaugh give meticulous attention to the details. They are happy to customize your stay whether you reserve the entire house or the dream-come-true honeymoon suite. You will be pampered with fine linens, Aveda bath products, gourmet chocolates and fresh flowers. Breakfast includes champagne and freshly squeezed orange juice served in your room, the dining room or on the patio. The Dillabaughs cordially invite you to relax and unwind in their Vancouver Island paradise.   573 Ebadora Lane, Malahat BC
(250) 743 - 9378 or (877) 887 - 8834
www.prancinghorse.com

Executive House Hotel

Victoria is on the southern tip of Vancouver Island, protected from the ocean weather, but with a climate moderated by the sea. Executive House Hotel commands a spectacular view of Victoria from its penthouse suites. Executive House is strategically located with easy access to the nearby Inner Harbour, the Victoria Conference Center, business and shopping areas. Modeled after a European boutique-style hotel, Executive House provides guests with world class hospitality and full service facilities. The penthouse suites feature living and dining rooms, separate bedrooms with private Jacuzzi atriums, fireplaces and balconies. All 181 rooms offer a grand view and complimentary high speed Internet access. Pets are also welcome at Executive House Hotel. The Fitness Centre contains two workout rooms, an outdoor sundeck, whirlpool and steam room. Superb food is provided in four excellent venues. Barkley's Steakhouse is the elegant home of fresh seafood and charbroiled steaks. The Polo Lounge, complete with fireplace, is perfect for pre-dinner drinks. For cheerful casual dining, Caffe d'Amore serves all three daily meals. Bartholomew's Bar & Rockefeller Grille is a lively British-style pub with heated outdoor patio, live entertainment and delicious food. Doubles Oyster Bar offers a cozy evening by the fire for romantically inclined travelers and the best oysters in town. With all the excellent choices, Executive House Hotel is capable of fulfilling any need and welcomes your stay.

777 Douglas Street, Victoria BC (250) 388 - 5111 or (800) 663 - 7001 www.executivehouse.com

Dream Weaver Bed & Breakfast

Jo McMurray's enchanting Dream Weaver Bed & Breakfast is located in the picturesque, seaside village of beautiful Cowichan Bay on Vancouver Island. About a forty-five minute drive north of Victoria, it is situated right in the heart of wine country. Each of the three suites, Magnolia, Primrose, and Rosewood, is uniquely decorated with Victorian-style charm. All of the suites have their own cozy fireplaces, jetted tubs and private ensuite bathrooms. The Magnolia occupies the entire top floor of the house! A romantic four-poster bed and a private balcony offering superb ocean views of Cowichan Bay make it an ideal bridal suite. There are a variety of attractions in the area known as the Cowichan Valley. Among them are numerous vineyards producing some excellent wines. Cowichan is a Native word meaning "the warm land." Also available are kayaking, whale watching, hiking, fishing, and many excellent restaurants and quaint shops to discover. Whether serving the delicious daily breakfasts or advising you on the best local attractions, Jo will make sure that you're treated as an honored guest during your stay at Dream Weaver Bed & Breakfast.

1682 Botwood Lane, Cowichan Bay BC (250) 748 - 7688 or (888) 748 - 7689
www.dreamweaverbedandbreakfast.com

The Bedford Regency Hotel

As befits its name and location, The Bedford Regency Hotel represents Victoria's golden era of small, elegant hotels. Of the once numerous hotels on Government Street between the Inner Harbour and Johnson Street, only The Bedford Regency remains. It wasn't originally a hotel; the Hibben-Bone Building that now houses The Bedford Regency, built circa 1910, hosted a book and stationery store at first. The Bedford Regency incorporates an even older piece of Victoria's history, the Garrick's Head Pub, which first opened for business in 1867 and continues to draw customers from around the world. The Pub is appreciated for its great West Coast menu as well as its excellent selection of local draft and imported beers, which you can enjoy indoors or on its patio overlooking the square. The Bedford Regency's forty air conditioned rooms offer plush, old-fashioned service and hospitality, with coffee brought to your door in the morning and many similarly thoughtful touches, as well as modern conveniences such as Jacuzzis, mini-fridges and fireplaces. The Bedford Regency also provides convenient access to the most popular attractions in Victoria, from Bastion Square to the Inner Harbour and the Royal B.C. Museum. If you're interested in something a little more offbeat, The Bedford Regency Hotel plays a prominent role in Victoria's popular Ghostly Walk tours. It seems the hotel may have a few guests who never leave. 1140 Government Street, Victoria BC (250) 384 - 6835 or (800) 665 - 6500 www.bedfordregency.com

Mermaid Cove Resort

Mermaid Cove is a family-oriented oceanfront resort located at Ladysmith on Vancouver Island. Family is a key element at Mermaid Cove, run by June Morry, whose parents, George and Frances Brooke, founded the resort. Though Frances passed on in 2004, George continues to work there. Mermaid Cove offers four cabins, each with a full kitchen and an outside deck facing the Strait of Georgia. If you have a camper or RV, there are RV sites with electrical hook-ups. Each site has a fire pit and there's one on the beach as well, plus a large barbecue house that campers are welcome to use. There are also facilities for showering. Ladysmith is known for its great swimming, beaches, canoes and paddleboats, all of which are just minutes away from Mermaid Cove. If you love communing with nature, you can explore the local tide pools or simply relax and enjoy the quiet and serene atmosphere. The cabins and campsites are available during the summer from June 15th to September 15th, and the rates are pleasantly affordable. Mermaid Cove Resort is accessible by highway from Victoria and by ferry ride from Vancouver. 3400 Laguna Vista Road, Ladysmith BC (250) 245 - 3000

Whalers on the Point Guesthouse

Located right on the waterfront in downtown Tofino, Whalers on the Point Guesthouse offers private rooms as well as family and shared rooms, and many amenities including a sauna, game room and Internet kiosk. If you love surfing, you'll be pleased to know that surfboard and wet suit storage and a rinse station are also available. Part of the Hostelling International network of worldwide backpackers hostels, Whalers on the Point Guesthouse in Tofino has garnered substantial acclaim since its construction in 1999. Providing a comfortable yet cost-effective center for hikers, cyclists and others who prefer to explore the Clayoquot Sound area under their own steam, the Guesthouse has been named the Best Hostel in Canada by the *Lonely Planet* guidebook series. In 2001, owners Rob and Debbie Cooper received the Ivy Devereaux Award for Best Canadian Hostel. Rob and Debbie would love to have you as their guests, however they emphasize the importance of making reservations well in advance.

81 West Street, Tofino BC (250) 725 - 3443 www.tofinohostel.com

Traveller's Inn

Traveller's Inn wants to be your hotel finder in the Victoria area. Offering a guarantee of the best priced hotel in Canada, Traveller's Inn, with eight locations in the Garden City, offers a discount for online reservations. The range of options provided includes extended stay, express hotel and vacation rentals. All rooms feature business working desks with fax, Internet and data ports. Guests can also choose to stay in Jacuzzi spa suites with VCRs. Traveller's Inn encourages preview travel. A virtual tour allows guests to see what the room will look like long before they arrive.

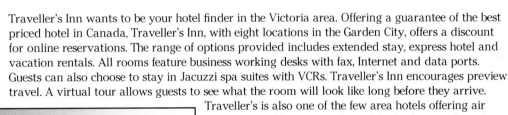

Traveller's is also one of the few area hotels offering air conditioning. Upgrade packages like the Serenity have been designed to add a touch of luxury to your stay: Rogers Chocolates paired with a bottle of wine from Cherry Point Winery, and bath salts. There are also Stay and Play golfer packages offering one night's stay, one round of 18-hole golf and a power cart rental. Large groups such as teams or businesses can qualify for group discounts, and reward points are given for each stay, redeemable toward future accommodations. See website for all locations.

Victoria BC (888) TRAVELLERS (872 - 8355)
www.travellersinnn.com/location.htm

Oak Bay Beach Hotel & Marine Resort

Kevin Walker, the current owner of Oak Bay Beach Hotel, is a third-generation hotelier who grew up on the coast of British Columbia. These days, he brings history with a family feel to one of Victoria's best-loved landmarks. The Oak Bay Beach Hotel has been in business since 1927, and though it suffered a setback when the original buildings were destroyed by fire in 1930, it was immediately rebuilt and has been operating continuously ever since. As befits a beloved traditional institution, hospitality based on personal touches is characteristic of customer service at Oak Bay. Guests enjoy complimentary continental breakfasts and hot chocolate with cookies served by the fireplace every night. General manager Brian Hobson worked in almost every position there before assuming managerial responsibilities in 1991; he looks forward to welcoming new and returning guests (though he sometimes claims that he's "forgotten more about our resort than most people know"). In addition to traditional hospitality, Oak Bay also offers unique marine resort activities. You can enjoy kayaking at sunset, and whale-watching excursions, to name just two. Guests can also enjoy the glorious views of the Haro Strait while they dine at Bentley's, or take the Sunset Dinner Cruise, available from April through October.
1175 Beach Drive, Victoria BC
(250) 598 - 4556 or (800) 668 - 7758
www.oakbaybeachhotel.com

Painted Turtle Guesthouse

Angie Gottenberg and Bruce Barnard will welcome you to Painted Turtle Guesthouse, Nanaimo's favorite place to stay. World travelers themselves, Angie and Bruce have created a place that combines the best features of their favorite lodgings around the globe, what they call lifestyle-oriented, with "funky Canadian style and fair dinkem Australian hospitality." Painted Turtle blends the trappings of a boutique hotel, the comfort and personal touches of a bed and breakfast, and the affordability and cosmopolitan flavor of an international hostel under one roof in the heart of the downtown Arts District. In addition to fine lodgings, Painted Turtle is a historic business, Nanaimo's oldest lodging and first licensed pub, built in 1875. Angie and Bruce have preserved the building's special character while adding modern conveniences including high-speed Internet stations and a fully appointed kitchen where guests are welcome to prepare their own meals. As a combination hotel/hostel/B&B, Painted Turtle offers private suites, family suites, and shared suites for the budget-conscious traveler, twenty suites in all. Incidentally, if you're a member of Hostelling International, you'll receive a nightly discount on your already-low room rate, and Painted Turtle is open year round. On their stylish website, you can get a sneak preview at Painted Turtle Guesthouse's rooms. 121 Bastion Street, Nanaimo BC (250) 753 - 4432 www.paintedturtle.ca

Estuary Estate B&B

Birders and nature lovers alike are instantly attracted to the lovely Estuary Estate B&B. For more than nine years, visitors have loved their stays at Estuary Estate. This comfortably appointed house features three guest rooms, each with a private bath and sitting area, and the private and romantic Koi Cottage (perfect for honeymoons and anniversaries). Situated at the point where Holland Creek meets the ocean, Estuary Estate offers its guests oceanfront views as well as ready access to hiking, kayaking, fishing, golfing, bird watching and beachcombing. While there you'll want to explore Ladysmith's Historic Heritage buildings and visit nearby Chemainus Theatre. The warm hospitality at Estuary Estate B&B includes a full gourmet breakfast in the formal dining room. 302 Roland Road, Ladysmith BC (250) 245 - 0665 www3.telus.net/estuaryestate/

Marifield Manor Bed & Breakfast

In 1910, Colonel Irton Eardly-Wilmot returned to Ireland from India after thirty years of service. He gathered his family and set sail for Vancouver Island. There, in the stunning Cowichan River Valley, he built a grand Edwardian mansion, complete with tennis court and tea pavilion. Perched on a hill above

Shawnigan Lake, the estate has been carefully restored to its original splendor. Now Marifield Manor Bed & Breakfast, it retains its original elegance and extends genteel hospitality to a lively mix of local and international patrons. Convenient to Victoria and accessible by float plane and rail, this is a delightful retreat. The impressive Marifield breakfast affords a hearty beginning to a leisurely day on the verandah or one full of activity in the beautiful surroundings. Kayaking or strolling along the lake, hiking, cycling, golfing, or touring British Columbia's burgeoning wine country, all are conveniently close at hand. When it comes time to retire, you will find serenity and every comfort in your handsomely appointed room. Host Shelagh John and the friendly and helpful staff invite you to enjoy the breathtaking beauty of the area and experience the luxury and charm of Marifield Manor Bed & Breakfast.
2039 Merrifield Lane, Shawnigan Lake BC
(888) 748 - 6015 www.marifieldmanor.com

Cable Cove Inn

Jennifer and Philip van Bourgondien's Cable Cove Inn is the only place in Tofino that is "couples only." The emphasis here is on honeymoons, anniversaries and romantic getaways. The Inn features seven beautifully decorated rooms, each with a fireplace, private deck facing the ocean and either a marble Jacuzzi or a private hot tub with an ocean view. But there are no televisions to detract from the romance. You'll enjoy a superb continental style breakfast delivered to your room, and if you want to go out exploring on the beach on a misty day, Jennifer and Philip will be happy to lend you binoculars, boots and rain gear. Cable Cove offers the service of a truly devoted staff, and remarkably, all of the staff have been there since the Inn opened eleven years ago. Jennifer and Philip live next door. This enables them to give full attention to their guests' needs while preserving their guests' privacy. If you're looking for romance, bear in mind that Cable Cove Inn has received the highest rating from the *Best Places to Kiss in the Northwest* guide. Start planning your getaway today! 201 Main Street, Tofino BC (250) 725 - 4236 or (800) 663 - 6449 www.cablecoveinn.com

Rondalyn Resort

With 35 acres of woodland situated along beautiful Haslam Creek, the Rondalyn Resort offers everything your family could want on a camping vacation. While all essential services are nearby, you will still feel far away from the hubbub of city life. Surrounded by mountains and forest, there are hiking and biking trails and great opportunities for fishing, fossil hunting and horseback riding. Deer and elk are abundant as are the birds and small animals of the forest. Whether tent camping or staying in a luxurious RV, you can immerse yourself in the wilderness experience or engage in a variety of activities offered by the resort. There is a stocked trout pond where you and your children can practice catch-and-release fishing. There is also a swimming pool, a hot tub, a nine-hole golf course, a playground, a clubhouse and an arcade-games room sure to please the kids. Cable television and Internet connections are available, as are a store and on-site laundry. There are many attractions nearby such as sea kayaking, the Trans-Canada Trail Suspension Bridge, The Bungy Zone, Nanaimo Casino, theatres and museums. Open year-round, Rondalyn Resort is a delightful getaway for the whole family.
1350 Timberlands Road, Ladysmith BC
(604) 245 - 3227 or (800) 643 - 7552
www.rondalynresort.com

Sooke Harbor House

Known as the *little white inn by the sea*, Sooke Harbour House has been owned by Frederique and Sinclair Philip for the past 25 years. *Travel and Leisure* magazine has rated them as "One of the top ten hotels in the world." Their easy access to fresh seafood and their organic, edible garden that tumbles down to the sea with berries, greens and over 250 kinds of edible flowers and herbs, paired with their culinary knowledge, makes it no surprise they have been rated "Best Restaurant in the World for Local Authentic Cuisine." Their menu changes daily to reflect the seasonal variations in products received from local organic farmers, gardeners, foragers and fishermen. Meals are savoured in a simply elegant dining room with views of the lavender beds leading to the ocean and mountains beyond. In addition, the wine cellar contains over 2,700 selections and 15,000 bottles of wine. Sooke Harbour House is one of only 88 restaurants in the world to have been awarded the *Wine Spectator* Grand Award. Most months they offer a wine tasting on the last Saturday which is lead by one of their in-house sommeliers. The hotel, restaurant, gallery and spa is housed in a restored and expanded white clapboard inn originally built in 1929. The twenty-eight rooms feature stunning ocean views, wood burning fireplaces, soaker or jetted tubs and steam showers for two. Each room is an adventure in itself, filled with local antiques, collectables and original art. Step onto your private balcony, the perfect location for watching sea lions, otters, seals and eagles go about their normal activities. The Sooke Harbour House also welcomes weddings, corporate retreats and family reunions. Guests can golf, whale watch, hike, fish for salmon or halibut year round or they can choose to revel in all the beach has to offer. All are worthwhile activities and they are within a short distance of Sooke Harbour House. A former guest once aptly described their stay by saying, "The Sooke Harbour House is bliss defined."
1528 Whiffen Spit Road, Sooke BC
(250) 642 - 3421 www.sookeharbourhouse.com

Queen Victoria Hotel & Suites

Built in 1965, the Queen Victoria Hotel & Suites is managed by Anthony Hartnell, whose family founded the business and began the tradition of warm hospitality and excellent service that Mr. Hartnell proudly continues. Guests of the "QV" enjoy a splendid selection of spacious rooms and suites, and all guests are invited to take advantage of the hotel's many amenities, from the indoor pool and sauna in room safes, valet laundry and guest coin operated laundry. Superb dining is available for guests at the hotel's celebrated restaurant, Samuel's by the Park, which offers breakfast, lunch, dinner and Sunday brunch in a gracious yet casual setting complemented by views of Thunderbird Park. The hotel is also just a few steps away from Victoria's 162-acre Beacon Hill Park, which features walking trails, a petting zoo, lovely ponds and many other attractions. The QV is convenient to Victoria's other popular attractions too. In fact, it's directly across the street from the Royal B.C. Museum and An Imax Theatre. The combination of luxurious amenities, better than reasonable prices and central location makes the Queen Victoria Hotel & Suites a true treasure and Mr. Hartnell and his staff are committed to keeping it that way. 655 Douglas Street, Victoria BC (250) 386 - 1312 or (800) 663 - 7007 www.qvhotel.com

The English Inn Resort

The Grand Manor House of The English Inn and Resort was once known as Rosemeade, built in 1906. Yorkshire realtor and developer Thomas Henry Slater, hired artisans from Scotland and England to work on the manor. Victoria's Samuel McClure designed the home and it features his trademark expansive roof, large front gables, bracketing finials, stone bas, tapering columns, large paneled front hallway and grand staircase. Many prominent citizens lived in the house. It also served as a naval officer's Stag house, the Olde England Inn, and finally, the five star resort boutique hotel it is today. In 2006, the manor will celebrate its 100th birthday! The manor is one of a village collection of English manors on this five-acre garden estate, surrounded by lush scented gardens and water features. It is surprisingly close to downtown Victoria, which is made easily accessible by harbour ferries. A wedding center and Anne Hathoway's conference centre are obtainable for guests planning an event. Wireless and high-speed Internet access is also available. There is a laundry service, dry-cleaning and an area for children to play. The Rosemeade dining room offers bold West Coast cuisine with executive chef Richard Luttman, and a spectacular view of the gardens. After your meal, relax in a four-poster canopy bed near a warm brick fireplace in one of the crown suites, or nestle into a cozy garden suite, a two-room townhouse suite, or a spacious estate suite.

429 Lampson Street, Victoria BC
(866) 888 - 4353

Dominion Grand Hotel

Originally built in 1876 and remodeled in 1990, the Dominion Grand Hotel is Victoria's most notable landmark. This local favourite showcases what first class amenities should look like. Once here, you'll be pampered and impressed by the hospitable, efficient staff. The Dominion Grand has concierge services, free parking and an on site bar and grill. Located in the heart of downtown Victoria, the Dominion is merely footsteps from the inner harbour, many exciting attractions and various other dining establishments and, of course, some of the best shopping in the world! For those who must work, there are data port connections in every room. Come visit one of British Columbia's most amazingly beautiful legends. Once you do, you'll go home feeling like you've really lived!

759 Yates Street, Victoria BC
(250) 384 - 4136

The Manor Guest House

In an Edwardian Heritage House built in 1902, Brenda Yablon runs one of the finest bed and breakfasts in Canada. Guests at The Manor receive more than a comfortable room, attentive service, and delicious, healthful breakfast. The Manor is also the first place to stop for complete information about Vancouver. There's virtually nothing about the city that Brenda and her staff don't know, and they'll be happy to provide anything from a full overview to a map or restaurant recommendation. Guests from around the world are welcomed; Brenda is fluent in English, French and Hebrew, and can speak conversational Spanish, German and even a little Russian. The Manor is centrally located within walking distance of attractions like Granville Island, Chinatown, Queen Elizabeth Park and Gastown. The view from the porch is breathtaking and the interior is decorated with lovely antiques, including a piano guests can play that's as old as the house. The Manor is the only bed and breakfast in downtown Vancouver that accepts children of all ages. In addition to breakfasts, guests can request custom dinners specially prepared by the resident chef. Be sure to visit The Manor's website for a virtual tour of The Manor and much more, including texts in German and Japanese. 345 West 13th Avenue, Vancouver BC (604) 876 - 8494 www.manorguesthouse.com

The Granville Island Hotel

The Granville Island Hotel is an island retreat in the heart of one of the busiest cities in North America. Easy to get to, but hard to leave, The Granville Island Hotel is ideally located for business travelers, vacationing families and couples on a romantic getaway. Everyone is welcome here, even companion animals. They'll love the island location and the hotel's specialty store for pets. There are eighty-two rooms, each one a cut above the ordinary. The suites and penthouses feature floor to ceiling windows and panoramic water views. Other rooms have beamed ceilings and marble floors with Persian rugs and soaker tubs. All rooms include complimentary high-speed Internet access, in-room coffee makers, telephones with data ports and voicemail, mini-bars and much more. The waterfront setting makes this hotel an unusual and exciting location for meetings and gatherings, and the conference rooms can host groups from eight to 80. Natural light and on-site catering are just two of the features that make the meeting rooms at The Granville Island Hotel special. For dining, the hotel offers The Dockside Restaurant. Open for breakfast, lunch and dinner, The Dockside can accommodate a party of two or two hundred! If you'd rather relax with a pint, The Dockside Pub features a fireplace, televisions and live entertainment on Friday and Saturday nights. 1253 Johnston Street, Vancouver BC (604) 683 - 7373 or (800) 663 - 1840 www.granvilleislandhotel.com

Wedgewood Hotel and Spa, Bacchus Restaurant & Lounge

In Vancouver a luxurious boutique hotel has become a unique landmark, so much so that it recently placed fourth for "World's Best Service" by readers of Travel & Leisure magazine. Other awards won recently by the hotel include Smart Meetings: Platinum Choice Award 2004, Conde Nast Gold List: World's Best Places to Stay 2005, and CAA/AAA: Double Four Diamond Award. All of these represent tangible evidence the hotel has captured many hearts in a city where choices abound. Committed to excellence and value, owner Eleni Skalbania opened the Wedgewood Hotel & Spa in 1984. This beautifully appointed hotel includes a second-floor spa, added in 2003, which features treatments using the Epicurean Discovery Skin Treatment System, voted best overall prestige skin care line by In Style magazine. While at the hotel, enjoy the romantic setting and exceptional food in the Bacchus Restaurant and Lounge, where executive chef Lee Parsons presides. His unique style of modern French cuisine is exemplified by offerings like the roasted fraser valley duck breast, confit duck leg, Savoy cabbage, roasted salsify shemiji mushrooms, and a lentil and sherry vinegar sauce. For reservations at Bacchus Restaurant call (604) 608-5319. The elegant lounge and piano bar is the perfect setting for cocktails or for High Tea. So treat yourself by making a visit to the Wedgewood Hotel and Spa, Bacchus Restaurant & Lounge. 845 Hornby Street, Vancouver BC
(604) 689 - 7777 or (800) 663 - 0666
www.wedgewoodhotel.com

Alma Beach Resort Bed & Breakfast Manor & Spa

In the heart of Kitsilano and Point Grey. Enjoy the beaches, a huge saltwater pool and both the Alma Beach Heritage Manor* and the Alma Beach Bed and Breakfast. The Manor is a completely renovated 1912 Heritage Home, filled with original artwork, treasures from Thailand and richly diverse furnishings. The suites range from a studio to three bedrooms, some with lovely ocean and mountain views. In the full service B&B, after a restful sleep under 350 thread count linens, guests start their day with a savoury, hot, three course gourmet breakfast including fresh fruit, chocolate cranberry muffins, bismarks and soufflés among other personal creations. The Manor and B&B are superbly located with less than a five minute walk to beaches, shops, entertainment, restaurant dining, bird watching, tennis and biking. Other activities to enjoy nearby are ocean kayaking for the more adventurous soul, while sailing and swimming offer a more traditional day out in the sun.   Amenities include high speed Internet access, cable television/DVD and private in-suite baths. Owners Carol and Manfred invite you to enjoy the soothing 'absolutely fabulous urban spa', an award winning day spa in Vancouver. Spa guests are greeted by the traveling Buddha and treatments open with a Thai-style herbal foot treatment plus a cup of hot ginger tea. The spa offers special VIP pricing to the guests of Alma Beach Manor and B&B. Ask about their all-inclusive packages or the full range of services. Come rest your mind and rejuvenate your body at the Alma Beach Resort Bed & Breakfast Manor & Spa.
3756 West 2nd Avenue, Vancouver BC
(604) 221 - 1950
www.myspa.ca www.almabeachvancouver.com

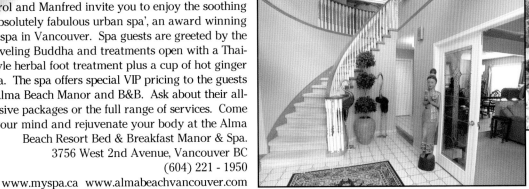

The Palms Guest House

Heidi Schmidt's guest house in West Vancouver has rapidly become one of British Columbia's favourite bed and breakfasts. A longtime resident, Heidi was lucky and found the perfect building in which to realize her dream of opening a B&B – a stunning contemporary mansion, where the finest accommodations and attention await you. At The Palms, each of the three suites, the Governor Room, the Princess Room, and the Ambassador Suite, is beautifully decorated with antique furnishings and feature Internet access, a full bathroom and a private balcony with spectacular views of the city and the ocean. The Ambassador Suite, with its canopied bed, double Jacuzzi tub and fireplace, is a favorite among honeymooners. A special Honeymoon package includeing champagne, chocolate and flowers is available. In the morning enjoy a hearty breakfast and then enjoy the area's many attractions. The beach and the seawall are a short stroll away, as are a variety of delightful shops and excellent restaurants. A ten-minute drive takes you to the ferries of Horseshoe Bay and Vancouver, and the Whistler Ski Resort is just over an hour away. If you need advice on what to do, just ask Heidi, she knows and loves the area and, by the way, she speaks Spanish and German in addition to English.
3042 Marine Drive, Vancouver BC
(604) 926 - 1159 or (800) 691 - 4455
www.palmsguesthouse.com

Pleasant Stay

For short or long-term rental rooms and apartments in New Westminster, Pleasant Stay offers affordable pet and child-friendly accommodations. The location is one block from transportation and close to all kinds of amenities: library, restaurants, shops, banks, park, school, a recreational center and movie theatre. New Westminster boasts seven recreational facilities, riverboat tours, a wide range of restaurants, museums, art galleries, golf and a long list of festivals and community events. Pleasant Stay is 30 minutes from most other destinations such as downtown Vancouver, the airport, the ferry or the U.S. border. Minimum lengths of stay vary by type of room, with some negotiable rates for less than the minimum length. The Bed and Breakfast option is very affordable for the budget-conscious traveler. For just a little more, the Homestay offers three meals a day. All rooms include heat and cable television hook-up and use of bathroom and kitchen facilities. Furnished or unfurnished rooms and apartments are also provided for limited leases. Laundry facilities, television sets, DVD players and Internet service are available for an additional fee, as is service to and from the airport. Accommodations are simple, comfortable and convenient. Luiza, George and Haidy are thoughtful hosts and will do their best to make sure you enjoy Pleasant Stay.

901 and 907 Fifth Street, New Westminster BC
(604) 540 - 9194 or (604) 512 - 2046
ca.geocities.com/mllumllu/PLEASANT_STAY

ThistleDown House

When Rex Davidson and Ruth Crameri acquired a beautiful Craftsman-style house on Capilano Road, they were simply looking for a home. They had thought about opening a bed and breakfast some time in the distant future but, while on a trip to Scotland, they made a spontaneous decision to convert their home into a bed and breakfast when they returned. Six months after they got back, ThistleDown House was opened. It's been full of delighted customers ever since. Rex did all the woodwork in the house himself, and Ruth did all of the interior design, an eclectic mix of sophistication and warmth. Each of the five guest rooms has a unique personality brought about by special features within and without, like the lovely mulberry tree just outside the Mulberry Peek room. ThistleDown House offers full concierge service twenty-four hours a day and many other amenities, including a communal library and high-speed Internet access. Ruth's gourmet cooking is a strong draw in its own right, with breakfasts featuring dishes like Crepes Primavera in chantilly sauce. Afternoon tea, with a selection of European pastries, chocolate indulgences and flans made with fresh fruit, is another reason customers flock to ThistleDown House. Reservations should be made well in advance.

3910 Capilano Road, North Vancouver BC (604) 986 - 7173 or (888) 633 - 7173
www.thistle-down.com

Hillhouse Bed & Breakfast

This 1910 Heritage home sits atop a New Westminster hill overlooking the mighty Fraser River from B.C's oldest neighborhood. Nicknamed the "Royal City", New Westminster was the first capitol of B.C. and retains a lively spirit as the hub of Vancouver's lower Mainland. Hillhouse bed and Breakfast was once a home to a family of 13 and now welcomes guests from around the world. Owners Denny and Don thoroughly enjoy their lifestyle and the chance to make each visitors stay a great experience. Denny says operating a B&B is the "Ultimate in sharing." "We travel the world around the breakfast table every morning". "Our photo gallery has pictures of thousands of smiling guests…including Alpaca salesmen from Peru to Beekeepers from Wyoming". This cozy B&B is a great base for exploring Vancouver with close access to rapid transit, great local antique stores and riverfront markets. Best of all its more than a cookie cutter hotel room. 358 Simpson Street, New Westminster BC
(604) 524 - 3060 www.hillhousebedandbreakfast.com

Pan Pacific Vancouver

Imagine yourself looking out over one of the spectacular views of the harbor, the city or the beautiful mountains which surround the Pan Pacific Vancouver. This hotel has a AAA Five Diamond award-winning fine diner called the Five Sails. There is also the Cafe Pacifica with a venue of North American and Japanese cuisine. With 504 luxurious rooms and suites, the Pan Pacific is sure to have exactly the right setting for your mood. The fully appointed Pan Pacific's rooms are complete with high-speed Internet connections and the views are worth writing home about. You probably won't be spending much time inside your room since there's a 2000 square foot fitness club, a heated pool with sun deck and a Jacuzzi on site to enjoy. Later you can relax in the Cascades Lounge for an after dinner drink or just to unwind from your busy day. There are elegant meeting and banquet facilities available for your special occasion or business needs, and the excellent staff are among the best in the world. To see their menus or to make reservations, visit their web site. For a truly delightful experience, visit the Pan Pacific Vancouver and see what a room with a view really should be.
300-999 Canada Place, Vancouver BC
(800) 663 - 1515 www.dinepanpacific.com

Photo by: Katie Bianchin

Opus Hotel

Opus Hotel is not your ordinary accommodation. In fact, *Conde Nast Traveler* magazine says they are, "one of the world's best places to stay." This incredible Vancouver landmark opened in 2002 and has become the place to stay while you're in British Columbia. Throughout the 96 stunning guestrooms and suites there are five unique decor schemes. Whether you appreciate a modern or more minimalist look, there are accommodations to suit your personality. While outside you can enjoy a leisurely walk along the waterfront seawall which stretches for over nine miles. This member of the Small Luxury Hotels of the World is unlike any place you've ever stayed before. A fine dining restaurant and bar are available for those who prefer to stay in, but this contemporary boutique hotel is located in the Yaletown district of downtown Vancouver. It's within walking distance of an eight square block heritage preservation zone, lounges, spas, fashion boutiques and Vancouver's finest area restaurants. For a stay worth remembering visit the Opus.
322 Davie Street, Vancouver BC (866) 642 - 6787 www.opushotel.com

The Fairmont Hotel Vancouver

For over sixty years The Fairmont Hotel Vancouver has been a landmark in the heart of the city. This longtime area landmark has two award-winning restaurants, a fitness center, data ports in every room, a swimming pool, spa, and they even allow your family pet to stay there too. Kings, queens and Hollywood royalty alike continue to visit The Fairmont Hotel Vancouver year after year. The Fairmont is rich in history, yet immediately puts visitors at ease with its incredible style and personal services.   For the opportunity to stay at one of Vancouver's most famous hotels, come to The Fairmont and see why this legend continues to dazzle every visitor who walks through its doors.

900 West Georgia Street, Vancouver BC

(604) 684 - 3131

Photo by: Geoff Richardson

Traveller's Hotel B&B

The colourful history of Traveller's Hotel B&B began in 1887, when entrepreneur Bill Murray, no relation to the comedian decided to provide accommodations for travellers heading for the Caribou gold fields. In its early days, the hotel's guests included miners, merchants, high court judges and at least one train robber, the legendary outlaw Billy Miner. For modern-day travellers, the hotel is a heritage-site destination. It is also a five-star accommodation, a place where the best of the past and present combine to create an outstanding experience. Over the past few years, Traveller's Hotel B&B has become a special favourite for honeymooning couples. Hosts Wally and Sharon Martin provide special amenities for honeymooners; it's no trouble to order tea or coffee brought to your room in the morning or arrange to have your favourite beverage,

chilled in an ice bucket, waiting for you when you check in. Traveller's doesn't sell alcoholic beverages, but you're welcome to provide your own. A special honeymoon package of additional high-quality appointments for your room is also available. Wally and Sharon are friendly hosts who will be happy to welcome you to Traveller's Hotel B&B, whether for a once-in-a-lifetime wedding celebration or a visit to soak up the history of the area.

21628 – 48th Avenue, Langley BC (604) 533 - 5569 www.travellershotel.ca

Best Western Kamloops Hotel

Kamloops' Best Western Hotel has something that puts it above the rest. As part of its mandate to be as natural as its setting in the heart of "Super, Natural" British Columbia, the hotel has installed hybrid solar water heating and heat recovery systems that give it real "bragging rights" when it comes to environmentally responsible business practices. The Swiss-designed equipment reduces the hotel's greenhouse gas emission by over 600 tons per year, the equivalent of taking 289 cars off the road. Nor is that all this Best Western has to be proud of. With over 200 rooms, Forster's Conference Center and Restaurant on the premises, an indoor courtyard with an abundance of lush tropical plants and a solar-heated swimming pool, this hotel is the best in its class. The Spirits Lounge is a great spot for cocktails. And then there's the setting. Kamloops is a city that offers the best in outdoor recreation, be it skiing, wilderness hikes, trout fishing or golf tournaments. The Best Western offers special packages to help you take advantage of these activities, all year round. Whether you're there for a meeting or a vacation stay, you'll love the facilities and the time you spend enjoying the panoramic view of the city from the Best Western Kamloops' patio.
1250 Rogers Way, Kamloops BC (250) 828 - 6660 or (800) 937 - 8376 bestwestern.kamloops.com

The Plaza Heritage Hotel

Winner of the 2002 Commercial Heritage Achievement Award, Plaza Heritage Hotel exemplifies the glory days of British Columbia's history. Built in 1928, this meticulously restored jewel offers luxurious yet affordable elegance. Enter the exquisite, wood-paneled lobby and step back in time. Each of the 66 guest rooms are designed as a unique expression of the luxe aesthetic of the 1920s. Rich, warm period styling is joined by every modern amenity to envelope you in comfort, beauty and convenience. You may decide to start your day with breakfast in the charming coffee shop, then you could wander through the galleries and boutiques in the heart of the city. Or you needn't venture too far to enjoy the spectacular scenic gifts of the area. Thompson River runs straight through town and is a favourite location for white-water rafters, Adams River draws visitors from around the world just to view the amazing sockeye salmon runs, Sun Peaks Resort beckons skiers to its more than 80 groomed runs; and within 15 minutes of the Plaza, you can play any of the five championship golf courses in the area. In the evening, settle in for an exceptional meal in the fine dining room. Whether you are planning an event, a conference, or some much-needed personal leisure, Plaza Heritage Hotel will fulfill your every expectation. 405 Victoria Street, Kamloops BC (250) 377 - 8075 www.plazaheritagehotel.com

Hampton Inn Kamloops

The Hampton Inn Kamloops offers a full range of accommodations, from standard and business rooms to large suites and Jacuzzi rooms. The Inn also offers free airport shuttle service, a fitness center, indoor pool, hot tub and excellent amenities. High-speed Internet connections are available in the lobby and in all guest rooms, so you can stay as hooked-up as you wish. But if getting away from it all is on your agenda, the Inn is within a half hour of some of the best skiing, golfing and fishing in the province. There are beautiful hiking trails nearby and the area is considered one of the best in Canada for mountain biking. The Hampton Inn offers a full complimentary breakfast every morning to get your day off to a good start. The friendly and professional staff is committed to your satisfaction. In fact, they guarantee it. Everyone, including your pet, is welcome there. The Hampton Inn Kamloops invites you to "Explore our world of adventure."

1245 Rogers Way, Kamloops BC
(250) 571 - 7897 or (866) 571 - 7897
www.hamptoninnkamloops.com

Four Points by Sheraton

The Four Points by Sheraton in Kamloops is a luxury mid-class hotel that has much to offer. General Manager Ray Strome is proud of the hotel's reputation as the best in Kamloops, one that sets standards above the others in guest service and housekeeping. Not only are they the best, they have won awards highlighting those services. He can also point to the opinions of their business clients, who love the "Starwood" rate program. An annual survey in *Business Travel News* put Four Points ahead of the other hotels in its class in appearance and in overall relationship between price and value. Always keeping the business traveler in mind, the Four Points has traditional rooms, but also deluxe rooms with kitchenettes, perfect for families, and best of all, Jacuzzi suites. Four Points is a place to have fun too, with an indoor pool and water slide, as well as fitness facilities. Ric's Grill is adjacent for fine dining in an intimate, relaxing ambiance. Everything you need and want in a hotel is there for you at the Four Points by Sheraton. 1175 Rogers Way, Kamloops BC (250) 374 - 4144 www.fourpointskamloops.com

Prestige Harbourfront Resort & Convention Centre

The elegant, four and a half star Prestige Harbourfront Resort and Convention Centre, situated on the shores of Shuswap Lake and within walking distance of downtown Salmon Arm, offers unrivalled accommodations, luxurious amenities and impeccable service. Beautifully appointed lakeside rooms offer spectacular views of Shuswap Lake and Bastion Mountain. Each guestroom features luxurious furnishings, deluxe amenities, high-speed Internet access and pay-per-view movies. Unwind in your very own deep soaker tub or glass walk-in shower. For that special get-away or celebration, treat yourself to one of the lavish theme Jacuzzi suites. Many unique romance packages will make your stay extraordinary. Fully equipped kitchenettes and beautiful executive suites are also available for guests requiring an extended stay. Guests will enjoy a visit to Forster Prime Rib House, renowned for their prime rib, seafood and pasta. The lively atmosphere of Spirit's Bar and Grill is the perfect place to mingle with friends. The two waterfront patios with magnificent views provide an unforgettable setting for that business luncheon or friendly get-together. Moorage is also available at the marina which is accessible from the resort waterfront walkway. Guests can take a leisurely stroll in City Park and around the waterfront nature trail adjacent to the resort. Guests wishing to experience the wonderful combination of relaxation and revitalization inside the resort, can rejuvenate their body with a workout in the Prestige Athletic Club, a swim in the indoor/outdoor swimming pool then a soak in the outdoor hot tub. Indulge yourself with the ultimate pampering of an aromatherapy body massage or treatment in the exclusive day spa. For your convenience and pleasure, quaint boutiques are featured in the shopping promenade, where you can enjoy a specialty coffee or dessert, purchase a unique gift, select a distinctive piece of jewelry, rent a car from Budget Car & Truck Rentals or have a fashionable hairstyle created just for you. The Prestige Harbourfront Resort & Convention Centre offers convention facilities for up to 600 delegates. Golf and ski packages are also available, and outdoor activities such as swimming, boating, fishing, cycling and hiking are all easily accessible from the resort. The Prestige Harbourfront Resort & Convention Centre is your perfect year-round destination choice. 251 Harbourfront Drive, Salmon Arm BC (250) 833 - 5800 www.prestigeinn.com/salmonarm

Best Western Sunrise Inn

Osoyoos, British Columbia is home to world-renown vineyards, first-class golf and many other recreational wonders. The Best Western Sunrise Inn, located on Main Street, offers visitors the perfect place to stay while they explore all the area has to offer. This well-appointed hotel is known for having the friendliest staff in the area. Excellent customer service is a focal point for owners, Lucky Gill and Charan Rai. They offer the old-fashioned, "bend over backwards" sort of service you don't often see today. Visitors can choose from 66 different standard, deluxe or kitchenette suites. Each room comes with a television, in-room coffee/tea maker, iron and board, hairdryer, and in most rooms, high-speed Internet access. Guests are also provided with complimentary on-site parking and a great continental breakfast. When you're done with your day's adventures take advantage of the Sunrise Inn's pool, Jacuzzi and fitness room. The hotel boasts two dining options for your convenience: a Quizno's sandwich shop, which is a great place for a quick bite, or the restaurant, a lovely place to enjoy a quiet meal at a more leisurely pace. The Best Western Sunrise Inn has also compiled several accommodation and recreation packages that allow you to make the most of your stay. One such package is the Ultimate Golf and Wine Holiday for Two. Come, relax and enjoy the fabulous service and amenities that the Best Western Sunrise Inn has to offer.

5506 Main Street, Osoyoos BC
(877) 878 - 2200 www.bestwesternosoyoos.com

Prestige Hotel & Convention Centre Vernon

The four and a half star Prestige Hotel & Convention Centre Vernon is located close to business, recreational and shopping areas. The Prestige Hotel features beautifully appointed guestrooms and spacious two-level loft suites. For the extended-stay traveller or guests requiring the convenience of home, fully-equipped loft kitchenettes are available. Guests can celebrate that special occasion with a stay in one of the luxurious theme Jacuzzi suites. Every guestroom is equipped with deluxe furnishings and amenities, high-speed Internet access and pay-per-view movies. A guest laundry is also available for your convenience. Experience the wonderful combination of relaxation and revitalization right inside the hotel. Rejuvenate your body with an energetic workout in the fitness centre, swim in the indoor pool and then relax in the soothing warmth of the hot tub. Revitalize your body from the inside out with a visit to Essential Elements Day Spa. Visitors to the Prestige Hotel & Convention Centre Vernon will also enjoy the many dining options available. Savour the culinary delights in Forster's Restaurant, open for breakfast, lunch and dinner. Mingle with friends in Spirit's Bar and Grill or treat yourself to a specialty coffee or freshly-baked dessert in the Gourmet Coffeehouse and gift shop. Convention Centre facilities can accommodate up to 400 delegates. The Prestige Hotel & Convention Centre Vernon offers golf and ski packages to many of the surrounding world-class golf and ski resorts.   Explore the provincial or city parks, spend a day relaxing at a nearby beach, enjoy a museum, a winery or an orchard tour. Outdoor enthusiasts will discover water activities, fishing and cycling are all located nearby. You are assured of a memorable stay at the Prestige Hotel & Convention Centre Vernon.

4411 – 32nd Street, Vernon BC V1T 9G8 (250) 558 - 5991 www.prestigeinn.com/vernon

Holiday Inn Express Vernon

"Stay Smart" is the promise of Holiday Inn Express Hotel and Suites, a modern hotel for travelers who want to make common-sense choices. Vernon's Holiday Inn Express offers complimentary continental breakfast, coffee, tea, morning newspapers and high-speed Internet access. You are also welcome to enjoy their heated pool, hot tub and fitness centre. For the sports enthusiast, they offer special ski and golf packages. The north shore of Kalamalka Lake is where you can relax on the spectacular beach and enjoy the lush scenery. The Inn also has board rooms and meeting rooms. A kid-friendly Inn, children under 18 stay for free when accompanied by an adult. The friendly and accommodating staff will be happy to assist you throughout your stay.

4716 – 34th Street, Vernon BC
(250) 550 - 7777 or (866) 677 - 1111
www.vernonexpress.com

Best Western Inn Kelowna

For thirty years The Best Western Inn Kelowna has been at the center of it all. Dynamic Kelowna, Canada's answer to Hawaii, offers visitors a wealth of recreational possibilities. Within a short walking distance from the hotel you will find playgrounds and picnic areas at Mission Creek Regional Park along with numerous restaurants and miles of walking paths. Okanagan Lake is only 10 minutes away with its many beaches and water activities. Three shopping centers are within easy reach and three world-class skiing areas are only an hour and a half drive. Guests of the hotel are treated to top-notch, friendly service at every turn. Amenities include a wellness spa, gift shop, rooftop terrace, two outdoor hot tubs, an indoor pool, steam room and a fitness centre. Guest rooms include complimentary newspapers, Internet access, refrigerators and/or mini-bars, bathrobes, slippers, and walkout balconies. Meeting and conference spaces totaling over 4,500-square feet are available along with event planners to help you choose a floor plan and meeting area to fit your needs. The entire facility is wheelchair accessible and full catering services are available for the conference area. Daily complimentary continental breakfast is served along with tea and coffee, also the 97 Street Pub is located onsite. Visit The Best Western Inn Kelowna on your next trip to the Okanagan Valley, it's a vacation within a vacation. 2402 Highway 97 N, Kelowna BC (888) 860 - 1212

www.bestwesterninnkelowna.com

Hume Hotel

The Hume Hotel in Nelson is the place to go when you need to relax and get away from it all. Nelson, known as the Queen City of the Kootenays, has 350 Heritage buildings, including the Hume Hotel. Established in 1898 by J. Fred and Lydia Hume, this hotel prides itself in its long history of excellence and exemplary hospitality. The hotel offers 43 rooms that will fill you with a strong sense of nostalgia for the days of old. Each room has its own special theme and the more rooms you see, the more you'll want to keep looking. The General Store Restaurant provides guests with a full complimentary breakfast to help start the day and it also serves a terrific Sunday brunch. Taffy Jack's Nightclub is a fun and funky cabaret that is decorated everywhere with a fantastic collection of sports memorabilia and historical artifacts. There is also Mike's Place Pub, or if you are looking for a quieter, more intimate place to pass the time, go to the Library Lounge. This elegant and magnificently restored room features a beautiful, original brick fireplace that was discovered during renovations. Here you can snuggle up in a cozy seating area for two or sidle up to the carved oak bar. The Hume Hotel has meeting and banquet rooms as well, which are perfect for special occasions and corporate gatherings. Come enjoy the old world tradition, ambiance and service you'll find at the Hume Hotel in historic Nelson. 422 Vernon Street, Nelson BC (250) 352 - 5331 or (877) 568 - 0888 www.humehotel.com

Residence Inn Marriott Trickle Creek

Boasting the very best activities and located in the beautiful scenic mountains Residence Inn Trickle Creek is a cut above the rest. With the golf course just moments away and the chair lift right outside the doors there is plenty to do and see. Wonderful scenery, accommodations and friendly staff make your stay enjoyable and memorable. Stay indoors and cozy up to the gas fireplaces, or walk out on your balcony to view the pristine mountains and amenities galore. On site you'll find: Kelsey's Lounge & Restaurant for relaxing, fitness facilities including a pool to help you stay in shape and there's even a complimentary European breakfast available. After a long day of sight seeing, working out, hiking, biking and golf you can relax with a swim or soak in one of the hot tubs. Come to the Residence Inn Marriott Trickle Creek and experience British Columbia's best kept secret.
500 Stemwinder Drive, Kimberley BC
(250) 427 - 5175
www.tricklecreek.com

Prestige Inns Rocky Mountain Resort & Convention Centre

The four and a half star Prestige Rocky Mountain Resort & Convention Centre is part of the Prestige Hotels & Resorts chain of first-class properties. Situated adjacent to the Canadian Museum of Rail Travel, the resort features deluxe rooms, executive suites, fully equipped kitchenettes and luxurious theme Jacuzzi suites. Each guestroom is equipped with deluxe furnishings and amenities, high-speed Internet access and pay-per-view movies. Guests can rejuvenate their body with a workout in the Prestige Athletic Club followed by a swim in the indoor swimming pool and a soak in the soothing warmth of the hot tub. Visitors can then escape to a world of relaxation with a visit to the spa at the Prestige and experience an aromatherapy body massage or other replenishing treatment. The creative stylists in Kutter's Korner hair salon present the latest in hair designs. Visitors to the Prestige Rocky Mountain Resort will enjoy the many dining options available. Hot Shots Cappuccino Bistro offers an array of specialized coffees, freshly baked items, light lunches and beverages. Munro's Restaurant, open for breakfast, lunch and dinner, features a luncheon buffet and tantalizing dinner selections which are sure to please every appetite. Chattanooga's Bar & Grill is an upbeat, fun place to mingle with friends, and outdoor patio seating is available. Convention facilities can accommodate up to to 600 delegates. The Prestige Rocky Mountain Resort offers golf packages for Cranbrook Golf Club, in addition to Bootleg Gap, St. Eugene Mission, Kimberly, Trickle Creek and Creaston Golf courses. Packages include a deluxe room, 18 holes of golf and a shared power cart. The resort offers easy access to every activity the region has to offer. Choose the Prestige Rocky Mountain Resort for a memorable stay.
209 Van Horne Street South, Cranbrook BC (250) 417 - 0444 www.prestigeinn.com

Prestige Inn Radium Hot Springs

Located in downtown Radium Hot Springs at the intersection of Highways 93 & 95, this four and a half star full-service hotel features superior guestrooms and suites. Each guestroom is equipped with deluxe furnishings and amenities. For a special get-away or celebration, guests may choose to stay in one of the luxurious theme Jacuzzi suites. You can experience the African, Egyptian or New York Suites. Guests also requiring an extended stay may choose a fully equipped executive suite or kitchenette. As a guest of the Prestige Hotel Radium, you are assured of the highest standard of customer service. Radium Hot Springs offers an abundance of activities for the outdoor enthusiasts. Visitors can relax in the therapeutic hot springs located just a short distance away, or challenge themselves to a round of golf, skiing, hiking, snowmobiling, fishing, cycling or sightseeing. Golf and ski packages are always available. Guests wanting to relax in the hotel will enjoy the indoor swimming pool, hot tub and Prestige Athletic Club. For ultimate relaxation, guests can discover the essence of an aromatherapy body massage or other replenishing treatment in the Bare Hands Day Spa. La Cabina Ristorante offers delectable menu selections for people of all ages and a visit to Carrington's Olde English Lounge is the perfect place to mingle with friends. Conference and banquet facilities are also available. (250) 347 - 2300 www.prestigeinn.com

Prestige Lakeside Resort & Convention Centre

Located on the shores of the West Arm of Kootenay Lake in the heart of downtown Nelson, the four and a half star Prestige Lakeside Resort and Convention is the perfect year-round destination choice. Enjoy spectacular views of Kootenay Lake and Elephant Mountain from the private balconies of the beautifully appointed lakeside rooms. For that special get-away or celebration, guests can choose one of the resort's luxurious theme Jacuzzi suites. Discover the wonderful combination of relaxation and revitalization right inside the resort. Revitalize your body with a workout in the fitness centre, followed by a swim in the indoor pool and a

soak in the soothing warmth of the hot tub. Experience the essence of a therapeutic body massage or other replenishing treatment in the exclusive Shalimar Health Spa. Visit the professional stylists at Waves on the Lake Hair Design for a fashionable new look. Guests and visitors at the resort can enjoy culinary delights in Munro's Restaurant which is open for breakfast, lunch and dinner. Manhattan's Waterfront Lounge is the perfect place to meet friends for great food and fun times. The two waterfront patios provide an unforgettable setting for business luncheons or get-togethers. Visit the Lakeside Coffee Cup and sample one of many specialty coffees and delectable desserts. Guests can moor their boats at the full service marina also offering boat rentals, seadoos, canoes and wakeboard lessons. Prestige Fishing Charters can provide you with the thrill of world-class fishing on the Columbia River or Kootenay Lake. The Prestige Lakeside Resort features convention facilities for up to 450. Golf and ski packages are available. Plus many other outdoor activities.
701 Lakeside Dr., Nelson BC V1L 6G3 (250) 352 - 7222 www.prestigeinn.com/nelson

Treasure Cove Hotel and Casino

It's time for relaxation, excitement, great food and fun! Visit Northern BC's newest Treasure and you will find all of the above in one fantastic place. The Treasure Cove Hotel gives priority attention to meeting all of your accommodation needs. Every room and suite is fully equipped and includes the amenities of individual climate control, mini fridges and wired high speed Internet. European complimentary continental breakfast buffet is served daily in the Breakfast Room. After relaxing in the sanctuary of your room, you may want to explore the Aqua Center. Refresh yourself in the sparkling pool, try the twisting waterslide or rejuvenate in the Fitness Room and revitalizing Jacuzzi. Now, are you ready for some excitement? Adjoining the hotel is the Treasure Cove Casino, the largest casino north of the lower mainland. Enter the Tuscan themed setting, where a beautiful fountain and impressive architectural design await you. You can try your hand at a game table or one of the 350 slot machines. The Casino includes a Las Vegas style Show Lounge and world-renowned entertainment. The Publik Drink House and Eatery offers a delicious menu. Just a few steps from the hotel are the Prince George Golf, the Curling Club and major shopping facilities. Nearby local attractions are the Prince George Railway and Forestry Museum, The Exploration Place and the University of Northern British Columbia. If relaxing is more your desire, the Araina Day Spa is located in the lobby of the hotel. Great spa packages are available to help you unwind after a long day. Whether you're on a business or a pleasure trip, your visit to Treasure Cove Hotel and Casino will more than meet your expectations. 2005 Highway 97 South, Prince George BC (250) 614 - 9111 or (877) 614 - 9111 www.treasurecovehotel.net www.treasurecovecasino.net

Red Coach Inn & The Lodge Conference Center

In the 1860s, gold was discovered in the creeks of Barkerville. Because of that, a gold rush trail called the Cariboo Wagon Road was established. It ran from Lillooet to Barkerville with a series of rest houses along the way. Each rest house was named after the mile where it was located, thus began the life of 100 Mile House. This former roadside stop for the stagecoach has become a bustling community of 1900 residents with an immediate trading area of twenty thousand people. As the village grew, the original 100 Mile House Hotel was destroyed by fire and was replaced by The Lodge which in turn was replaced by the Red Coach Inn. The Lodge, heritage treasure of the Caribou, has been wonderfully maintained and is still situated, directly behind the newer hotel. In 1966 the Red Coach Inn, named for a stagecoach on the Barnard Express line was built. That particular coach was the last to ride from Yale to Soda Creek and is still displayed behind the Inn. Featuring a restaurant, dining room, full size indoor pool, hot tub and catering facilities Red Coach Inn has 49 charmingly-appointed guest rooms that are inviting and comfortable. The family style restaurant is open year round and features a traditional menu that is sure to please. The Red Coach Inn and Lodge Conference Center is suited for conferences of up to 300 people. You can host small, intimate gatherings or larger events including business meetings and company conferences. Meeting facilities and unique accommodations are also available at the Lodge Conference and Retreat Centre, which offers additional accommodations. Surrounded by scenic forests, meadows and the Exeter Lake Bird Sanctuary, it is the perfect place for weddings, spiritual retreats or family reunions. The Inn Shoppe offers delightful clothing, books, jewelry and souvenirs to commemorate your visit. Red Coach Inn is the place to stay in the South Cariboo. 100 Mile House BC (800) 663 - 8422 www.bcadventure.com/redcoachinn

White Cap Motor Inn & RV Park

The White Cap Motor Inn & RV Park in Wells, in the heart of the Cariboo Mountains, is only eight kilometers from the historic town of Barkerville and 28 kilometers from Bowron lake. It is open seven days a week year round and offers a family-based approach to service highlighted by a warm welcoming atmosphere and clean comfortable rooms. Many of the motel's guest rooms are in the form of two bedroom suites with their own kitchen and living rooms, providing ideal accommodation for families. All rooms have their own bathrooms, color television and direct dial telephones. Amenities include an on-site laundromat, coffee shop with Internet access, children's playground and even an outdoor hot tub that provides an extraordinarily refreshing way to warm up in the wintertime. The RV park is directly across from the motel and offers water, electrical and sewer hook ups for RVs. It has its own washrooms and shower facilities. There are fire pits, gas barbeques, and both covered and open picnic areas for use by RV or motel guests. The town of Wells is just a two-minute walk away. Originally established as a gold mining town in 1930, Wells has maintained its tradition of brightly colored buildings to stand out against the white winter snows. Although some gold mining still continues, more recently it has become the home of a small community of talented artists. There are galleries displaying paintings, photographs and pottery, and during the summer season the town hosts numerous musical concerts and recitals. The school building is used during the summer to provide painting and music classes including a highly-regarded harp school. There are hiking and mountain biking trails for the summer and ski and snowmobile trails in the winter, all leading off into the mountains with their awe-inspiring scenery.

3885 Ski Hill Road, Wells BC (250) 994 - 3489 www.whitecapinn.com

Best Western Tower Inn

Located in the heart of the town of Quesnel, the Best Western Tower Inn is committed to providing travellers a home away from home. Every comfort is provided for and every amenity is available. There is high-speed Internet access in every guestroom, a full-service business center, a fully equipped exercise room, and all areas of the Inn are accessible to people of all physical abilities. With superb customer service and the highest standards of housekeeping, you will feel very well cared for. The Inn's restaurant, Begbie's Bar & Bistro, named for the famous Judge Begbie of Gold Rush days, is a favorite of Quesnel locals. There is a full menu of fine dining, including long-time favorites and innovative new preparations. The restaurant recalls historic Barkerville, a must-see during your stay. Close at hand is the beautiful riverfront walking trail and the Inn is within walking distance of the casino, theatres, parks, sports and recreation venues and an international array of restaurants. When visiting Quesnel, the place to stay is Best Western Tower Inn. 500 Reid Street, Quesnel BC (250) 992 - 2201 or (800) 663 - 2009 www.bw.towerinn.ca

49

Attractions

Orca Spirit Adventures

In the mood for adventure? Orca Spirit Adventures is an educational and exciting sightseeing tour for people of all ages. Safety is their number one priority, not only for their passengers, but also for the whales. They use four-stroke Yamaha motors, renowned for quiet performance and ultra low emissions, on their Zodiac boats. They participate in whale watching associations, dedicating themselves to protecting the marine environment. Certified naturalists and biologists narrate every trip. They know the individual whales by number. The high success rate of sightings is due, in part, to the large, fast boat that is necessary to get to the whales quickly. The other factor in their success rate is a sophisticated whale spotting network they initiated and still operate. Every step to exceed government regulations is taken to ensure the quality of your trip and the safety of the whales. When you first enter the gift shop and check-in office, you get the feeling of being under the ocean. Large underwater murals depict very real pictures of Orcas and other marine life. There is also an educational room with maps, wildlife books and an introductory video to watch before each trip. For the most rewarding whale watching experience you can find, Orca Spirit Adventures is sure to satisfy. 146 Kingston Street, Victoria BC (250) 383 - 8411 or (888) 672 - ORCA (6722) www.orcaspirit.com

Romper Room Indoor Climbing Center

Looking for something different and fun the whole family can have a blast doing together? Perhaps something just for you, to burn off some stress and help get you in shape? Look no further than Romper Room Indoor Climbing Center. Even if the nature channel is the closest you've ever come to the great outdoors, there is a rock in there with your name on it! There are special climbing groups for kids, teens and adults to join, and the instructors are awesome professionals who want everyone to enjoy the thrill of rock climbing, no matter what your skill level is when you walk in the door. It's a fun way to work out, make new friends and learn something new about yourself. It's also a great place to throw a party.

Your kids will love inviting their friends for a birthday party that is definitely not the same old thing. With over 7,000 feet of climbing surface and patient, enthusiastic instructors, you have to finally give rock climbing a try! Give Romper Room Indoor Climbing Center a call for information on specials, memberships and individual lessons. You'll be happy you did. 4385-B Boban Drive, Nanaimo BC (250) 751 - ROCK (7625) www.climbromperroom.com

Jamie's Whaling Station & Adventure Centres

Land, sea and sky! Jamie's Whaling Station offers a wide variety of marine, land and air tours from its stations in Tofino and Ucluelet. It is the oldest and largest whale watching tour company in British Columbia. With a fleet of seven boats, Jamie's Whaling Station carried over 30,000 whale watching enthusiasts on tours last year. Jamie's Marine Manager Bruce Adams says the 65-foot Leviathan II and the 65-foot Lady Selkirk make whale watching accessible to seniors and small children and helps account for the popularity of Jamie's. They also provide whale watching and bear watching on 29-foot Zodiac-style vessels for the adventurous. Hot Springs tours and Hot Springs Sea to Sky, boat up fly back tours are also available. Surfing lessons, kayak tours and rentals, Harbour tours, Meares Island Big Tree Trial transfers and Family Fun Fishing are some of the other tours available through Jamie's. Jamie's also provides scenic air flights in and around Clayoquot Sound, Barkley Sound, Pacific Rim National Park and Bedwell Glacier. If you want to see the area from another perspective, you can try a 4X4 guided land tour. The Tofino-Clayoquot Sound and Ucluelet-Barclay Sound areas have become a Mecca for whale, bear and wildlife watchers from all over the world. Jamie's has a specialty tour to view the thousands of Stellar's and California sea lions that congregate in the Broken Group Islands in the Pacific Rim National Park during August and September. Other wildlife that may be sighted on all tours includes harbour porpoise, black bears, deer, wolf, otter, mink and raccoons. There are over 450 species of birds passing through the Pacific Rim area, and the tours are a bird watcher's delight. Bring warm clothing and don't forget your camera and your binoculars. There's something for everyone at Jamie's Whaling Station! 606 Campbell Street, Tofino BC (250) 725 - 3919 or (800) 667 - 9913 www.jamies.com

Long Beach Golf Course

Keith Gibson, Director of golf at Long Beach Golf Course, invites you to play a round at one of the most challenging courses in Canada. Located in the Clayoquot Biosphere Reserve in part of the Pacific Rim National Park, the course formerly had a reputation for being more punishing than challenging because of thick overgrowth in the landing areas. When Keith took over, he instituted a first-grade maintenance program to clear out the bush, and the golfers who come to play in the annual Long Beach Amateur event are unanimous in their praise for the success of his efforts. Though the brush is not the hazard it once was, Long Beach is by no means a wholly domesticated course; when you play there, you may get to say "hello" to Earl, the local bear. If you enjoy camping, the course also offers 58 campsites available for summer fun. If you'd rather not cook your own meals while camping out, stop by the course's lounge restaurant. Capable of accommodating up to 130 people, the restaurant can also serve as a very enjoyable center for a golf retreat, corporate conference or family event.

1850 Pacific Rim Highway, Tofino BC (250) 725 - 3332 www.longbeachgolfcourse.com

Bungy Zone Adrenaline Centre

Regarded as one of the most beautiful bungy-jumping sites in the world, the Bungy Zone Adrenaline Centre has been challenging thrill-seekers since 1990. You might decide to simply enjoy the fourteen acres of manicured grounds and the natural beauty of the Nanaimo River, cook a hotdog at the barbecue pit, join in a sedate game of volleyball or you can take a flying leap off the 143-foot Saunders Bridge. It was North America's first legal bungy bridge, built specifically for the sport. But that's not the only rush in store, there's also a 140-mile per hour Ultimate Swing considered one of the most terrifying rides on the continent and the Flying Fox, a zip line traversing a 600-foot deep arc along the canyon. You can go on your own if you wish, or plan ahead for corporate or other private parties. There are dining, lodging, skydiving and camping facilities nearby. For an experience you will not soon forget, Bungy Zone Adrenaline Centre is where it's at!

Nanaimo BC (250) 753 - JUMP (5867) www.bungyzone.com

Surf Sisters Surf School

Can it get any better than this? That's what surfing students say about Surf Sister Surf School. Canada's only all-women surf school began in Tofino in 1999. Founded by Jenny Stewart, longtime Tofino surfer and Canadian women's surfing champion, the school is dedicated to promoting women's surfing in Tofino and worldwide. Their goal is not to exclude men from their lessons, but rather to make sure that women feel included when trying to surf in Tofino for the first time. Surf Sister introduces women and men of all ages and abilities to the sport of surfing in a safe, fun and supportive environment. The instructors are friendly, down to earth and fun. All Surf Sister instructors meet the requirements for safety and training as set out by the British Columbia Association of Surf Instructors and hold certificates for Standard First Aid, CPR and Lifesaving. Safety is a priority. No surfing experience is required, but

all students should be able to swim and feel comfortable in the water.

You can choose from the many lesson structures and programs they offer. Classes are held on the fabulous beaches near Tofino. These beaches are some of the most spectacular and pristine in the world. They are surrounded by a majestic temperate rainforest, the perfect backdrop for your surfing lessons. 625 Campbell Street, Tofino BC (250) 725 - 4456 or (877) 724 - 7873 www.surfsister.com

Great Pacific Adventures

Andrew Skinner knows something about marine adventures, having spent 22 years as a marine tour operator before owning Great Pacific Adventures, but he's not blasé. He knows the ocean is anything but predictable. With partner Rod King, Andrew offers a fascinating variety of opportunities to experience the wonders of the North Pacific and its astonishing inhabitants, such as the mighty orcas. Whale watching excursions are perennially popular, and Great Pacific's are excellent, with operators who are certified marine biologists and naturalists. The excursions follow the established guidelines for Responsible Whale Watching, bringing people into contact with whales in a safe, non-exploitative manner. In addition to orcas, Great Pacific offers excursions to view the other wildlife around

Vancouver Island such as seals, sea lions, porpoises and bald eagles. Travel in comfort on the M.V. King Salmon, a 45-foot cruiser, or on one of the open aluminum-hulled Zodiacs for an unforgettable outdoor experience. Each Zodiac passenger is outfitted with a full-length cruiser suit. Great Pacific also offers you the opportunity to create your own adventure by renting a kayak, canoe or powerboat. If you'd rather not leave dry land, you can rent hiking equipment or bicycles. No matter how you choose to experience the wonders of nature in coastal British Columbia, Great Pacific Adventures will see that you have the adventure of a lifetime. 450 Swift Street, Victoria BC (250) 386 - 2277 or (877) SEE - ORCA (733 - 6722) www.greatpacificadventures.com

Tofino Bus

Tofino's proximity to unspoiled wilderness largely accounts for its increasing popularity as a destination for travelers, but that same proximity has created a problem for people seeking easy transportation to this remote community. Dylan Green, the owner and operator of Tofino Bus, saw that problem as an opportunity. Since 2002, he has been providing a solution. With daily express service from Vancouver, Victoria and Nanaimo, running comfortable coaches at reasonable fares, Tofino Bus has enjoyed enough success to add three new buses in 2005. It has expanded its schedule to include sightseeing tours to view such nearby wonders as the ancient old-growth forest of Cathedral Grove. Even on the regular runs the drivers will be happy to provide interpretive commentary as you pass by raging rivers and majestic mountains, so feel free to ask. Tofino Bus is also committed to maintaining an environmentally sensitive presence on Vancouver Island. Its buses are currently fueled by a 25% mixture of biodiesel fuel derived from vegetable oil. Dylan's ultimate goal is to run the buses on 100% biodiesel fuel, recycling the cooking oil from Tofino's many restaurants.

564 Campbell Street, Tofino BC (250) 725 - 2871 or (866) 986 - 3466 www.tofinobus.com

Cowichan Bay Maritime Centre

As you stroll along the 350 foot 107 meter pier of the Cowichan Bay Maritime Centre, breathe in the rich salty air and imagine yourself in days past when the docks were teeming with the activity of ships and boats coming and going. A time when seafaring vessels were the livelihood of Cowichan Bay. Scavenger hunts and toy boat building will keep children entertained as you view the maritime culture displayed in the four unique buildings built along the pier. The Centre is run by the Cowichan Wooden Boat Society, a non-profit organization

dedicated to the preservation of maritime history. The Society is open to new membership, and is always seeking new cronies to come on down and join in the fun. There are always restoration projects in the works to check out in the boatbuilding shop, and traditional wooden boatbuilding courses are offered. Every summer the Centre is host to the Cowichan Bay Boat Festival, highlighting the Fast and Furious Boatbuilding Competition. This rollicking celebration has grown over the years to include various exhibits, games, silent auction, mural painting competition and the Best Chowder in the Bay competition between local restaurateurs. Other events throughout the summer include a Kids' Bullhead Fishing Derby and a sailing regatta. The Centre also hosts the Cowichan Valley Dragon Divas dragon boat team. These tenacious breast cancer survivors can often be seen training for racing season in the Bay. As the Cowichan Bay Maritime Centre's motto says, "Come by road or sea!" You will certainly be glad you accepted that invitation. 1761 Cowichan Bay Road, Cowichan Bay BC (250) 746 - 4955 www.classicboats.org

Craigdarroch Castle

Built in 1889, Craigdarroch Castle was the dream estate of Robert Dunsmuir, a Scotsman born into a family of coal masters. He immigrated to Vancouver Island in 1851 and eventually discovered a mother lode of coal near Nanaimo. He was a tenacious and canny businessman whose operations made him the richest man in western Canada. Dunsmuir died before the completion of Craigdarroch, which is sited on a hill overlooking Victoria. His wife resided in the Castle until her death in 1908. It served as a military hospital, a college, and later a music conservatory before it was ultimately placed in the hands of the Craigdarroch Castle Historical Museum Society. Now designated a National Historic Site, the Castle is visited annually by over 140,000 people from around the world. It has been carefully restored to its original Victorian opulence, featuring fine and exotic woods, stained and leaded glass and period art and artifacts. The Castle Society is a vibrant and evolving organization that encourages interesting uses for the Castle. For example, January brings a celebration of poet Robert Burns and in December there are magical Victorian Christmas festivities. A highlight of the Castle's periodic evening events is "innovative environmental theatre" during which the audience moves from scene to scene staged throughout the Castle. Visitors love exploring the scores of rooms and the tower with its stunning views. This may not have been part of Robert Dunsmuir's dream, but he would surely be delighted by his legacy. 1050 Joan Crescent, Victoria BC (250) 592 - 5323 www.craigdarrochcastle.com www.thecastle.ca

The Whale Centre

Whale watching is one of the most popular vacation options for visitors to Vancouver Island. And John Forde's Whale Centre in Tofino offers the most comprehensive tours you can find there. A seasoned veteran with over 18 years experience and a professional photographer as well, John provides the only tours that include a photo shoot of the trip for you to take home. The Whale Centre has recently acquired a new 30-foot covered aluminum craft that provides considerable comfort for up to 13 passengers on the cruises through Clayoquot Sound. More adventurous travelers can ride in the 28-foot open Boston Whaler. During the two-and-a-half-hour tour, you'll visit the whales' feeding grounds. During the early spring, the world population of Pacific Grey whales, estimated at some 19,000, migrates northward along the west coast of Vancouver Island. Then in September, the whales return to their calving grounds off Baja California. Other whales you may see include humpbacks and orcas. These waters are also home to sea lions, porpoises, sea otters and other wildlife. In addition to whale watching tours, The Whale Centre can offer you bear watching and bird watching excursions, and even surfing lessons. The Centre itself also houses a

free museum of exhibits donated by Tofino locals over the past 25 years, including a complete 40-foot gray whale skeleton.
411 Campbell Street, Tofino BC (250) 725 - 2132 or (888) 474 - 2288
www.tofinowhalecentre.com

Sea Trek Tours & Expeditions

Whales, sea lions, seals, eagles and more! Who knows what you may see? Every trip is a new adventure. Sea Trek is a marine wildlife tour company offering educational and recreational ocean adventures for all ages. All of Sea Trek's guides are professional mariners and are happy to share their knowledge with you. Just a few minutes north of the Pacific Rim National Park, Sea Trek is located in Tofino on the western coast of Vancouver Island. This area also contains the reserve of the Tla-o-qui-aht First Nations, who began cultural tours offering the Aboriginal perspectives about whale watching. They network with other First Nations companies in a desire to share the Aboriginal knowledge and history of the area, as well as their views concerning the environment and information behind phenomena such as the social structures of clam beds and fish runs. Their stories relate to the original whale watching. Cruise the sheltered inlet of Clayoquot Sound at low tide and you may see black bears foraging for food on the beaches. Although sightings are not guaranteed, their success rate is very high. Experience Hot Springs Cove in Maquinna Provincial Park. Glide through the waters in Sea Trek's glass bottom boat to Meares Island and witness the largest known living red cedar, the hanging garden tree. Tours operate in the calm sea seasons from April to October.

455 Campbell Street, Tofino BC
(250) 725 - 4412 or (800) 811 - 9155
www.seatrektours.bc.ca

Duncan Meadows Golf Course

Working with his father Frank on Meadow Gardens Golf Course in Pitt Meadows, Ming Hui learned what makes a golf course great. When Frank sold Meadow Gardens, Ming was hired to oversee a refurbishment and redesign of the course, which he completed with great skill. The result was a course that's now one of the top public courses in the Lower Mainland. But sadly for Ming, it no longer felt like the course he had grown up on. He decided it was time to leave the past

behind and discover his own course, which he found in Duncan, a little town in the Cowichan Valley on Vancouver Island. When Ming and his wife Grace took over the Duncan Lakes course in 1996, they found a diamond in the rough, a well-designed course in a beautiful setting in the shadow of Mount Prevost. But it was a course that had fallen into disrepair. With the help of Dave Brummitt, who had been Ming's course superintendent at Meadow Gardens, the Huis revived the course and renamed it Duncan Meadows. It's now thriving under their care, attracting both professional and amateur golfers excited by the unusual challenges awaiting them at this full 18-hole, par 72 facility. In 2004, Duncan Meadows turned a corner in its history when it hosted a Royal Canadian Golf Association Championship series, bringing it national attention. With its newly completed clubhouse, Duncan Meadows Golf Course looks forward to a bright future. 6507 North Road, Duncan BC (250) 746 - 8993 www.duncanmeadows.com

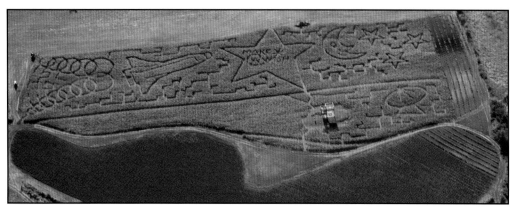

McNab's Corn Maze

Saving the family farm through diversification and public education, are words to live by for Murray McNab and his family. They have been farming sweet corn since 1960 and change has been the one thing they could count on. So, in 2002, they did some changing for themselves. The result is a spectacular seven-acre maze of corn that's twelve feet high! Its design changes each year and has portrayed alien signs, a detailed farm scene, and a massive Mayan composition, complete with the Aztec sun. From the top of the viewing platform, you can appreciate the whole of the design, as well as the farm and the surrounding countryside. But down in the maze you might just as well plan on getting lost, especially spooky if you're there at night. Adding to the fun, there are seasonal hay rides to the giant pumpkin patch where you can buy a pumpkin of your own. A favorite event is the Halloween bonfire with hot dogs and marshmallows for roasting over the flames. Groups are welcome and the McNabs even host a 4-H day. There are barbecues, fire pits and picnic tables on the grounds. It is such a great place for parties, birthdays or any special occasion. Don't forget that this is not a fun park, it's a farm! Visit Mareena's market at the maze and pick up the freshest produce you can find anywhere, as well as honey, crafts, refreshments and more. The McNabs invite you to join them for family fun in the country. 4613 Yellowpoint Road, Ladysmith BC (250) 245 - 0666 www.mcnabscornmaze.com

Hatley Park National Historic Site of Canada

On the ocean, amidst the forest, by the castle, in the gardens, Hatley Park is one of the most beautiful and unusual properties in Canada! Sweeping down to the Pacific Ocean, this stunning Edwardian Estate is criss-crossed by walking, cycling and hiking trails and is home to peacocks, deer and other wildlife. It is located in Victoria, the capital city of British Columbia, just 20 minutes from the heart of downtown. The 1908 Hatley Castle sits prominently in the centre of the estate, adjacent to the Italian, Japanese and rose gardens. More than 15 kilometers of trails welcome guests to experience nature, explore our preserved forests and enjoy the spectacular vistas that over look the Esquimalt Lagoon and the Strait of Juan de Fuca which stretches across to the majestic Olympic Mountains in the U.S. state of Washington. This 565-acre property is truly a unique example of Canada's natural and cultural heritage and was designated a National Historic site in 1999. The Honourable James Dunsmuir,

premier of British Columbia, built Hatley Castle as a retirement home in 1908. From 1940 to 1995, the property was the home of Canada's Royal Roads Military College, a training school for military officers. Since 1995, the property has taken on a new purpose. It is now home to Royal Roads University, renowned for its educational excellence. It's well known as a special-purpose institution focusing on the educational needs of mid-career professionals. The kaleidoscope of visitor activities are dynamic, engaging and highly personalized, ranging from historical castle tours to soap making, to garden workshops and modern day high tech treasure hunting, more commonly known as geocaching. This is truly a historical site with many fascinating stories to tell!
2005 Sooke Road, Victoria BC
(250) 391 - 2666 or (866) 241 - 0674
www.hatleypark.ca

Capilano Suspension Bridge

In the late 1800s, George Mackay built a hemp-rope and cedar-plank suspension bridge to his cabin. The cabin was built on the edge of a canyon wall. Dubbed Capilano Tramps, by friends of Mackay, the bridge has been reincarnated several times. It was first replaced by a wire cable bridge in 1903, then reinforced by additional cables, and was finally rebuilt with concrete encasings in 1956. The bridge sways hypnotically 230 feet above the Capilano River. Reaching the other side requires crossing 450 feet over the scattered mist below. It is an unforgettable experience of immeasurable splendor. The bridge and park are hedged by a 300-year-old cedar-scented rain forest, imbuing the site with a magical air. The bridge is surrounded by a host of other attractions. Enter into Totem Park to enjoy the colorful sight of authentic totem poles and life-sized Depression era cedar statues. Shop at the trading post gift store, filled with regional treasures such as spirit masks, Inuit soapstone, clothing and collectibles. The interactive living forest display, picturesque trout ponds, and free history and nature tours give guests a beautiful glimpse into the natural world. First Nations artists demonstrate their heritage of carving skills in the Big House Native Carving Centre. The Canyon Café, Loggers Grill, and Bridge House Restaurant provide diverse refreshments to renew your body and spirit. Capilano Suspension Bridge is open every day except Christmas. Seeing it is an experience you will never forget.
3735 Capilano Road, North Vancouver BC (604) 985 - 7474 www.capbridge.com

Grouse Mountain

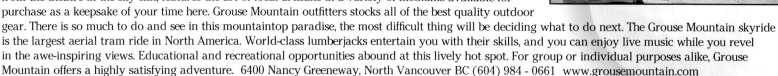

The North Shore Range has always drawn curious climbers from Vancouver. One of its most unusual characteristics is that it is situated in an east to west orientation instead of north to south. On the summit known as Grouse Mountain, a four-season resort by the same name makes ascending this mountain more than just a journey to the top. All the best of British Columbia is represented in this incredible destination. View the stone and timber architecture up close and the city and ocean from afar. Grouse Mountain has outdoor mountaintop ice-skating, snowboarding and skiing, with top-notch instruction provided for its extreme snow sports. Dining options range from casual to elegant. The spirit gallery gift shop, accessible from the theatre in the sky exit, features the art of local artisans in a variety of mediums available for purchase as a keepsake of your time here. Grouse Mountain outfitters stocks all of the best quality outdoor gear. There is so much to do and see in this mountaintop paradise, the most difficult thing will be deciding what to do next. The Grouse Mountain skyride is the largest aerial tram ride in North America. World-class lumberjacks entertain you with their skills, and you can enjoy live music while you revel in the awe-inspiring views. Educational and recreational opportunities abound at this lively hot spot. For group or individual purposes alike, Grouse Mountain offers a highly satisfying adventure. 6400 Nancy Greeneway, North Vancouver BC (604) 984 - 0661 www.grousemountain.com

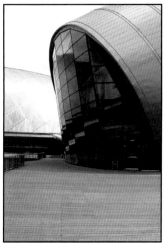

CN IMAX Theatre

The Image Maximum (IMAX) system was first viewed in 1970 at an Expo in Japan. The impressive system was developed by a trio of Canadians. Graeme Ferguson, Roman Kroitor, and Robert Kerr had been working on a multi-projector large screen system, but the difficulties encountered with that process led them to develop IMAX. A system capable of producing huge, high-resolution images. Because the viewer's field of vision is filled with the images produced, it is an immersion event that can create physical sensations of movement in the viewer. It's a "you are there" feeling of virtual reality. Some viewers actually experience motion sickness! The CN IMAX Theatre is located at Canada Place, an exciting venue built on the Burrard Inlet waterfront. Canada Place is a Vancouver landmark that's instantly recognizable for the building's striking white sails. The theatre is the first IMAX 3D theatre in the world. It was originally built for Expo '86, with a 440-person capacity. Once inside the theatre, patrons experience a profoundly powerful visual and auditory adventure. The screen is five stories tall, and the six-channel wraparound digital sound adds to the realism. Most movies are about 45 minutes in length. The stories onscreen become moving poetry, as they create an extraordinary encounter between the senses and film art. Step into the CN IMAX theatre and enter a realm of suspension and disbelief.
201-999 Canada Place, Vancouver BC (604) 682 - IMAX or (800) 582 - 4629 www.imax.com

Royal City Star Riverboat Casino

Roulette, baccarat, blackjack or slots, whatever your game of choice, Lady Luck is sure to be at your side as you board the Royal City Star Riverboat Casino. With all the beauty and charm of her authentic riverboat ancestors, she is thoroughly modern in her amenities and excitement. Your most difficult decision will be where to try your luck first! But take time to treat yourself to a superbly prepared meal at Fraser's Restaurant, or try The Sand Bar or Café Royale Bar and Deli when it's time to take a break from the action. There is always something fun happening, so call or check the event calendar on their website for upcoming happenings, such as comedy revues, outstanding musical performers and special holiday extravaganzas. For a night to remember, be sure to ask about booking the Showboat Lounge or the Poker Room for your next party or banquet. As they say, "Odds are you'll have a great time!" 788 Quayside Drive, New Westminster BC
(604) 519 - 3660
www.royalcitystar.bc.ca

63

Science World

Long before procuring the Expo Centre building, the seed that would grow into Science World was already a success. Under the tutelage of Barbara Brink, the Junior League of Greater Vancouver and the City of Vancouver, the temporary Arts, Sciences & Technology centre managed to deliver outreach programs to 400,000 recipients and exhibit hands-on displays to ever-burgeoning crowds. After acquiring the Expo in 1987, a massive campaign rallied enough support to refurbish the building with five new hands-on gallery exhibits and the largest OMNIMAX screen ever seen. Progressive creativity has thrust this centre into the limelight more than once. Alcan Inc. and Science World partnered to produce several notable OMNIMAX films. One of these, The Living Sea, was nominated for an Academy Award. Science World has hosted renowned individuals such as Her Majesty Queen Elizabeth II, Former Soviet Union President Mikhail Gorbechev, and physicist Dr. Stephen Hawking. In recent years, Science World has continued to expand and progress with the times. Continually updating the galleries and developing traveling exhibitions has kept the centre fresh, and contributed to the enhancement of all science-

Photo by: Emanuel Lobeck

oriented exhibition facilities. Wonder at the marvels of the human body in the new BodyWorks Gallery. Exhibits such as this one embody the purpose of this non-profit organization, fostering understanding and knowledge of the world and everything in it. Bring the family or just yourself, and become immersed in the newly enlightened modern world of science.

1455 Quebec Street, Vancouver BC (604) 443 - 7443
www.scienceworld.bc.ca

The Vancouver Aquarium

The non-profit Vancouver Aquarium Marine Science Centre has become the largest aquarium in Canada, as well as one of the top five world-wide. This adaptable, cutting-edge facility employs over 280 people and hundreds of volunteers, all dedicated to the vision of display, education, research and responsible action. In 1997, the Vancouver Aquarium Conservation Foundation was formed to manage funds for the centre's far-reaching programs. The Vancouver Aquarium serves as a window into an exotic underwater world of color and grace. Intriguing displays encourage interaction with our planet's water dwellers. The aquarium is internationally recognized for an effective Marine Mammal Rescue and Rehabilitation Program. Recognition of their excellence has resulted in accreditation by the Canadian Association of Zoos and Aquariums and the American Zoo and Aquarium Association. The Canadian Federal Government named the enterprise Canada's Pacific National Aquarium. Recently, two Pacific white-sided dolphins rehabilitated in Japan joined the aquarium. The dolphins had sustained injuries in an accidental fishing net mishap, rendering them unable to be safely released to the open ocean. Happily, they will make ideal companions for an 18-year-old resident male dolphin of the aquarium. In addition to the commendable work done by this organization, it is also a fun place to go. After a show, stop at the UpStream Café for refreshments. Wrap up your adventure with a visit to the ClamShell Gift shop, full of keepsakes and original gift ideas. Stanley Park, Vancouver BC (604) 685 - 3364
www.vanaqua.org

Photo by: Martin Baldwin

Queen Elizabeth Park & Bloedel Conservatory

On the top at the highest point of the city of Vancouver, the Queen Elizabeth Park sits like a jewel on the crown. Dazzling visitors with spectacular 360-degree views of Vancouver, the park is also host to a variety of intriguing activities and points of interest. The land has been completely transformed from its early days as a stone quarry into a marvel of gardens and fun features. Tree lovers will be thrilled to wander through an arboretum with nearly all of Canada's native trees, as well as exotic selections from other countries. The North Quarry Garden, developed in 1961, is a dry garden with oriental influences. Beautiful sculptures grace the park, providing another magnificent facet of representation of the three-dimensional arts. On the southern section, pitch & putt golf, tennis, roller court, basketball court areas and Frisbee golf are readily available for lively groups. A small rose garden of experimental rose plantings is located on the southwestern perimeter. Over 100 species of birds fly about freely within the triodetic dome of the Bloedel Floral Conservatory. The display of flowers, plants, koi fish, and colorful birds within the dome make this a dazzling backdrop for the many weddings which take place in this climate-controlled environment. For a burst of regenerating energy take a break at the Seasons Hill Top Bistro. For unparalleled views and fun take a trip to this royal park! Cambie and 33rd Street, Vancouver BC (604) 257 - 8584 www.city.vancouver.bc.ca/parks/parks/queenelizabeth/index.htm

Photo by: Brad Dosland

Pier's End Adventure Centre Ltd.

Whale sightings are guaranteed or your next trip is free! Owners Jamie and Jock Bray are among the pioneers in the field of whale watching with over 25 years of adventure tour experience. Their staff is marine safety certified and bring nautical experience you can count on, all with a smile. Pier's End Adventure Centre Ltd., is strategically located at the closest launch point to the South Gulf/Puget Sound Orca (Killer Whales) viewing grounds, White Rock, just minutes from the "Peace Arch" border crossing into Washington State, a quick 40-minute drive south from Vancouver. The Centre's 47-foot Coast Guard certified Phantom Hawk IV will take you from the pier in White Rock for an unforgettable whale watching experience. Relax in the heated cabin with wraparound windows or enjoy the outdoor viewing deck and the vistas of a coastal landscape that is second to none. During your journey you will be entertained by their fun and educational commentary. The Centre also operates the Saturna Island and Gulf Islands National Park Reserve Shuttle. Their convenient morning and evening departures allow for exciting day trips that will suit the whole family. Kayaking is available on the island. Bring your bikes and your packs. It's island hopping made easy.

1160 King George Highway, White Rock BC

(604) 535 - 5455 or (888) 535 - 5455 www.piersendadventures.com

Fort Langley Historic Site

The Hudson's Bay Company is the oldest chartered trading company in the world. In 1670, the company began a history that would span three centuries. Built in 1827, Fort Langley was one of the Hudson's Bay Company's trading posts in Western Canada. The Fort traded in fur, fish and cranberries, served as an import-export centre, and developed the first all-Canadian route from the coast to the regions west of the Rockies. The Fort was named in honor of a company director, Thomas Langley. At Fort Langley the company men married native women and brought their families to live at the fort, creating a truly multi-cultural living experience. Fort Langley went through several stages of use, from fur-collecting to provisioning, to an industry of salmon salting and packing. Langley farm once covered 800 hectares and supplied a variety of agricultural meat and produce. In 1858, Fort Langley became the starting point for the Fraser River gold fields, bringing it world fame. Later that year, the British Parliament revoked the Company's monopoly, signaling Langley's decline. In 1923, it was declared historically important and it became a National Historic Park in 1955. Fort Langley is now the site of interpretive history performances by costumed narrators and it is also the location for many special events. One original building remains on the site, along with several reconstructed buildings. Experience the wonder of Fort Langley's history first hand.

23433 Mavis Avenue, Fort Langley BC (604) 513 - 4777 www.pc.gc.ca

Whistler Alpine Guides Bureau

Providing top notch mountain guiding and instruction since 1992, Whistler Alpine Guides Bureau is a family-owned and operated guiding company. Directed by Rob McCurdy, Whistler Alpine Guides Bureau's mission is, To provide our guests with an awesome outdoor experience, to support them in overcoming challenges and to educate them with the knowledge and skills necessary to play in a mountain environment. They and their team of highly qualified and knowledgeable career guides offer a full complement of programs suitable for all ages and abilities. Daily excursions are offered year round. Summer activities include glacier hikes, trail hikes, rock climbing, mountaineering and via ferrata, a one-of-a-kind engineered vertical pathway with cables and ladder rungs to the top of Whistler Mountain. Once at the top, be sure to feel the adrenaline rush of face forward rappelling down a 140-foot sheer rock face on the new, unique tour called rap jumping. Winter activities include backcountry skiing, snowboarding and ice climbing. For those inclined to take up rock climbing, ice climbing, mountaineering, backcountry skiing or snowboarding as a more serious pastime, formal courses and clinics are offered. Whistler Alpine Guides Bureau also leads extended trips far from the beaten path in British Columbia and in South America. For real adventure in Whistler and other beautiful parts of the world, call on Whistler Alpine Guides Bureau.

113 – 4350 Lorimer Road, Whistler BC (604) 938 - WAGB (9242) www.whistlerguides.com

Bowlertime and Chilli's Bar & Grill

Bowlertime and Chilli's Bar & Grill are a match made in heaven. Good food and good fun are at your fingertips. Bowlertime offers, you guessed it, bowling! But that's just for starters. There are also video games, pool tables, pinball games, and keno.

There are regular bowling leagues and leagues for the physically or developmentally challenged, as well as the Bowlertime Birthday Club for twelve and unders. Chilli's Bar & Grill cooks up authentic Mexican meals, the best quesadillas in town, homemade Chilli Chips, chicken strips and a nice range of pub fare. They can cater your private meeting on the premises or cater out your event for up to 100 people. In Kamloops, Bowlertime and Chilli's Bar & Grill is "party central" for Christmas parties, birthday parties, teen parties, company parties and there is public bowling every day and night. One thing is certain, when you come to Bowlertime you'll enjoy great food and a fun time, guaranteed.

1200 8th Street, Kamloops BC (250) 554 - 1610

McArthur Island Golf & Gift Shop

Doug Sinclair, co-owner of McArthur Island Golf & Gift Shop, is a member of the Canadian Pro Golfers Association with 30 years' experience. Since some of his students have been members of Canadian and U.S. Pro Golf tours, it's safe to say Doug knows golf better than most. That's what makes his shop an exceptional place to go when you're looking for outstanding golf clubs and equipment, apparel and accessories. The shop is part of the McArthur Island Golf Plex that also includes a restaurant, a 40-stall driving range, a miniature golf course and nine-hole executive course. Gift items range from beautiful jewellery and First Nations crafts to original works and prints by local artists such as Georgia Lesley, whose works have been acquired by fine art collectors from around the world. Co-owner Diane Kupo oversees that aspect of the business. Together Diane and Doug have created an outstanding shop that offers something for everyone from golf pro to non-golfing art lover. You will find it all at McArthur Island Golf & Gift Shop.

846 Caroline Street, Kamloops BC (250) 554 - 3575

Mount Paul Golf Course & Driving Range

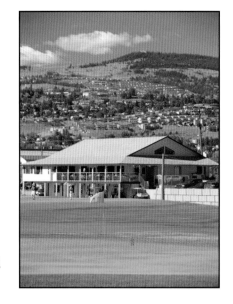

All golfers can appreciate Mount Paul Golf Course & Driving Range. The beautiful surroundings and gently rolling grounds afford several kinds of challenge appropriate for all skill levels. This is a nine-hole course, designed to provide the casual golfer an enjoyable round. The fully stocked shop has everything you will need to play, carts are available, and CPGA professionals are on staff for lessons and pointers. The driving range is a superior practice facility. 18 of the 20 stalls are under cover and each is appropriate for left or right-handed golfers. The restaurant is open daily serving breakfast, homemade soups, salads, sandwiches and burgers. It is also a popular banquet facility offering extraordinary dining, gracious service, a full bar and dance floor. All course facilities are available for your special occasion. Mount Paul has a friendly and welcoming staff who always do their best to help you enjoy your visit. 615 Mount Paul Way, Kamloops BC
Pro Shop: (250) 374 - 4653   Restaurant: (250) 374 - 4672 www.mountpaulgolf.com

Hell's Gate Airtram

Hell's Gate is an awesome display of nature's power. Millions of gallons of rushing Fraser River water forcefully push through the gorge on a determined journey to the Pacific Ocean. The River's namesake, Simon Fraser was the first European to explore this region. He crossed through Hell's gate on his hands and knees, holding tight to a bark ladder made by the aboriginals. The year was 1808, and Fraser's quote is well-known; " surely we have encountered the gates of Hell." and many who came after must have agreed. The narrow, deep water and a rockslide caused by the expansion of the railroad through the area has caused crisis to traveling salmon, but eight fishways have eased the situation. The gorge was once successfully navigated by a blind cow that had been chased into the water by some frisky dogs. The cow, Rosebank Rosie had been blinded by chewing on a battery and was mother to a calf when she went for the ride of her life through Hell's Gate. Miraculously, Rosie survived and went home, no doubt a little changed by her incredible journey. As for human travel through the gate, now it can be done in magnificent style in one of two 25-passenger gondolas on the Hell's Gate Airtram. From a vantage point high above the turbulence, the gorge can be viewed in all its glory. Surely Rosie would have appreciated the gentle ride.
43111 Trans Canada Highway, Boston Bar BC (604) 867 - 9277 www.hellsgateairtram.com

Ropes End Climbing Gym

Learn to climb with your friends! At Ropes End Climbing Gym you will find a whole menu of climbing adventures, from birthday parties and other kinds of get-togethers to serious training classes. This is an indoor climbing facility that has all the safety equipment and training you will need to have a wonderful time learning a new skill or developing one you already have. This activity is for everyone. Any age is welcome, you don't have to be an athlete either. There are special events and a summer climbing camp for kids. Ropes End Climbing Gym's mission is to provide a supportive and entertaining environment for people to experience the thrill of mountain climbing. It's also a place where the whole family can have fun together. You can get a day pass, a bouldering pass, become a member by the year or for a few months, by yourself or with your whole family. Or you can just come in for a really unforgettable party. Ropes End Climbing Gym even has real rock climbing and outdoor programs, but remember reservations for those activities are definitely necessary.
954 B Laval Cresent, Kamloops BC (250) 372 - 0645 www.ropesendgym.com

Predator Ridge Golf Resort

Calling all golfers, living in paradise is now an option. Tucked away between the Okanagan and Kalamalka Lakes in Western British Columbia you will find Predator Ridge Golf Resort, a community unlike any other. This award winning golf resort offers two accommodations and four dining choices. Guests can stay at the lodge and spa, located in the centre of the village overlooking the Osprey and Peregrine courses, or in private cottages. Both provide kitchens, lovely spacious rooms, guest robes and down comforters. All have the additional benefits of three pools and hot tubs. Dining choices include the Predator Ridge Clubhouse, featuring the Vista Terrace, The Gallery Dining Room and The Sand Trap Sports Lounge, or you can create your own gourmet meal from the cottage barbeque menu. For those who wish to turn a Predator Ridge vacation into a permanent lifestyle, elegantly-designed, master-planned neighborhood homes are available. Residents enjoy all of the same luxury amenities as resort guests but never have to unpack again. Owners David and Herb Patterson know man cannot live on golf and fine dining alone, so they have built a system of hiking trails that allow guests and residents alike a chance to explore all 1,200 beautiful acres that make up Predator Ridge. Over 60 wineries dot the Okanagan landscape offering a kaleidoscope of vintages to sip and miles of arbors to explore. For those who prefer the nightlife, both Vernon and Kelowna have performing arts centers. Predator Ridge, your home or home away from home.

301 Village Centre Place, Vernon BC (250) 542 - 3436 or (888) 578 - 6688 www.predatorridge.com

Nk'Mip Canyon Desert Golf Course

Oliver plays home to a wide selection of recreational opportunities. Among these is the delightful Nk'Mip Canyon Desert Golf Course. This 18-hole championship course is open to the public and includes a driving range, putting and chipping greens, practice area and three practice holes. A brand new clubhouse provides all the amenities for relaxing and socializing before or after the game. The Canyon Restaurant and Bar is open seven days a week during golf season and provides a large inside dining area along with outdoor patios and decks. It offers breakfast, lunch and dinner along with a choice selection of Southern Okanagan wines and mixed drinks from the lounge. It is also a great place to host your own event, family gathering or business meeting. The

restaurant can cater for 20 to 120 people and specializes in custom-designed buffets. The pro shop features a fully-stocked CPGA store along with club fittings, sales and repair, clothing and accessories. You will also find power or pull-carts, as well as club rentals. Golf lessons are available and golfers, from novice to expert, will delight in this stunning par-72 course that is full of surprises. It consists of four courses in one: forward, mid, back and championship tees. Successful play on many holes calls for a discerning eye and a steady hand. Annually, over 2,000 hours of sunshine beams down on the Nk'Mip Canyon, making this course a boon on every golfer who believes a day not spent swinging a club is a day not living up to its potential. 37041 – 71st Street, Oliver BC (250) 498 - 2880 or (800) 656 - 5755 www.inkameepcanyon.com

The Harvest Golf Club

Attention golfers! The Harvest Golf Club course is an impeccable 7,109 yards on nearly 300 acres of Kelwona's southeast hills. Designed by internationally renowned architect Graham Cook, the course has sweeping panoramic views of the Okanagan that rival the beauty of the Napa Valley. General Manager Gilles Dufort successfully oversees all aspects of this excellent club. Harvest Golf Academy practice facility boasts 16,000 square feet of grass tees, target greens, putting and chipping greens and sand bunkers. You can sharpen your game with one-on-one or group instruction with certified CPGA instructors. Video analysis is also available. Always willing to customize a program for you, The Academy specializes in corporate entertainment. No group is too big or too small. 87 beautiful acres of the property are devoted to a working orchard of apple, cherry, pear, apricot and nectarine trees. An additional 10 acres are set aside for wine grapes that are used exclusively by award-winning Calona Wines. Also the recipient of awards are the club's two superb dining rooms, the Harvest Dining Room and the Harvest Grille. Relax and enjoy exquisite cuisine from Executive Chef, Paul Cecconi. Their extensive wine collection features world renowned vintages and a large selection of Okanagan's best. After dinner you can enjoy a stroll by their beautiful waterfall and ponds. In combination with Sun Peaks Resort, The Harvest Golf Club is well on its way to becoming one of Canada's premier destination points. 2725 K.L.O. Road, Kelwona BC (250) 862 - 3103 (800) 257 - 8577   www.harvestgolf.com

Skaha Meadows Golf Course

Skaha Meadows Golf Course in bustling Penticton offers a terrific venue designed for players of all skill levels. The friendly and knowledgeable staff at Skaha Meadows is available to assist you whether you simply want to improve your game or set up a tournament of your own as a corporate outing or family get-together. Skaha Meadows strongly believes in encouraging junior players, as they are the future of golf. Just as importantly they support players of all ages and abilities. The flat and well-groomed landscaping allows for easy walking. Motorized wheelchairs are allowed on the course to insure access for mobility-impaired members. The course currently boasts about 900 members, currently aging from five to 96 years old. The relaxed and comfortable atmosphere is evidenced by the casual dress code and happy smiles. Skaha Meadows offers several weekly events including Ladies' Day on Tuesday mornings and Wednesday evenings, Men's Day Wednesday morning and Thursday night. Juniors' Night on Monday evenings also features snacks and prizes for the participants. This family-friendly and affordable course provides a terrific way to enjoy this noble and rewarding sport.
#113-437 Martin Street, Penticton BC
(250) 492 - 7274

LocoLanding
Adventure Park

Known for its vivid landscapes and an abundance of recreational opportunities, popular British Columbia is a Mecca for outdoor enthusiasts from around the world. Penticton, located in the south Okanagan Valley, offers visitors a wealth of options mixed with inspiring beauty. LocoLanding Adventure Park combines the best of both worlds on its impressive grounds, offering spectacular landscaping and

the ultimate in family fun. At LocoLanding, you will find an exciting 18-hole miniature golf course complete with waterfalls, caves and misting stations. After your game of mini-golf, head out to the crazy Bumperboats equipped with water guns and enjoy bumping and spraying others. To dry off, get the gang together for a game of Aeroball, a combination of volleyball and basketball on a trampoline, or try competing to be the first to make it to the top of the park's 25-foot rock climbing wall. Another awe-inspiring attraction of this park is its award-winning gardens, featuring more than 150 different varieties of plant life. You can also see a vast array of waterfalls and ponds filled with water lilies, and a kaleidoscope of vines, bushes, flowers and buds that will leave you smiling for hours. Lesley and Adolf Steffen, owners of LocoLanding, along with partner Gary Senft, built this incredible park as a tribute to the memory and spirit of their fun-loving son Mike. LocoLanding is considered one of Western Canada's leading attractions and a must-see for garden lovers everywhere. It is open May through October seven days a week and on weekends after Labor Day. Celebrate landscape design and family fun at its finest at LocoLanding Adventure Park.
75 Riverside Drive,
Penticton BC
(250) 770 - 1896
www.locolanding.com

Fairmont Hot Springs

There's no other place quite like Fairmont Hot Springs Resort. The four and a half star resort has one of Canada's largest all-natural, hot mineral spring water pool complexes and is open every season of the year. Fairmont is perfect for families, honeymooners, golf getaways, business conferences, ski trips and fine dining. Guests at the resort golf in summer, ski in winter, relax in the resort's Spa, and swim all year-round. They go horseback riding, hiking, play tennis, beach volleyball, and partake in a host of other activities. Fairmont Hot Springs Resort's RV Park is the highest rated in the Canadian Rockies, with 311 sites offering services ranging from cable television and Internet hookups, through to a playground, central fire pit, laundromat and many others. Located 20 minutes south of Invermere, BC on Highway 93/95, Fairmont Hot Springs Resort is truly a four-season playground.

5225 Fairmont Resort Road,
Fairmont Hot Springs BC
(800) 663 - 4979 www.fairmonthotsprings.com

St Eugene Mission Resort

Just minutes away from the Cranbrook International Airport is a breathtaking place called the St Eugene Mission Resort. For six years this beautiful and luxurious resort has been home to some of British Columbia's most amazing scenery. Starting as a premier golf destination, St Eugene Mission expanded into a casino in 2002, then added a hotel in 2003. With spectacular views of the Rockies and St Mary's River this turn of the century stone building is as welcoming as it is majestic. As one of the top three Best New Canadian Golf Courses designed by Les Furber the focus of St Eugene's Mission is to be a leader in their industry with plans to maintain that status by always offering clientele superior services and great amenities.

7731 Mission Road, Cranbrook BC

(250) 417- 3417

www.steugene.ca

East Kootenay Fly Fishing Adventures/
The Framed Fish Studio

Professional fly-fishing guide Mike Labach and fish artist, Mya DeRyan are a couple that offer their clientele the best of the Kootenays and a unique portrayal of exclusive memories. You will fly-fish for wild West Slope Cutthroat trout while drifting pristine Rocky Mountain rivers. World class dry, fly-fishing for the beginner to the expert, and the adventure doesn't stop at flyfishing. Expand your experience with the unique thrill of river snorkeling where you get to peer into the world of the Cuthroat Trout. Mike also offers scenic river drifts with natural interpretation for families and groups up to 12. A beach picnic is included. For more information about these adventures, visit Mike's website. By combining nature and art, Mya has arranged it so you can take with you more than memories of your adventure. Mya is perhaps the only Gyotaku artist that specializes in fish

rubbings of fresh water sport fish as well as salt water species. She has developed a technique and the discipline to extract even the finest detail from her fish subject. Each of the multiple rubbings pulled from a single fish are as unique as a finger print. Once the ink has cured, Mya then masterfully applies the colorations and surface markings combining technical accuracy with creative license. This enables you to have an original fish rubbing likeness created from a photo of your catch and release prize fish. Mya's rubbings are commissioned and collected internationally and are becoming a new trend in trophy art as well as a decorative alternative to taxidermy You can also purchase one of Mya's original fish rubbings of local sport fish from many regional galleries or view her online gallery on her website. You may visit Mya's studio by appointment if you are in the Kimberley area.

323-8 Ave, Kimberley BC (250) 427 - 4006
(877) We Drift (933 - 7438)
Mike's: www.flyfishingtrout.com
Mya's : www.theframedfish.com

Richbar Nursery Golf & Garden

Barendina Wiersma and Peter Josephy, natives of Holland and Germany, were horticulturalists who emigrated to Canada in 1948. In 1957, they built a small lean-to greenhouse close to their home on a scenic property overlooking the Fraser River near Quesnel. From such modest beginnings Richbar Nursery Golf & Garden has flourished, growing to encompass 120 acres that includes 24,000 square feet of greenhouses, a splendid par-33, nine-hole golf course, and the 24 Carrot Cafe, known as one of the best places to go for great homestyle food. Still owned and operated by the Josephy family, Richbar Nursery Golf & Garden is now a beloved local institution. The family's commitment to quality has earned them awards, most recently the British Columbia Landscape Architects Landscaping Award. Specializing in plants that thrive in the challenging climate of the Cariboo area, the Josephys take pride in the fact that they have been helping to beautify the Cariboo for the past 48 years. Committed to the community, the Josephys are proud sponsors of many local charities. Richbar Nursery Golf & Garden shares the knowledge accumulated by its staff, offering seminars during the spring and summer months that include hands-on training and projects that participants can take home.

3028 Red Bluff Road, Quesnel BC

(250) 747 - 2915 www.richbarnursery.com

Candy, Ice Cream, Coffee & Bakeries

Trafalgars Bistro & Sweet Obsessions

Sweet Obsessions was Stephen Greenham and Lorne Tyczenski's initial venture in the early 1990s. It is a cake shop with made-from-scratch recipes and painstaking preparation that have earned widespread praise. *Vancouver Magazine* lauded it as "upper Kitsilano's best pâtisserie." In 1998, they added Trafalgars Bistro,

expanding to include fine dining as well as fine desserts. The combination showcases Stephen and Lorne's passion for the entire food experience. Modeled after French bistros, Trafalgars features strong Canadian influences as well. Executive Chef Chris Moran, who trained at the George Brown School of Hospitality, uses locally-grown fresh produce to whip up spectacular dishes. The menu is seasonal. The wine list also shows a strong local influence, with superb selections from popular British Columbia wineries such as Burrowing Owl. Naturally,

Trafalgars has an extensive dessert menu thanks to Sweet Obsessions. The restaurant has a loyal following and diners travel from all over the lower mainland for a truly exceptional dining experience. Stephen and Lorne are engaging hosts, happy to come out and share gossip with the many local customers who count Trafalgars among their favorites. They also offer catering, with set menus as well as custom creations for more adventurous gatherings.

2603 West 16th Avenue, Vancouver BC (604) 739 - 0555
www.trafalgars.com

Planet Java

With its comfortable, home-like atmosphere, Planet Java is a popular meeting place for local families and friends. The large patio offers an extraordinary view of the famous Golden Ears Mountains. Indoors, you will find a warm welcome. Long-time employees Lorraine Jensen and Charlie Wang bought Planet Java and, together with a great staff, they continue the tradition of excellent service in pleasant and friendly surroundings. Planet Java features a wonderful selection of coffees from around the world. Their Kenyan House Blend has been a hit with customers for many years. Rich with the smell of coffee, the air is also redolent of fresh-baked muffins, scones and delectable desserts. The Early Riser breakfast is a great way to start your day. An open-faced bagel topped with cream cheese, ham, fluffy eggs, tomato and cheddar, grilled and served with fruit. The various bagel melts are popular lunch items too and an evening mocha pairs beautifully with dessert. Seasoned travelers know the best place to go where the locals go, and in Langley that place is Planet Java. 20999 88th Avenue #205, Langley BC (604) 882 - 0339

Marina's Gelato

Being the entrepreneur behind an extraordinarily successful baking supplies company might be enough for some people, but Paul Ravensbergen and his wife Marina wanted more. Specifically, they wanted to run their own ice cream parlor. In 2002 they opened the first Marina's Gelato shop in Maple Ridge. The same skills that enabled Paul and Marina to create a business in a foreign country, they're natives of Holland, enabled them to make Marina's a hit, and in March 2004 they opened a second shop in Fort Langley. Gelato is ice cream in the Italian style, batch-frozen instead of churned, giving it a richer flavor. Marina's offers a tempting variety of homemade flavors such as chocolate, almond, bubble gum, and mango: 45 flavors in all. Marina's gets the ingredients directly from Italy, and also imports delicious Torrefazione coffee for specialty drinks. Try the European pastry specialties too. Paul grew up in a pastry shop and baking is in his blood. All these delicious treats can be yours at Marina's Gelato.
9180A Glover Road, Fort Langley BC
(604) 881 - 1193
www.marinasgelato.com

Fort Langley Bakery

Shirley and George Garai met while working in the bakery department of a national supermarket chain. They joined their lives and their talents and went into business for themselves. They have been baking from scratch in this same location since 1980. Just walking into their bakery is a meal in itself. The aroma of so many fresh-baked goods is intoxicating. Shirley and George bake a great variety of breads including wheat-free and organic spelt breads. In honor of Fort Langley they created the whole-grain Fort Bread, a delicious favorite of locals and visitors alike. Along with their

many fine pastries, they are known for their genuine ecceles cakes, made with currants, cinnamon sugar, and puff pastry. One of the greatest draws is the more than twenty varieties of cookies. Who can walk out the door without a few? The Garai's have created an all-Canadian bakery with an emphasis on wholesome goodness to satisfy people from all walks of life. They invite you to drop in any time, but remember, you won't leave empty-handed. #6 - 9110 Glover Road, Fort Langley BC (604) 888 - 2668

Petra's Arts Kafe

Petra's Arts Kafé is nothing short of a brilliant idea charmingly realized. It is a cozy and comfortable place to paint ceramics that has also been voted Tsawwassen's best coffee shop for seven consecutive years. Long-time local residents Petra and Bruce Tetreault provide a light and airy, homelike setting for crafting while enjoying a snack. Bruce's fine woodwork, including the pine cabinetry and plank floors, glows in the light from large corner windows and the warmth of the fireplace. On your first visit you may decide to paint a cup or a bowl but the aromas and flavors of goodies baked from scratch, delicious soups, and really good coffee will have you planning an entire service for twelve. This is a wonderful place to meet friends and make new ones. Bring your artistic bent and your appetite to Petra's Arts Kafé.
1200 56th Street,
Tsawwassen BC
(604) 943 - 0409

Steiger's Swiss Pastries & Café

The Swiss are duly honored for their way with pastries. This 25-year-old pastry shop, now owned by Ursula and Max Romann, has long been tempting palates with extraordinarily delicious baked goods and confections. What might you find in their showcase today? Well, how about meringues, tiramisu and raspberry tortes, napoleons, streusel, tarts, cakes, cookies, strudel and pie. Oh, my! Their truffles and candies are made with the finest Swiss chocolate and they make breads with crusty crusts and tender centers like the best breads of Europe. It's little wonder that for 11 straight years, Swiss Pastries has received the Readers Choice Award for their desserts. Their cozy café also offers continental breakfast, soups, salads and sandwiches made with their delicious homemade bread, buns and croissants. To accompany your meal, they have a nice selection of Espresso drinks and ice creams. Steiger's Swiss Pastries & Café, open Tuesday through Saturday, is a charming place to eat or to browse for that perfect treat to take home.
359 Victoria Street, Kamloops BC
(250) 372 - 2625

Zack's Exotic Coffees, Teas & Gifts

Daniel and Deborah Zacharias' goal in opening Zack's was to make the customer feel like a guest in their home. Home, in this case, being a coffee shop on Victoria Street, in the heart of downtown Kamloops. And a very homey coffee shop it is, with Daniel doing the coffee roasting and blending and Deborah making cakes of all kinds from scratch. Daniel and Deborah's daughters help out too, making fresh Italian gelato at Zack's Old Style Sweet Shoppe, a next-door annex to the main shop. Zack's is located in a building that began life in 1914 as a drugstore. Daniel and Deborah have gone out of their way to preserve the rich environment of the original shop, including some of the original apothecary equipment and other interesting antiques. When you're in the store, it's worthwhile to take a moment and scrutinize your surroundings AS there's always another fascinating detail to find. The latest addition to Zack's is the Royal Victorian Teahouse, on the corner of 4th and Seymour, in a century-old Heritage Home that Daniel and Deborah have restored. It has been transformed into an intimate setting for classic English High Teas, complete with an outdoor patio overlooking a rose garden. 377 Victoria Street, Kamloops BC (250) 374 - 6487

Urban Oasis Java & Juice Bar

Freshly squeezed orange juice or the cool, sweet, delicious taste of a fruit smoothie. These and more can be part of your day with a trip to Urban Oasis Java & Juice Bar in Kelowna. Find out how they can enhance your body, mind and spirit. Enriching your life with her products and presence is owner Cherisa Patton's passion. Her personal touch will stay with you as you savor one of her healthy delicacies and then move on into your day. Dedicated to healing people with

foods and positive choices for their lives, Cherisa and her assistant Sarah Mcdougall chose having an urban oasis as their way of touching people with healing philosophy. It's hard to believe treats this scrumptious can be good for you. You will find organic ingredients in their awesome salads including fresh greens, tofu and chicken. Boosters can be added to their homemade soups and breakfast wraps. Urban Oasis is vegan friendly and if you have special requests, just ask. Urban Oasis is also about education. Cherisa and Sarah know that eating well and organically has made a difference in their lives and they want to share their knowledge and the benefits of a healthier lifestyle with you. Urban Oasis has been featured in several top-notch health and entertainment magazines. Sip a delicious smoothie for a satisfying breakfast while you find out how good nutrition can change the quality of your life. You don't have to move to the farm, there's a new healthier you just waiting to be discovered at Urban Oasis Java & Juice Bar.

1567 Pandosy Street, Kelowna BC
(250) 762 - 2124

Sweet Gestures Chocolate Shoppe

In the rainforests 2,000 years ago, chocolate from the seeds of the cacao plant were used to make a bitter, but highly prized drink. It slowly made its way around the world, being sweetened in Spain, and was made into a creamy candy when the technology became available. The largest chocolate bar ever made was a 5,026 pound giant displayed in Turin, Italy in March of 2000. A 2,002 pound slab of fudge was once made in Ontario. Did you know the melting point of cocoa butter is just below human body temperature, so it literally melts in your mouth? A well-known mood lifter, chocolate releases the same chemicals in your brain that create bliss when you fall in love. Chocolate lovers everywhere love facts about how chocolate is created, displayed and, of course, consumed. Sweet Gestures Chocolate Shoppe is happy to provide their perfected personal creations of the gift of chocolate. Michelle and Brent Shypitka and their staff operate this elegant yet quaint business with quality workmanship, plus a good deal of fun. Their truffles are created from hand-dipped Belgium chocolate. They develop their own authentic recipes, and the word is spreading. The heritage town of Fort Steele carries Michelle's creamy chocolate fudge. Fun shapes like the peppermint piano and the lemon butterfly crème add visual delight to these gourmet taste treats. All of their candy is temptingly beautiful, and Sweet Gestures can make an irresistible gift box to your exact specifications. Michelle and Brent would love to help you find the perfect treat for yourself or someone else, so stop in and see what they can do for your sweet tooth.
1115 D Baker Street, Cranbrook BC (250) 417 - 3199

The Pixie Candy Shoppe

Two thousand years before the Aztec or the Inca civilizations, the Kootenay (water people) Indians lived in the area that now bears their name. The area was inaccessible to Europeans, until the Hudson's Bay Company and Northwest Trading Company laid the fur trading routes. As time went on, precious metals and land brought in a population that built the 350 historic buildings, some of which you'll find still standing. This part of Nelson's history is evident in the buildings on Baker street. The Nelson Trading Company is the location of an indoor shopping center here, and it is the home of the Pixie Candy Shoppe. Angel Stuyt aims to please in her nostalgic all-ages Candy Shoppe. Angel creates a fun atmosphere and enjoys being part of your experience. She will deliver, worldwide to your door. The Pixie Candy Shoppe carries lollipops weighing up to three pounds and retro tin lunch kits,

some featuring your favorite comic book heroes. They have ice-cream and magnets, 1950s style candy and a large selection of pop just waiting for you in an old- fashioned cooler. Then there's imported British candy, Dutch licorice, local Nelson chocolate and licorice all calling to your sweet tooth.   The 16 flavours of saltwater taffy are always fresh as it comes from nearby Creston. There are at least 50 different sugar-free items for health concerned and diabetic individuals. Nelson gelato is served up with a smile and there is extensive stock of nostalgia candy from the 1940s through to the 1970's. Bag your candy in fun sacks or walk away with a loot bag of retro toys. If you don't see it here, ask, because Angel will try to get it for you.
107-402 Baker Street, Nelson BC (250) 354 - 1122 www.pixiecandy.ca

The Yellow Umbrella/Thyme for Tea

The Yellow Umbrella/ Thyme for Tea is built on historic ground dating back to the 1800's when the promise of gold lured many people to the Cariboo country. While certainly a different venue than the old roadhouses provided, Linda and Norm strive to provide country hospitality and service to their customers. The tea house carries over 50 teas to enjoy on premise or to take home to brew. A gift selection changes with the seasons and the garden art will stand the test of thyme. The entire staff works as a team to provide outstanding repasts for their customers. The food is made from scratch in the tea house kitchen, the menu changes daily and includes comfort foods such as pot pies, quiche, scones, yummy soups and beautiful desserts. Linda and staff love all the seasons and enjoy creating a new atmosphere for each one. Although only two years old the gardens have already become a place to stroll through while enjoying friends or a time of solitude. Hosting special events such as birthday parties, anniversaries etc., have become a regular event and requests for events are always welcome. Come enjoy a cup of tea served in china tea cups, let the staff pamper you, enjoy a stroll through the gift selection and the outdoor setting. Enjoy country hospitality at its finest. The Yellow Umbrella is located right next to a 1900s restored schoolhouse at 150 mile house. 3075 Hwy 97, 150 Mile House BC (250) 296 - 4235

Galleries

Orveas Bay Gallery

Photo by: Ya-Tang Yang, Taiwan

Stunning ocean views and delightful, imaginative art come together at the Orveas Bay Gallery. This charming gallery is located on a llama farm on the southwest coast of pristine Vancouver Island and also boasts a lovely courtyard vacation suite. A professional ceramic artist, Glenys Marshall-Inman works in many forms of clay art, including porcelain and earthenware functional pottery, sculpture and paperclay paintings. Dr. Stanford Perrott, former head of the Alberta College of Art Academy, is quoted as saying, "She is among the top 20 students I have encountered during a 50-year career teaching art from primary school to university." Guests at the Orveas Bay Gallery are able to see functional pottery being made and fired, or watch as sculptural pieces come to life in Glenys' private studio and display area with the magnificent Pacific Ocean as a backdrop. International Academy of Ceramics Vice President Les Manning says of Glenys, "I do not know any other artist that is more committed, more consistent and none more passionate about the material and her personal identity as a ceramist than this artist." Owners Glenys and Basil Marshall-Inman, a professional wood craftsman, opened the Vancouver Island gallery seven years ago with the desire to supply clients with original works that are available only through their gallery. Visitors who wish to stay awhile can take advantage of the beautifully-appointed, smoke-free, private courtyard suite at Orveas Bay Gallery. 4568 Otter Point Road, Sooke Harbor BC (250) 642 - 5555 www.marshallinman.com

Mary Fox Pottery

Mary Fox is known for creating ceramics of beauty and distinction, whether in her line of functional stoneware or in her exceptional art pieces. Since her early teens, Mary has expressed an original sensibility through her work. She develops her own glazes and experiments with glazing and firing techniques. What she achieves in color and textural effects, you won't find anywhere else. Believing that the most beautiful shapes are the simplest, Mary creates contemporary vessels based on classic shapes. Her work has been exhibited at the largest international ceramics exhibition in the southern hemisphere in Shepperton, Australia and was part of the 53rd International Contemporary Ceramics exhibitions at the Museum of Ceramics in Faenza, Italy. Her elegant vase became part of the Museum's permanent collection following the exhibition. Mary's work has appeared in the former Canadian Craft and Design Museum, and the Canadian Clay and Glass Gallery in Waterloo, Ontario. Mary invites the public to visit her studio. You will see her works in progress and she will be pleased to help you find that one-of- a-kind piece that will add inspiration to your home or office. Mary Fox Pottery, original artwork that will stand the test of time. 321 3rd Avenue, Box 35, Ladysmith BC (250) 245 - 3778 mfp@islandnet.com

Jo Vic Pottery

Jo Vic Pottery represents a blend of the talents of Jo and Vic Duffhues. While they share in the glazing and decorating of their pieces, Jo produces their slab-ware line and Vic makes most of the wheel-thrown pottery. They produce high-quality functional stoneware including vases, tiles, ikebana pots, pitchers and dinnerware. Collectors can request custom pieces in their special patterns. The Duffhues' art pottery is exquisite. Jo crafts architectural ceramics and Vic makes mochaware decorated with landscapes. The two also make original garden art. Individually and together, they continue to pursue new directions in their craft. Characteristic of their distinctive and colorful work, many of Jo's pieces feature sgraffito, the carving away of a surface layer to reveal a contrasting ground. They also do raku and give frequent demonstrations of this ancient firing technique. Having received a wedding gift of a potter's wheel from Vic, Jo says, "I acquired a husband and a career at one and the same time." This gifted couple credits the magnificence of Vancouver Island for their glaze development and the beauty of the pieces they produce together. You too will delight in the surroundings and in the fine work you will find when you visit Jo Vic Pottery.

4781 Shell Beach Road, Ladysmith BC
(250) 245 - 8728
www.jovicpottery.com

'Chosin Pottery

Robin Hopper and Judi Dyelle, internationally acclaimed potters, live and work in paradise. Their two and a half acre garden is Robin's award-winning 30-year work in progress. Loosely based on various models, including traditional Japanese gardens, Robin terms it "Anglojapanadian" in style. This serenely beautiful setting contributes to 'Chosin Pottery's popularity as a destination for artists and customers from around the world. Robin was the first recipient of the Bronfman Award. His work includes beautiful functional pottery for everyday use in the home, as well as painterly one-of-a-kind art pieces in porcelain. Both artists began working with clay at an early age, mixing their

own clay bodies, making thrown and hand-built pieces, and studying the medium and its masters. Both were also long-time teachers of ceramics prior to their partnership and marriage. Judi, who studied with Tatsuzo Shimaoka (one of Japan's National Living Treasures), specializes in very fine porcelain, sometimes carving or piercing patterns into her pieces. She has done extensive work with Oriental and microcrystalline glazes and achieves subtle color and textural effects. Robin and Judi continue their arts education commitment with the Metchosin International Summer School of the Arts. A visit to 'Chosin Pottery is a visit to a world of living art, tranquility and inspiration.

4283 Metchosin Road, Victoria BC
(250) 474 - 2676 www.chosinpottery.ca

Eagle Aerie Gallery

Roy Henry Vickers, owner of Eagle Aerie Gallery, is one of the best-known Canadian First Nations artists. A recipient of the Order of British Columbia, Roy was commissioned by the province to create an original painting, "A Meeting of Chiefs," which was presented to Queen Elizabeth II in 1987. Eagle Aerie Gallery was conceived to honor his heritage. Designed as a traditional Northwest Coast longhouse, the gallery features a carved and painted cedar plank exterior with doors made of beaten copper. As you enter, the 40-by-50 foot main hall you'll notice the soft lighting and restful music that create an atmosphere of harmony and peace which many visitors have likened to church. In addition to displaying Roy's original paintings and limited edition prints, the Aerie encourages visitors to spend time learning about the native art and culture of the Northwest Coast. A wide selection of books on the subject are available. Eagle Aerie Gallery welcomes over a hundred thousand visitors every year.
350 Campbell Street, Tofino BC (250) 725 - 3235 www.royhenryvickers.com

StoneAge Art Company

The outstanding beauty of Zimbabwean art is unique. Since June 2003, StoneAge Art Company has been bringing it to the people of Vancouver. The gallery features the work of the oldest tribe in Zimbabwe, the Shona. Traditionally styled the guardians of King Solomon's Mines, the Shona stone carvers are known as the People of the Mist. They believe that every rock contains a spirit essence that influences the way the stone will be shaped and transformed during carving. Crafted from serpentine, opalstone, red jasper and other native stones, the sculptures produced by these artists display great individuality. Each piece is an original to be valued by the astute collector. StoneAge Art Company is co-owned by Peter and Angie Vickery, who were both born at the same hospital in Harare, Zimbabwe, though they did not meet until years later in another country. Now citizens of Canada, they started their gallery on Granville Island because they wanted a place where

visitors could experience a touch of Africa through authentic art sculptures in a relaxed atmosphere. Two words that are taken very seriously at StoneAge Art Company are, customer service. Peter and Angie take great care in helping their customers find the right artwork for their personal tastes and budget. #11, The Creekhouse, 1551 Johnston Street, Vancouver BC (604) 801 - 5108 or (888) 801 - 5108 www.stoneageartcompany.com

The Art Emporium

Andrew Wyeth, 24 x 19

Alexander Calder, gouache, 30 x 44

Who can you trust for great art? How about a gallery that has had a successful track record for more than a century? The Art Emporium has been at the center of Vancouver's art scene since 1897. Now it continues its service to the community under the ownership of Torben Kristiansen. As one of the country's most highly respected art dealers, he offers a wealth of fine paintings as well as expert services such as appraisals. The Art Emporium carries well-known artists from the past and present, from the Impressionists to Cornelius Krieghoff, J.W. Morrice, Emily Carr, David Milne, Tom Thomson and all members of the Group of Seven. The paintings range across distinguished, world-renowned artists from Andrew Wyeth and Calder to Appel, Dufy, Picasso, Utrillo and Montague Dawson. Expert advice is one of the most important services you'll find at The Art Emporium. Here are the answers to all your questions about collecting art. The knowledgeable staff can suggest creative ways for anyone to invest, no matter what the budget. Bring home a piece of art that will enrich your life, with the confidence that you have made a great investment.
2928 Granville Street, Vancouver BC
(604) 738 - 3510
www.theartemporium.ca

Emily Carr, oil, 38 x 13

Lawren Harris, oil, 12 x 15

Lattimer Gallery

Lattimer Gallery is an impressive showcase for Northwest Coast art of First Nations peoples. Visitors are welcomed to browse works of art at their own leisure in the open, warm atmosphere of the gallery, which captures the ambiance of a West Coast longhouse. Traditional and contemporary art in a variety of media is featured in the gallery. You will find gold and silver jewellery; sculptures in cedar, soapstone and argillite, masks and drums; prints and paintings. Lattimer Gallery represents artists and cultures throughout British Columbia. The gallery was founded in 1986 by Leona Lattimer. Her grandson Peter Lattimer now operates the gallery with a commitment to developing strong client relationships, and with an emphasis on continuity. The large number of loyal, repeat customers is a testament to this. The friendly, knowledgeable staff strives to answer every question and meet every need. Peter also carries on Leona's tradition of supporting young artists, encouraging them and promoting their work. The Lattimer Gallery is open seven days a week and worldwide shipping is available. 1590 West 2nd Avenue, Vancouver BC (604) 732 - 4556 www.lattimergallery.com

Jacana Gallery

A Jacana is a colorful migratory bird from Asia and Dany Filion thought it was the perfect name for a distinctive store. She and her husband, Peng Liu, have filled a tranquil space with an ever-changing mixture of the ancient and the contemporary. They have created a fluid but peaceful space, where one-of-a-kind pieces of Asian furniture and art are at home with contemporary works by local artists. A sense of peace, and a happy awareness that you are in the presence of great art and design from the past and terrific contemporary art. This is what you will find at Jacana. Jacana's effect is the result of the owners' strong personal styles and artistic discretion, and they are exceptionally knowledgeable about every piece in the store. Peng travels throughout Asia in search of pieces for their collection. It is a store designed to bring you the clean, elegant lines of Chinese and Tibetan furniture and of designs and artisans from across the centuries, as well as strong contemporary abstract works. They complement each other as they please us. At Jacana, you will have all the time you need to browse and enjoy the impressive works. Visit Jacana Gallery to experience for yourself a place that many have found "like a temple."

2435 Granville Street, Vancouver BC (604) 879 - 9306 www.jacanagallery.com

Douglas Reynolds Gallery

The genesis of Northwest Coast art lies in the ceremonial life of the Native people who traditionally inhabit the coastline of British Columbia. Early contact with Europeans brought a market for native curios that generated a demand for smaller works, sometimes in media that were not traditionally dominant on the coast, such as argillite and European-introduced precious metals. The twentieth century saw significant changes in Northwest Coast art with the growth of tourism in British Columbia and a demand for everything from souvenir totem poles and baskets, to canes and even lampshades. Beginning in the 1960s, public institutions showed renewed interest in Northwest Coast art, featuring exhibits that highlighted contemporary works as an extension of the primarily historical focus of their collections. By the close of the century, contemporary Northwest Coast artists were carving not only new versions of older pieces, but had redefined their art to encompass new media and fresh approaches to traditional forms. As we enter the 21st, Northwest Coast art continues to grow and reach out in new directions, while always maintaining a grounding in the past. Located in the heart of Vancouver's main gallery district, the Douglas Reynolds Gallery is one of Canada's leading specialists in historic and contemporary Northwest Coast art. Featuring carved wood masks, bent boxes, totem poles, panels and hand crafted gold and silver jewelry, the gallery also carries a variety of baskets, prints, and bronze and glass editions. The year 2005 marks the gallery's 10th anniversary, with works by leading artists including Don Yeomans, Larry Rosso, Rick Adkins and Robert Davidson on display. 2335 Granville Street, Vancouver BC (604) 731 - 9292 www.douglasreynoldsgallery.com

Ian Tan gallery

Photo by: Lisa Henriques

ian tan gallery offers important contemporary Canadian ceramic and glass art in addition to paintings and photographs by established and budding artists. Ian Tan's lifelong love of the arts led him to leave his scientific career in molecular evolution and open this beautiful space. The gallery's focus is showcasing timeless works that appeal not just to the eyes, but to the hearts and minds of their viewers. The artists represented are not trendy. They represent a wide range of personal expression that may be inspired by the primitive or the Renaissance, the mystical or the classic. Many have exhibited internationally and are recipients of honors such as the prestigious Saidye Bronfman Award. The gallery's clients are often people who frequent art museums, know what they like, and would like to own some of what they've seen. Dr. Tan offers expert personal consultation, often taking clients to the studios of artists whose work they admire. To view notable, contemporary Canadian art, don't miss ian tan gallery. 2202 Granville Street, Vancouver BC (604) 738 - 1077 www.iantangallery.com

Photo by: Jay MacDonell

Kurbatoff Art Gallery

Elena and Konstantin Kurbatoff met in the desert on the shores of the Red Sea. They soon discovered they had received Bachelor of Arts degrees at the same school, Kharkov State University in the Ukraine. Both were active in the art community and Konstantin was also an art journalist in Israel. Together they have created this warm and open space where people of different tastes and passions come to discuss art

and artists. On display are contemporary works by established and mostly Canadian artists. The Gallery also strives to give exposure to emerging artists. Dynamic and open-minded, the Kurbatoffs select pieces based on the mastery they demonstrate, a distinguishing characteristic of all the works they choose. With a wide spectrum of styles and directions in contemporary art, they exhibit many international influences. Artists hail from such disparate lands as Germany, Australia, Holland and Transylvania. The Gallery stages solo and group shows and provides personal consultations in order to find the right homes for works of art. Elena and Konstantin look forward to seeing you at "Destination #1" on Vancouver's Gallery Row.

2427 Granville Street, Vancouver BC (604) 736 - 5444 www.kurbatoffgallery.com

Amati Art Gallery

Amati Art Gallery is Amy Levinson's latest addition to her unique venue for the lively arts. Amy has turned the underground level of the Arbutus Shopping Centre into a popular haunt for the artistically inclined. In September of 2000, she opened Amati String Studio, offering instruction in violin, viola, cello, guitar, and piano. This music school is well-regarded and has students ranging in age from three to 80-plus. The studio also features performances by students and other local musicians. Amati Art & Books followed, supplying sheet music, art and music books and unusual gifts. Add to all that the new art gallery and this is an exciting place to be. With a different featured artist every six weeks, the focus is on new and emerging contemporary art. There is an annual Children's Art Show that will absolutely amaze you. Also available are hands-on arts and crafts and a large patio outdoors where you can relax and reflect on all you've seen. Amy's parents are important players in the business. Carla Levinson, a retired singing teacher, acts as curator. Ben Levinson is an architect and an accomplished pen-and-ink artist. If you are visiting or on vacation, this is the place to keep up with your music lessons, and you can also participate in Summer Camp. But whatever the season, you are sure to enjoy this delightful and original underground center for the arts. 4255 Arbutus Street, Basement Level B6, Vancouver BC (604) 736 - 9813 www.amatistringstudio.ca

Jennifer Kostuik Gallery

Jennifer Kostuik Gallery displays an aesthetic unlike any other gallery in Vancouver.

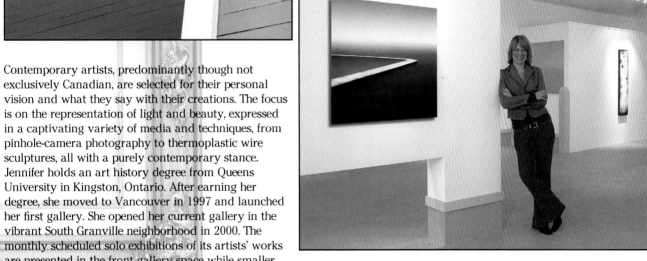

Contemporary artists, predominantly though not exclusively Canadian, are selected for their personal vision and what they say with their creations. The focus is on the representation of light and beauty, expressed in a captivating variety of media and techniques, from pinhole-camera photography to thermoplastic wire sculptures, all with a purely contemporary stance. Jennifer holds an art history degree from Queens University in Kingston, Ontario. After earning her degree, she moved to Vancouver in 1997 and launched her first gallery. She opened her current gallery in the vibrant South Granville neighborhood in 2000. The monthly scheduled solo exhibitions of its artists' works are presented in the front gallery space while smaller group exhibitions continue in the center and back gallery spaces. This allows for new work from its artists to always be on display whether they have a show scheduled or not. Almost all artwork available in the gallery is listed on the gallery website, keeping the site and the gallery current. The artwork selected can be explained as having a foot in the past yet presented in a contemporary format. The principles of open, balanced space and light embody the artists' work which carries into the gallery space. The gallery provides the service of visiting clients' home or office spaces personally, or through emailed images of their spaces, to assist clients in choosing and placing the artwork they have expressed interest in pursuing. This service enables the staff to help buyers find the artwork best suited to their personalities and spaces, whether they live in Vancouver or abroad. Jennifer Kostuik Gallery provides custom framing and shipping services. 2928 Granville Street, Vancouver BC (604) 737 - 3969 www.kostuikgallery.com

Spirit Wrestler Gallery

Spirit Wrestler Gallery specializes in master-level sculpture and graphics by acknowledged contemporary Inuit, Northwest Coast, Plains and Maori (New Zealand) artists. Located in the heart of historic Gastown in Vancouver, the gallery has an ongoing exhibition schedule that documents the work of individual artists or regions and has also created fusion exhibitions that explore similarities and contrasts between the cultures in an exciting and provocative

way. Under the direction of owners Gary Wyatt, Derek Norton and Nigel Reading, the gallery exhibits the work of many of the leading contemporary artists and explores themes of shamanism and transformation. Spirit Wrestler is open seven days a week and responsibly ships their artwork internationally. The gallery is housed in the oldest brick building in Vancouver.
8 Water Street, Vancouver BC
(604) 669 - 8813
www.spiritwrestler.com

Object Design Gallery

Together Sako Khatcherian and Tamara Clark, husband and wife, own and operate Object Design Galleries. Sako is a rare goldsmith, one who excels in all the aspects of his craft, designing, wax carving, casting and setting. He is a third generation goldsmith with over 20 years of "bench" experience. Tamara graduated from the Ontario College of Art in enameling and sculpture: elements apparent in her jewellery design. Her work unites a variety of precious and semi-precious gems with contrasts of gold, copper and bronze accents. Object Design began as the design label and

evolved into the gallery's name as Sako and Tamara pursued their dream of housing a number of local artists under one roof. The gallery opened in 2000, featuring five local jewellers. The number of local and international participating jewellers has grown to over one hundred. A range of other artists in photography, wood and glass are also featured now. With personalized service and custom designs, they offer exciting opportunities to partner with you to create one-of-a-kind jewellery that reflects the personality, character and uniqueness of the individual. Since opening, Object Design Gallery has become a valuable Artists' Resource Center. Besides serving as a home base for local artists who rent bench space, they have hosted many successful group and featured artist exhibits.

Unit 4, 1551 Johnston Street, Vancouver BC (604) 683 - 7763
Unit 110, 4295 Blackcomb Way, Whistler Village BC (604) 905 - 7768
www.objectdesigngallery.com

New-Small & Sterling

For the best contemporary designs in functional and sculptural glass, visit the New-Small & Sterling Studio on Granville Island in Vancouver. The organic forms and high-quality glass created by David New-Small are a unique synthesis of form, function, craftsmanship and color. The studio lines include Peacock perfume bottles, Ikebana vessels, Love Songs perfume bottles, Pousse Café vases, and David's signature Marine Reliquary series. Each

piece is one-of-a-kind, numbered and signed by the artist. David discovered hot glass as a teen and has been fascinated by the art ever since. In 1979, he studied at the Pilchuck School in Washington state and in 1983 established the studio on Granville Island. In the gallery attached to this dynamic studio, owners David New-Small and Nora Sterling also feature works from over 50 other Canadian glass artists, ranging from jewelry to sculpture. School tours are welcome. 1440 Old Bridge Street, Vancouver BC (604) 681 - 6730 or (888) 776 - 8839 www.hotstudioglass.com

Sculpture by Ju Ming

Sculpture by Lynn Chadwick

Buschlen Mowatt Galleries

Vancouver sits like a gleaming jewel beside the sea, so it is no surprise this setting provided the inspiration for a world-renowned gallery. Buschlen Mowatt Galleries was established in 1979 and from the beginning, embraced contemporary international art. The gallery showcases esteemed artists from all over the world, produces museum caliber exhibitions, and finds and identifies emerging talents. In 2001, a second gallery, larger than the first, opened in Palm Desert, California. Owner Barrie Mowatt continues to maintain an award-winning presence in the art world. He has received the Vancouver Business in Arts Award and the Ethics in Action Award, and

Sculpture by Sorel Etrog

was twice nominated for Western Canada's Socially Conscious Entrepreneur of the Year. His gallery supports the community through the Buschlen Mowatt Foundation, established in the memory of Don Buschlen to promote community art education. Buschlen Mowatt Galleries is a sponsor of Arts Umbrella, Canada's #1 visual and performing arts institute for youth, ages 5 to 19. Buschlen Mowatt is the primary sponsor and founder of the visionary Vancouver International Sculpture Biennale that features sculptures by major names in the art world from over 13 nations. Every two years along the bike and walking trails paths surrounding Vancouver's waterfront, world class sculpture is installed and enjoyed by all. The gallery invites you to discover the fine art of collecting at Buschlen Mowatt.
1445 W Georgia Street, Vancouver BC (604) 682 - 1234 or (800) 663 - 8071
45-188 Portola Avenue, Palm Desert CA (760) 837 - 9668
www.buschlenmowatt.com

Gallery Jones

Mark Reddekopp and Shane O'Brien created Gallery Jones in 2004 to combine their 18 years of collective experience in the art world. They built a space where the best in contemporary Canadian and International art can mix. The sophisticated art lover will have the opportunity to appreciate the immense range of talent displayed by British Columbia's finest artists. Gallery Jones displays works in a variety of media, including sculpture, painting and photography. The gallery received outstanding notices for a show of German-born painter and photographer Eric Klemm's astonishing Metamorphosis photographs, a series created in an auto graveyard on Saltspring Island. In the short time since it opened, Gallery Jones has already scored a major coup by becoming the exclusive Vancouver representative of Otto Rogers, the Saskatchewan native who has become one of Canada's most renowned artists, "an icon of Prairie Modernism." His works are on display at the National Gallery of Canada as well as the Museum of Fine Arts in Boston, and now in Vancouver. For a glimpse of their style, visit Gallery Jones' beautifully designed website, but it's best to go into the gallery and see the real thing. 1725 West Third Avenue, Vancouver BC (604) 714 - 2216 www.galleryjones.com

Elliot Louis Gallery

Located in the vibrant Waterfall Building, the Elliott Louis Gallery offers intriguing, eclectic works by both established artists and cutting edge newcomers. In an impressive scope of categories, both Contemporary and Historic, regular exhibitions showcase dynamic displays of fine art painting, sculpture and photography. Vancouver artists that include (to name but a few) Toni Onley, Jane Adams, Christian Nicolay, Peter Aspell and Jack Shadbolt, are joined by Montreal's Martin Brouillette and Philip Buller from California. Steel sculptor Cory Fuhr, recently commissioned to design the award for the Giller Prize, one of Canada's most prestigious literary awards, continues to forge his brilliance. Reflecting Vancouver's cosmopolitan personality, the gallery also features works by international artists including Post-Impressionist French painters Fernand Pinal and Joseph Le Tessier, Cambodian painter Mong Yen and Laotian painter Thep Thavonsouk. Intriguing in its own right is the gallery's architecture designed by world renown Vancouver architect Arthur Erickson, who also designed the Canadian Embassy in Washington, DC. The venue has been the scene of location shoots for scores of television shows, movies, commercials, rock videos and social events.

1540 W Second Avenue, Vancouver BC
(604) 736 - 3282
www.elliotlouis.com

Harrison Galleries

Harrison Galleries is proud to provide an unhurried, pleasant art experience (like stepping into a friend's living room), but one where you will discover a new treat with each visit. Every month the gallery presents a one-man show that runs for two weeks, so the gallery is constantly changing, from the layout to the color of the walls. Every visit brings a new experience and new artists for you to enjoy, both traditional as well as contemporary, in the heart of Vancouver's South Granville Rise area. Owner Christopher Harrison's father emigrated from England in the 1950s and originally worked as an art conservator and restorer. Christopher himself grew up in the gallery and has always been surrounded by artistic beauty. Now he heads up one of Canada's oldest family-owned and operated galleries, bringing art to the community with the help of his excellent staff, all long-term employees. Harrison Galleries has been at this location since 1978, with a mission to bring joy through art, and a special interest in showcasing Alberta talent. Regionally and internationally recognized artists are at home at the Harrison Galleries, and art lovers are too. 2932 Granville Street, Vancouver BC (604) 732 - 5217 www.harrisongalleries.com

Hills Native Art

North America's largest Native Art Gallery, Hill's Native Art in Vancouver features the work of more than 1,200 artists from every known tribe and nation of the Northwest Coast. It is the result of an effort begun in 1946, when Lloyd and Frances Hill acquired the Koksilah general store and post office and created an outlet for local Native artisans to display and sell their work. Celebrating over 50 years of quality service, Hill's offers beautifully sculpted carvings from Inuit and Native artists, expertly carved ceremonial masks illustrating stories or rituals, and exquisitely designed, hand-carved jewelry. You will also find Cowichan knits; warm hand-crafted knits with enduring signature images. Perpetuated by a small group of Coast Salish artists, the two-century old craft tradition of Cowichan knitting has graced the Hill's shops since 1946. In addition, you will find totem poles, bentwood boxes, blanket boxes, drums, feasting dishes, glass sculptures, leather crafts, woven baskets and much more. Hill's magnificent third floor gallery offers an inspiring atmosphere for native-themed receptions. Come visit this incredible showplace of beauty, inspired originality and tradition.
165 Water Street
Gastown,
Vancouver BC
(604) 685 - 4249
www.hillsnativeart.com

103

Dreamweaver Gallery House

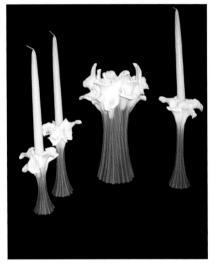

Joyce Falconer travels the world and brings it home to Tsawwassen. Her Dreamweaver Gallery House is full of hand-picked exotica from Africa, Europe and the Americas. There are etchings by Canadian Irene Klar, amber jewelry from Poland, gold and platinum trimmed collectibles from Uruguay, metal art from Haiti, and wood carvings from Africa and the Philippines. Whether local works or pieces from far away, the focus is on the beautiful, the intriguing and the unusual. From furniture and décor, accessories to jewellery, paintings and prints, every item is exceptional. You will be pleased with the prices, as well. Beautiful, high-quality gift wrapping is offered with every purchase, creating exquisite presentation. Joyce invites you to browse through Dreamweaver's distinctive collection. Just ask and she'll gladly share the story behind each piece.

5674 – 12th Avenue, Tsawwassen BC (604) 948 - 5788

Jenkins Showler Gallery

At Jenkins Showler Gallery every piece of art is original and every collector is unique. Established in 1990 and located in the heart of White Rock, the inviting ambience of the

gallery inspires both first time visitors as well as seasoned buyers. Representing traditional and contemporary Canadian artists, they continually strive to showcase innovative, original works of art. The knowledgeable staff is enthusiastic and happy to share their passion for art, assisting everyone in making informed purchases. Indulge yourself, experience the joy of art at Jenkins Showler Gallery.

1539 Johnston Road, White Rock BC (604) 535 - 7445 or
(888) 872 - 3107 www.jenkinsshowlergallery.com

Artful Things

Garrie Holmes and his daughter Lorrie are art lovers, and Artful Things is a warm reflection of their love. Everything in their gallery has been made by human hands. As Lorrie puts it, "We don't care what it's made of – canvas, metal, wood, clay, straw or whatever, or where it comes from, but it has to be hand touched in some way." Garrie and Lorrie's enthusiasm has given the gallery its reputation for discovering and attracting emerging artists; a wide range of local British Columbia artisans' work is

featured there. Other artists presented include internationally recognized painter Katsumi Sugita. Artful Things is the only authorized Canadian representative for Sugita's work. There are three essential elements to Artful Things, the gallery element, offering an eclectic range of affordable works; the museum element, offering museum-quality art prints and posters; and the entertainment component. Every weekend, Artful Things hosts an Artists at Work event, inviting customers to observe an artist as he or she crafts a new work and displays finished pieces. Garrie and Lorrie's goal is to break down barriers in the art world, living up to their belief that art is for the people. 840 – 3041 152nd Street, South Surrey BC (604) 538 - 9681 www.artfulthings.biz

Bellerophon's Equestrian and Antiques

A shop dedicated to equestrian art and antiques, Bellerophon's was named by owner Joan Blackhall's father for the hero of Greek myth who captured and rode the winged horse Pegasus. Jan, who has been a professional rider, trainer and riding instructor, has loved horses all her life. For many years she cherished the dream of finding a "horse" store. When the store of her dreams remained unfound, she and her family created it. Located at the end of a little Fort Langley street, picturesquely named Gasoline Alley, Bellerophon's offers original paintings and statuary depicting the beauty of horses and the glories of nature. The Langley area is the horse capital of British Columbia and artists not only display their works at the gallery but also come by on summer days and set up their easels outside, inviting the public to observe. Bellerophon's also features a wide variety of equestrian collectibles, from vintage Breyer horse models to antique rocking horses. The Blackhalls, who consider themselves collectors of beautiful things, have also stocked Bellerophon's with a splendid selection of hand-picked antique furniture, glass paperweights, rugs, raku and more.
9203 Glover Road, Fort Langley BC
(604) 882 - 6525

The Plaza Galleries

Recognized and respected around the world, The Plaza Galleries displays Whistler's largest collection of fine art. Owner Ann-Marie Little is focused on providing a place where locals and visitors alike can come to discover and learn about art. The gallery features artists from Canada and around the world. Works include the Parisian oil paintings of Kal Gajoum, David Lee's florals on silk, Emanuel Mattini's vivid abstract musical instruments, and the hand-blown Murano glass sculptures of Dino Rosin, who lived on Murano for many years. Little encourages emerging artists. For example 10 years ago, at the age of eleven, Romanian-born Jasmin Aldin began showing at The Plaza Galleries and her paintings are now collected worldwide. There are many other selections and the collection is continually infused with new work and new artists who know The Plaza Galleries' reputation for integrity and professional service. You owe yourself the pleasure of a visit to The Plaza Galleries, one of Whistler's treasures.

#22 – 4314 Main Street, Whistler BC (604) 938 - 6233 www.plazagalleries.com

Black Tusk Gallery

Bill MacGillivary learned about Northwest Coast art from his uncle who was a knowledgeable collector. He taught Bill about artistic intent and about the meanings of Native art. Bill opened this gallery to focus exclusively on the art of First Nations people. All of the artists exhibited there are of aboriginal heritage. The works reflect their respective histories and traditions. A few of the many accomplished artists represented at Black Tusk are Bill Henderson who carries on his father's legacy as a master carver, Susan Point who expresses Coast Salish themes, and Rande Cook whose work is informed by the Kwakwaka'wakw tradition. Sculpture, masks, panels, totems and hand-carved jewellery are all on display. MacGillivary is committed to providing a venue characterized by trust, respect and service. His commitment is to the broader community as well, supporting emerging artists and participating in Zero Ceiling, a program designed to assist aboriginal adolescents. For true appreciation of the rich history of this area and the artistry of its indigenous peoples, be sure to visit Black Tusk Gallery.

#108-4293 Mountain Square Art Gallery Row, Whistler BC
(604) 905 - 5540 or (877) 905 - 5540 www.blacktusk.ca

Photo by: Karen Leung

West Coast Art Gallery

Bill MacGillivary was an art collector long before he became a gallery owner. He actively promoted developing artists and his interests extended from local to international works. So in 2000, Bill broke new ground in the Whistler art community by opening his own gallery in the Pan Pacific Hotel where he features international as well as Canadian contemporary art. There you will find world-class originals as well as limited-edition paintings, glass works and sculptures in soapstone and bronze. Vancouver native Brent Heighton's landscapes and street scenes, plus Maya Eventov's brilliantly colored still-lifes and small Tuscan scenes, along with the deeply dimensional paintings of Samir Sammoun are among the featured Canadian works. The exquisite still-lifes by Angel (Dong Wen Jie) of Northern China are a fascinating counterpoint to the beautifully expressed faces in her figure paintings. These are just a sampling of the many fine artists whose work you will find here. Bill MacGillivary has an extraordinary eye, which means this West Coast Art Gallery is a real gift to the Whistler community and art lovers from around the world.

#123-4320 Sundial Crescent, Whistler BC (604) 935 - 0087 www.westcoastartgallery.com

Photo by: Mark Tullos

Tree Line Studios

One of the highlights of Sun Peaks Resort, just north of Kamloops, is Tree Line Studios. Founders George and Anne Terwiel were ski instructors who fell in love with the skiing, the people and this amazing area. Eventually they would move here in 1991. George and Anne wanted to convey that beauty in their gallery and the art they sell. Developed by Nippon Cable in 1993, Sun Peaks is a resort that includes a self-contained village where everything vacationers could want is available. Fine dining, community services and top-notch shopping abound, including Tree Line Studios. The studio features work by local artists using a wide variety of media to depict the mountains George and Anne love so well. Artists represented at Tree Line include oil painter Ken Farrar of Kamloops, who captures Sun Peaks in all moods; Pavel Barta, whose simple yet effective shadow boxes and creative sculptures embody the active lifestyle so easily pursued here, and Kendra Smith whose realistic watercolors illustrate the allure of the summer and winter at Sun Peaks. Beautiful jewellery, carvings and works in clay are featured here as well, making Tree Line Studios a must stop for skiers and other vacationers who come to stay at Sun Peaks Resort.

No. 3, 3240 Village Way, Sun Peaks BC
(250) 578 - 2674

Hampton Gallery

Grace Brown's lifelong love of art has led her to satisfy the need for a first-class gallery in Kamloops. She has created a space in the heart of downtown where high-quality original art is key and visitors can see a remarkably wide variety of styles and media. At Hampton Gallery, art lovers relax in a comfortable, easygoing setting while they view the range of works by many of the best artists in Canada. In this pleasant atmosphere, you can see works

such as First Nations artist Daphne Odjig's strikingly stylized designs, Rod Charlesworth's impressionistic landscapes, and the beautiful watercolour paintings of Toni Onley. In addition to paintings, drawings and original prints, the gallery also features works in glass and raku, and sculptures from the Western Arctic. As well as its regular displays, Hampton Gallery holds two special shows a year, in spring and mid-November. Grace also offers individualized consultation to help clients find the works best suited to their tastes. With the wide selection available, you never leave Hampton Gallery disappointed.

167 Fourth Avenue, Kamloops BC
(250) 374 - 2400
www.hamptongalleries.com

The Art Ark Gallery

Bursts of color challenge your eye, then moments later clean, graceful curving lines of bronze statuary allow you visual rest. The Art Ark Gallery in Kelowna offers 5,000 square feet of cleverly designed exhibition rooms, six in all. These spaces vary in size, content and theme to best showcase both established and emerging Western Canadian artists. As the largest gallery in British Columbia's interior, it provides a veritable feast for the senses. Guests to the gallery will find canvases that inspire, sculptures that charm, mixed media to stir the blood and photography that leaves you breathless. Other media have been shaped and molded to take the viewer into the minds of the artists themselves. Owners Peter and Brigitte Werner strive to match the work of contemporary artists to clients who are seeking those pieces. Peter states, "I am not an art dealer, I represent the artist." The Art Ark's calming and client-friendly atmosphere reflects an environment designed to encourage the viewer to learn about art. Contemporary art aficionados and those who are merely curious walk side by side through this thought-provoking, mesmerizing, inspiring ocular roller coaster and come out richer or the experience.

1295 Cannery Lane, Kelowna BC (250) 862 - 5080 or (888) 813 - 5080 www.theartark.com

Gallery 421

Gallery 421 in Kelowna offers patrons a stunning collection of world-class artwork. Featuring both regional and local artists, owners Susan Einerssem and Bev Jackson believe strongly in supporting and showcasing working artists. Their goal is to consistently provide a fun, art-filled environment, in which to learn about art. Mary Kozel, a key employee at the gallery, looks after all of the little details that individually may seem unimportant, but put together make a trip to Galley 421 a magical experience. Patrons will be delighted with the ever-changing displays filled with jewellry, blown-glass art, Raku, soapstone carvings, bronze and steel sculptures and much more. There is a particular focus on three-dimensional art in the gallery, pieces that will simply amaze you. Several of the artists featured at Gallery 421 are world renowned. You will find delightful stone carvings from crafter Vance Theoret along with passionate paintings from Julia Hargreaves. Artist Jeff Holmwood designs exquisite pieces of blown glass art and you will be astounded by the sculptures of Brian Kelk and Kenneth David MacKay. They are just a few of the talented artisans on display at Gallery 421. Committed to contributing to the community in which they reside, Susan and Bev participate in and host several events throughout the year. Whatever the season, you will be glad you stopped at Gallery 421. 100-421 Cawston Avenue, Kelowna BC (250) 448 - 8888 www.gallery421.ca

Mat & Mitre House of Framing & Art Gallery

Penticton boasts a thriving and diverse community of art lovers, wine connoisseurs and outdoor enthusiasts. It is there you will find Mat & Mitre House of Framing and Art. Owner, artist and picture framer Jerrlee Hack has been serving the Penticton and South Okanagan area for over 10 years and attributes her success to the marriage of her creative approach to framing with loyal clients who frequent the gallery. With a roster of over four thousand clients she has made a name for herself by consistently providing high quality expertise with first class service to corporate and individual alike. Conservation framing being the cornerstone of the gallery brings to mind the many objects and originals you can frame and preserve for future generations. Local art is featured all year round and in the summer months you can see local artists at work in the outdoor studio garden area surrounding Mat and Mitre House. To learn more about art and those who create it, visitors are encouraged to ask questions and connect with the artists. Jerrlee, an artist herself, strives for diversity and flexibility within her gallery and provides space in which change often occurs. Exhibits are rotated monthly and patrons are inspired to stop in frequently to see what's new. Jerrlee also takes an active role in the community by teaching art classes to local students and donating framing to budding grade school artists in the area. Mat & Mitre House of Framing & Art features incredible framing and artwork that can be found worldwide, or you can see it right here in Penticton.

196 Eckhardt Avenue West, Penticton BC
(250) 492 - 5855

Caprice Fine Art & Co Inc.

Caprice Fine Art & Co., Inc. Studio Gallery features original oil paintings by artist/owner Caprice. She invites you to come and watch the artist at work. Caprice's paintings capture the feeling and energy of the landscape which surrounds her. Caprice Fine

Shangri-la, oil on canvas

Art is happy to have the opportunity to give back by donating paintings to different organizations such as the Muscular Dystrophy Association of Canada, Wildsite Environmental Society, Canadian Foundation for Women's Health, Reaching E-quality Employment Services for the Disabled and the Variety Club of British Columbia. Caprice began painting in 1994 and had the great fortune to be mentored by several professional artists who honed her skills. Moving to Kimberley, British Columbia in 1997, put her in the heart of the mountains, trees and lakes she so loves to paint. Caprice's first solo exhibition in 1998 gave her the confidence to pursue painting as a full time career. Her works are now in corporate and private collections across Canada, the United States, England, Holland and New Zealand. On April 7, 2005 Caprice was honored to be inducted into the Lethbridge Collegiate Institute's Wall of Distinction, where she attended high school. Caprice now paints and sells her work from her studio gallery in Kimberley and welcomes visitors by chance or by appointment.

65 Boundary Street, Kimberley BC (250) 427 - 2556
www.capriceartstudio.com

As Above So Below, oil on canvas

Rocky Mountain ArtisaNiche Gallery

In 1591, Uffizi Gallery in Florence, Italy became the first gallery/museum to open to the public. The first shop gallery was constructed in Paris in 1786, by a nephew of King Louis XIV. He rented his garden to shopkeepers, to build little shops from which to sell their creations. Rocky Mountain ArtisaNiche Gallery in Cranbrook carries on the long tradition of the representation and enjoyment of artistic works, open, and for sale, to the public. The gallery name was taken from the word "artisan," people who create with their hands, and "niche," a unique or specialty market. The high-quality works are all made by local East Kootenay artists and artisans, with new and original pieces being brought in continuously. The building is a two-story, 2800 square feet display area, with contributions from over 90 artists. Raku, ceramic and porcelain pottery are all represented, along with glass lamps, soapstone carvings, oil, acrylic and watercolor paintings, hand-forged wrought iron and exotic wood works. Cardigans, sweaters and vests are created by the Kootenay Knitting Company. Metal art is also featured. Gift wrapping is always provided free of charge and packing and shipping services are available to destinations in North America. Because of the creative nature of this establishment, if you don't see what you want, check with ArtisaNiche about having it made to order. With over 5000 items to choose from, the only difficulty you will find is deciding which ones to take home with you. 107 3rd Street S, Cranbrook BC Corner of HWY 3/95 (250) 417 - 2787

Galleries   Northern BC

Direct Art

Direct Art, Inc., specializes in featuring both the artists and their work in the gallery, an unusual occurrence in the far north. Artists such as Steve Hanks and Robert Bateman have brought their pieces for exclusive shows at Direct Art. In addition to great exhibits, John Westergard and his partner Julie Lepage provide Prince George with a truly state-of-the-art frame shop. With the latest in computerized matte cutters, beautiful mouldings, and 20,000 saws for doing fillits, these master framers provide a caliber of service and product usually found only in major cities. Direct Art is also the only frame shop in town with access to the 23 carat yellow gold and

22 carat white gold used in high-end, fine-art framing. For viewing exclusive art showings and for the best possible framing of your important and precious artwork, Direct Art, Inc. is the gallery of choice.
1102 6th Avenue, Prince George BC (250) 561 - 2561

Gifts

Fiber Options Naturals

Gord Johns was just out of college and on his way to a career as a financier in Asia when he stopped in Tofino for a brief holiday in 1994. Prompted by the dispute between logging companies and environmental activists over the fate of the local old-growth rainforests, Gord began to consider the issue of finding alternative ways of meeting consumer needs without destroying irreplaceable resources. His career plans abruptly changed course as Gord decided to devote himself to sustainable growth. In 1997, with support from a progressive local investment company he opened the first Fiber Options store. Fiber Options is devoted to providing customers with a wide variety of good quality, consciously made, environmentally friendly natural clothing and earth-friendly products including recycled materials. Nominated for an "ethics in action" award by the government of British Columbia, Gord and his staff organize the annual "Bike to Work" week in Tofino, and they celebrate Earth Day every year with a big hemp pancake breakfast. In addition to the original store in Tofino, Gord has partnered with Peter Skeels of Whistler and opened another store. A third store opened in Victoria in 2000. Gord found his purpose in life, and if he has any regret, it can only be that he never has gotten around to taking that holiday he planned in 1994!
5-120 4th Street, Tofino BC (250) 725 - 2192 www.ecoeverything.com

Method Marine Supply, Stormlight Outfitters, Tofino Fishing & Trading

"Outfitting you for a West Coast adventure," Method Marine Supply, Storm Light Outfitters and Tofino Fishing and Trading have everything you could possibly want or need for adventuring on the west coast of British Columbia or anywhere else in the world. If you're thinking about reeling in the big one, Method Marine carries fishing gear galore. A fully integrated marine supply company, it carries charts, bait, ice, rods, boots, raingear and much more. If the "big one" keeps getting away, they can help you try your hand at something different. Method Marine carries scuba diving gear, tanks, airfills, floater jackets and kayaking equipment too. They also have limited moorage space and a marine fuel depot. You name it, Storm Light Outfitters has it! They carry the best in tents, sleeping bags, camping stoves, hiking pants and boots, compasses, binoculars, lifejackets and survival gear. They also offer equipment rentals, a great way to research and try out before you purchase. What you don't find at Storm Light or Method Marine you will surely find at Tofino Fishing and Trading. This retail store has provided loyal customers with quality outdoor clothing and accessories since 1997. Finding just what you want should be a cinch when you're choosing from lines such as Woolrich, Sierra Designs, North Face, Smartwool, Timberland, Far West and Blundstone Boots. Dream big, plan a great adventure and come to any one of their great locations for all of your outdoor adventure needs. Method Marine Supply: 380 Main Street, Tofino BC (250) 725 - 3251 Storm Light Outfitters: 390 Main Street, Tofino BC (250) 725 - 3342 Tofino Fishing and Trading: Campbell and 4th Streets, Tofino BC (250) 725 - 2622 www.tofinofishingandtrading.com

Escapades West Vacations, Ltd.

Escapades West Vacations, Ltd., specializes in Vancouver Island travel and exploration. This is a team of travel consultants who are experienced travelers, educated in hospitality, tourism, marketing, communications, and corporate event planning. They have personally experienced every accommodation, business and activity they recommend. Corporate clients appreciate the unique team-building packages planned especially for their staff. Every travel package is custom designed to provide discerning clients with a memorable and worry-free time away. Whether you are looking for extreme sports venues, wine tours, great outdoor adventures or a romantic getaway, Escapades West will provide you with an itinerary to satisfy your every wish. From kayaking, whale spotting and snorkeling with seals, to hiking, golfing, cycling and tours, you will enjoy value travel. Check in with Escapades West Vacations, Ltd., and check into a once-in-a-lifetime vacation. Box 702, Nanaimo BC
(250) 758 - 7040 or (877) 737 - 3771
www.escapadeswest.com info@escapadeswest.com

Artina's Jewellery

At Artina's Jewellery, you will find something that is exclusive to the place and time. This is a store where they carry only the best of Canadian artistry. Each piece of jewellery is

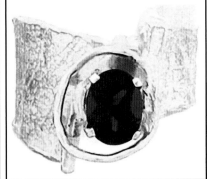

handmade and owner Lori is justly proud of the wearable art in her bright, attractive shop. They have created what they believe is the best venue for their artists to show and sell their works, and to inspire the loyalty of collectors. The artists are contemporary craftspeople, some of whom are also First Nations artists. Artina's well designed and colorful website not only has beautiful photos of dozens and dozens of individual pieces of gold and silver work, but also a special section on the legends of the First Nations. Many of the myths you will find described there are depicted on one-of-a-kind rings or necklaces in Artina's inventory. As well as a wide variety of artisan styles made of precious metals, semi-precious stones, beadwork and glass work, Artina's also offers the opportunity to commission a special piece. Their jewellery comes in all price ranges, and the store's gracious staff will be happy to help you. When you come in, you will also find that they have a special patient partner chair. 1002 Government Street, Victoria BC (250) 386 - 7000 www.artinas.com

119

Karl Stittgen & Goldsmiths

For more than 50 years, Karl Stittgen & Goldsmiths has been an institution on Granville Street. Generations of families have engaged the services of this boutique-style shop. Karl Stittgen earned an international reputation for his bold and elegant work with a distinctly European sensibility. Fine craftsmanship and fresh and timeless composition continue to be hallmarks here. The store offers one-of-a-kind pieces that are more than mere adornment, they are works of art. Crafted in white or yellow gold with fine gemstones, pearls or ancient Greek and Roman coins, each piece is a wonder. Diamond rings and wedding jewellery are custom-designed. Expert individual consultation is a most-important service and special orders are the norm. The sister store, Stittgen Fine Jewelry in West Vancouver, is of the same calibre. A few of its master goldsmiths trained under Karl and still produce some of his signature designs. For high-end, classic and custom jewellery, the trusted name is Karl Stittgen & Goldsmiths.
2203 Granville Street, Vancouver BC (604) 737 - 0029 www.stittgen.com

Favourite Things Art & Giftware

Favourite Things Art & Giftware has something for everyone. Owner Chris Jodoin believes in leaving a lasting impression with gifts and acknowledgements; ideally they should be out-of-the-ordinary and seem to have been created exclusively for the recipient. Favourite Things carries tasteful and unusual pieces that have been created by several talented local artisans. There is a fabulous collection of jewelry, locally made natural body care, cards, functional hand-blown glassware, pottery, artistically enhanced furniture, photography and home décor items. A new discovery awaits you in every corner of the shop. "Creatively Enhanced Designs" expresses Chris' artistic flair and love for funky decorations, recycled functional furniture and eco-friendly design. Chris wanted to create a business that utilized his interior design knowledge combined with his passion for art, so he also added an intimate gallery space to the shop's downstairs area. Crisp white walls and floors highlight the original artwork displayed there. The gallery is a great place to hold meetings, wine tasting and small parties. Favourite Things Art & Giftware offers design service and a free gift registry for special occasions.

614 Columbia Street, New Westminster BC (604) 519 - 1815 www.creativelyenhanced.com

Vancouver Architectural Antiques

In Vancouver, Eric and Judith Cohen offer a world class collection of architectural and decorative antiques. Specializing in Nineteenth and Twentieth century lighting, Vancouver Architectural Antiques enjoys a diverse and appreciative clientele worldwide. In addition to lighting, they are known for eclectic items like wind-up gramophones, high quality music boxes and all manner of decorative and architectural elements. If it is rare and unusual, they carry it. To name just two examples, they uncovered and restored a monumental crystal chandelier believed to have been from the Empress Hotel, and they acquired and sold a huge pair of Nineteenth century carved marble mantels originally from the London mansion of Lionel Rothschild. Recently they offered a rare, top of the line, Edison Open wooden horn. Whatever the item, if it is found at Vancouver Architectural Antiques, it is an example of the best of its period.
2403 Main Street, Vancouver BC
(604) 872 - 3131 www.vaaltd.ca

Vancouver Pen Shop

At the Vancouver Pen Shop, the sky is the limit when it comes to fine writing instruments. Owner Margaret Leveque has been in the pen business for more than 40 years and she knows quality. You will find Sheaffers, Pelikans, Montblancs, Parkers, Watermans and more. Pens made of gold and special metals, fountain pens, calligraphy pens; if you want it, they have it. Are you looking for a certain weight, a certain feel in the hand? This is the store that can help you. You can spend as much as $2,000 or as little as $4. Take your time; the staff will never hurry you. "We encourage customers to try different brands of fountain pens and nibs," says Margaret. "We're amazed at the people who would buy a quality pen without even trying it." The selection of pens, nibs, inks, bottles and converters is extensive. You will also find a wonderful selection of papers. After all, one must have good paper on which to use a good pen, eh? Post-sales support is stressed at the store, too. The Vancouver Tourism Office recently notified Margaret that a visitor to the city was so impressed with the enthusiasm, courtesy and caring displayed at the store that the visitor took the time to write and tell them about the experience.
512 West Hasting, Vancouver BC (604) 681 - 1612

Bionic Footwear

If you love shoes as much as you love comfort, Bionic Footwear has just what you need. At

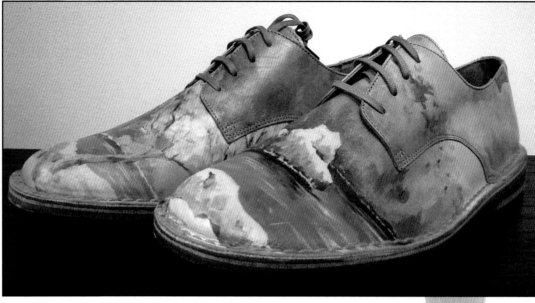

Bionic Footwear, the emphasis is on style and function, but the product must also be comfortable. They carry unique, quality footwear, perfect for people who want the latest fashions but must work on their feet. Bionic features limited edition shoes, so it is likely that you could be the only person in your city with a particular style. At Bionic you will find Cydwoq handmade European styled shoes and handbags, as well as Japanese limited edition Gravis and Puma Mahara products, made available only to Bionic Footwear in British Columbia. You will also find stylish and functional handbags, laptop bags, and travel luggage. With customers ranging in age from 19 to 90, Bionic Footwear prides itself on individual customer service with an emphasis on a relaxed buying experience. To find the perfect style for all of your footwear needs, Bionic is the place to see. 1072 Mainland Street, Vancouver BC (604) 685 - 9696
3065 Granville Street, Vancouver BC
(604) 731 - 9688

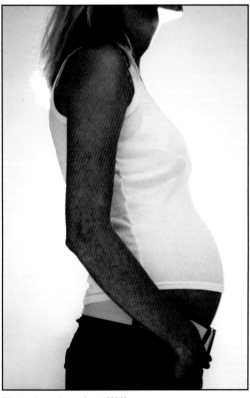

FoRMES

FoRMES was created in Paris in 1983 after economist Daniel Boudon observed that women he knew, who normally had no trouble finding attractive clothing, found the situation completely different when they became pregnant. The idea of providing stylish fashions for pregnant women caught on very quickly, and FoRMES now has an international network of 100 boutiques, including Vancouver since 1998. As Boudon put it, "Vancouver women have a strong sense of fashion and enjoy looking good. We are thrilled to give them the opportunity to remain en vogue while they are pregnant." FoRMES features fun, chic Paris fashions in two collections a year, spring and fall. The clothes are designed to be worn during all stages of pregnancy, from the first month through the ninth. These garments are made with such quality and ingenuity that they're often treasured and worn by women who aren't pregnant. Made from durable, elegant, long-lasting cottons and linens, there are FoRMES designs for every occasion, from casual to formal. You can see the current collection online at a website that is as attractive and engaging as the clothing, "… a sun filled collection for pregnant women." FoRMES Vancouver is a small, intimate boutique where personal service as well as style is always emphasized.
2985 Granville Street, Vancouver BC
(604) 773 - 2213 www.formesvancouver.ca

Photo by: Jonathan Willmann

122

Treasure Chest Antiques

Antiques have been Craig Morton's passion since early childhood and he bought his first antique chair at the age of 13. In 1993, he became owner of Treasure Chest Antiques, the oldest antique shop in West Vancouver, where he had previously worked as an employee. Treasure Chest Antiques is located in West Vancouver's charming Dundarave Village, renowned for its outstanding shopping, and Craig has ensured that the Treasure Chest fits right in. A wonderful place for browsers and serious collectors, it has the feel of a British antique shop from a generation ago. It features an

outstanding selection of carefully chosen antiques and collectibles ranging from silver tea services and English china teacups to 19th century hardwood dining tables and crystal vases. The store is laid out in the style of a private residence, with antiques throughout rather than in cabinets, so that customers can better visualize how the antiques will look in their own homes. With the help of his assistant Bari LeMare, Craig welcomes visitors every week from Tuesday through Sunday. Just a block from Dundarave Beach and within easy walking distance of Dundarave's fine restaurants, the Treasure Chest is a place you shouldn't miss on your next trip to Vancouver. 2465 Marine Drive, West Vancouver BC (604) 922 - 2982

Hill's of Kerrisdale

For fashionable, contemporary clothing and jewellery in the Vancouver area, you will want to visit Hill's of Kerrisdale. Hill's is the flagship store of a successful family of independent retailers, now run by third generation siblings Ross and Nancy Hill. The 8,000 square-foot specialty department store carries shoes, jewellery, fashion and casual men's and women's wear and is known for their great selection of designer brand denims. You will also find both a Blue Ruby Jewellery and Aritzia shop-in-shops at Hill's. Owned by Ross and Nancy, Blue Ruby has five additional locations in the lower Mainland, and each store has been uniquely modeled after a 1940s Elizabeth Arden showcase called the "Beauty Bar" that was discovered in a Los Angeles antique store. Blue Ruby carries original designer jewellery and fashion accessories made by artisans from around the world. The collections include a mix of earrings, bracelets, necklaces and rings, in addition to a variety of hair accessories, body jewellery, purses and belts. Brother Brian Hill runs the Aritzia boutiques, featuring trendy fashions for young women, with 15 locations across Canada. The Hill family's experience and dedication to quality and customer service has helped position the company as a leader.
2125 West 41st Avenue, Vancouver BC (604) 266-9177
www.blueruby.com
www.aritzia.com

Receptive Earth

Allison Wright founded Receptive Earth as a place where people can enjoy a friendly, eco-conscious boutique shopping experience. Originally located in Nelson, where Allison had moved to attend school, Receptive Earth relocated to Vancouver when Allison decided that it was time to reconnect with family and friends in her hometown. Specializing in hemp products and local designers, the store offers all-natural clothing from shirts and pants to tailored hemp/silk dresses and vegan-friendly shoes, in styles ranging from casual to haute couture. Receptive Earth offers 12 varieties of hemp-based oils and fragrances, and hemp twine is available undyed or in an extraordinary assortment of colors for jewellery, braiding and other craft projects. Allison's own special creations, Rainbow and Rasta multi-colored hemp twine, are available here. There are also unusual items like the hemp and cedar Rhythm Racks, designed to hold CDs but easily adapted for a lot of uses. Allison's commitment to encouraging the use of hemp fiber has led her to make her products available to wholesalers as well. A visit to Receptive Earth is a happy, rewarding experience. 4168 Main Street, Vancouver BC (604) 875 - 6198 or (800) 684 - 3189 www.receptiveearth.com

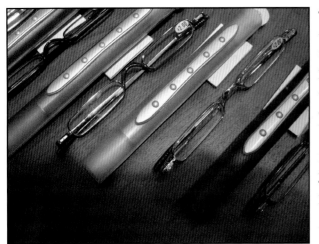

Readerwear

Wayne Yarrow and Benny Deis proffer a new concept in glasses stores, Readerwear, a shop focused solely on fashion reading glasses. Their goal is to create stylish, high-quality alternatives to the inexpensive and often low-quality reading glasses we've all seen on bargain displays. Their mission is to assure that style and quality are available to baby boomers with aging eyes. They reach out to the middle-aged who are experiencing the common problem of presbyopia, or increasing far-sightedness. Their glasses are made with the same care as prescription lenses, and Readerwear offers a wide selection of up-to-the-minute designer frames made from materials ranging from stainless steel to multilayered plastics. Customers can select comfortable, well-crafted frames that suit their face and their sense of style. Readerwear glasses have aspheric lenses: lighter, thinner and less distorting. They last much longer than common reading glasses, so they're well worth it. Located in Kitsilano, Readerwear features the largest selection of fashion and designer reading glasses in Canada. 2149 West 4th Avenue, Vancouver BC (604) 733 - 3801 or (877) 733 - 3801 www.readerwear.com

Puff Pipes

Imagine a place where you can find an eclectic mix of artisan-crafted smoking accessories, skateboarding gear and hand-crafted jewellery by local artists. Puff Pipes in Vancouver has a worldwide reputation for quality glass pipes and smoking accessories, hand-blown by area glass artists. Committed to supporting artists and designers, Puff Pipes carries an intriguing selection of locally crafted bracelets, pendants, and glass body jewellery too. But there's more! You will find a contemporary array of T-shirts and "hoodies" as well as skateboards in the long-board style, oversized old school skates, and "blast from the past" used vinyl records. In addition to supporting local artists, Puff Pipes also sponsors local events and enjoys being known as a local culture spot. Check out their online shop.

3255 Main Street, Vancouver BC (604) 708 - 9804 #14 – 712 Robson Street, Vancouver BC (604) 684 - PUFF (7833) www.puffpipes.ca

Miss Coquette Clothing Boutique

"Coquette: a woman whose behavior is intended to attract sexual attention by being playful and charming. A flirt." Leanne Dunic had ideas for starting her own business as far back as elementary school, so it was hardly surprising that she opened her store before she was 21. Featuring "Flirty, French and Feminine" clothing and gifts, in just a few years Miss Coquette has established itself as one of the most interesting and eclectic boutiques in Vancouver. The store specializes in dresses, with an emphasis on locally produced custom designs and jewelry. But you'll also find books, purses, bath products, stationery, and even teas for sale there. Leanne does not believe in limitations, and her store reflects her personal style. Miss Coquette also specializes in personalized customer care, with owner and staff getting to know each client's individual style and taste. The atmosphere is unhurried, warm and friendly. Come in and enjoy it yourself.

4372 West 10th Avenue, Vancouver BC (604) 221 - 2888 www.misscoquette.com

Tenthirtyeight Clothing Company

In 1987, Glyn Roberts moved from Manchester in the U.K. to Vancouver. Involved in the fashion industry for most of his life, it was only natural for him to open a clothing store; thus the avant-garde Tenthirtyeight Clothing Company was born. The knowledgeable staff at Tenthirtyeight avidly observe trends and styles, ensuring they'll have what customers want before they know they want it. Choosing environmentally conscious manufacturers like Patagonia and carrying many Canadian-made products, Tenthirtyeight specializes in street wear, active wear and outdoor gear. It's a flagship store for the increasingly popular Stussy line of casual wear, and carries Umbro and many other cutting-edge clothing lines and accessories in active sports and street style brands. At Tenthirtyeight every effort is made to guarantee customers receive the best service, whether they come from around the block or across the Pacific. Some of the staff are fluent in

Japanese and Cantonese, a great help to the increasingly large Asian clientele. The low-pressure service style of the staff is friendly and informative, and no matter what your needs are, you won't leave Tenthirtyeight disappointed.

1025 Mainland Street, Vancouver BC
(604) 669 - 6469
www.t38.ca

Dragon Space

Enter Dragon Space and you enter a world of wonders. The mystical, the magical and the mythological are the inspirations here. Celtic-themed giftware, finery, books, cards, and fantastic creations are all around. There are gnomes and dragons and faeries and trolls. There are items for Wiccans, aromatics and incense, T-shirts and gargoyles. Unique jewelry and figurines made by local artisans are also featured. You will find tarot cards and tarot readers. Since 1985, Jessica Pan has created an environment for exploring the great mysteries. Customers from around the world have found that this shop embodies the spirit of the genre. At Dragon Space, all eyes will find what they are looking for.

6 – 1551 Johnston Street, Vancouver BC
(604) 689 - 8931
www.dragonspace.ca

The Flag Shop

If Doreen Braverman had a nickel for every time she's been asked "Why a flag shop?" or "Who buys flags?" she would have a stack high enough to run a flag up. After 30 years in business she can confidently answer that, sooner or later, everybody buys flags. In 1975 she purchased Vancouver Regalia from Mr. And Mrs. Lyn Beard whose main clientele had been fraternal organizations, consulates and a few collectors who knew about the small fifth floor office. Several years later when Ontario flag suppliers could no longer meet her demands, Doreen felt it was time to expand. She purchased a building on 4th Avenue in Kitsilano and began experimenting with printing flags. At first she printed them with ink, however the "hand" of the print was so stiff it would crack if bent, so she had to learn how to dye-print. She was just in time for the run-up to Expo '86 where she won the honor of being the sole supplier of logo flags and banners. Now, with 13 locations across Canada, The Flag Shop has serviced scores of major events including Vancouver's 2010 Olympic Bid, the Calgary Stampede, and the APEC conference of 1997 The Flag Shop attempts to stock every national, provincial and state flag known as well as a selection of historical flags. Doreen also has a whimsical array of fun flags including baby-on-board and pirate motifs. The shop also supplies banners, pins, luggage tags, playing cards, decals, flagpoles and accessories. There's a lot more to the Flag Shop than flags! 1755 W 4th Avenue, Vancouver BC V6J 1M2 (604) 736-8161 www.flagshop.com

Beansprouts

It may sound like a health food store, but Beansprouts is actually Vancouver's most lively consignment shop for children's clothing and toys. Owner Angie Heintz has fostered a sense of community and togetherness in a retail setting. Local mothers also get into the act at Beansprouts by bringing in their own product lines such as handmade candy, locally produced videos and music are featured here as well. Estevan, Angie's precocious young son, can be found meeting and greeting customers and is always a willing play pal for visiting children. Merchandise at Beansprouts is organized by color and size within the store's wide open spaces. From skin care products to wooden toys imported from Poland, there is a rich array of goods to meet the diverse needs of growing children. A nursing chair and a play area allow mothers to shop unhurriedly. Angie has an art background and while providing children's art to stores, she realized a need existed for a classy neighborhood market to provide new and pre-owned products for children. Customers agree Beansprouts meets that need, and then some.
4305 Main Street, Vancouver BC (604) 871 - 9782 www.beansprouts.ca

Bodacious

This pretty pink shop is run by bodacious cousins, Lorna Ketler and Barb Wilkins They specialize in sizes 10 to 24 and have developed quite a following over the past five years by women who want to wear fun, funky and sexy clothing to celebrate their curves. This sassy store features local designers and one of a kind fashions. They also provide a wide variety of colourful accessories, hosiery and locally designed greeting cards. Get some girlfriends together and check out Bodacious for a fun shopping experience that won't leave you feeling bad about that dessert you had last night!
4393 Main Street, Vancouver BC (604) 874 - 2811 www.bodacious.ca

The Temple of the Modern Girl Boutique & The Art of the Inner City

At The Temple of the Modern Girl Boutique and The Art of the Inner City there is a lively mix of art, culture and fashion to be explored in this warm and inviting space. Denise daRoza began her Kind Clothing line in 1992 and her shop is a one-of-a-kind journey into the Vancouver fashion scene; a welcome respite from this age of endless imitation. With her eclectic, fun and funky aesthetic, daRoza designs new apparel and re-works vintage clothing. Neo or retro, it is certainly unique. There is a refined approach to modern style, emphasizing individuality and personal expression. You can

get a single piece or an entire wardrobe designed just for you. Jewellery of modern yet timeless design is also available as are quirky and beautiful accessories. For a fresh face in fashion, you will be delighted with the Temple of the Modern Girl.
2695 Main Street, Vancouver BC
(604) 484 - 4475

The Fort Toy Box

Patrick and Angela Reeves must have the best jobs in the world: they work in a toy box! The Fort Toy Box offers high-quality classic toys that you may have thought you'd never see again. These are not plastic toys manufactured to reflect current fads. They are the kinds of toys you remember from childhood and wish your children and their children could enjoy. What could be more evocative than a beautiful red Radio Flyer wagon? They originated in Chicago in 1917 and you can still have one. Classic red trikes, scooters and bikes, wooden puzzles, dolls and pedal cars; this store offers the kind of toy-shopping experience both children and parents love. Tops to tinker toys, tin whistles to whoopee cushions, paper dolls to cuddly stuffed animals, shopping at The Fort Toy Box is a lot of fun for the whole family. Patrick and Angela are always happy to search for the toys you remember and they have located many hard-to-find collectable and vintage toys for their customers. So stop in the tiny toy store with the great big heart, The Fort Toy Box. 9199 Glover Road, Fort Langley BC
(604) 882 - TOYS (8697) www.forttoybox.com

Durant Illusions Fashions & Art Gallery

An original concept from a very creative woman, Durant Illusions Fashions & Art Gallery is a one-of-a-kind boutique. In addition to featuring her own fashion designs, Karen Durant supports fellow artists by providing gallery space for their work. With exhibits changing monthly, Durant features many British Columbia artists, working in a variety of media. People visit regularly to see what's happening in the art scene. Karen is a gifted designer and seamstress. She creates her own line of clothing and also does custom work perfectly fitted to your shape, style, and wardrobe

requirements. When you see an item you want, Karen and her talented assistants can make it in your size in no time. The clothing is exquisitely made and expertly tailored to your personal specifications. Karen also offers carefully chosen ready-to-wear lines and she and her team provide skillful alterations as needed. Add the beautiful accessories on display, such as scarves, hats, shawls, capes and jewellery, and you can put together your personal fashion statement. Often called a unique boutique, Durant Illusions Fashions & Art Gallery is the place to go for an exceptional shopping and art experience.
33721 Essendene Avenue, Abbotsford BC (604) 852 - 1116

Village Antiques Mall

With ten thousand square feet of shopping space hosting 50 antiques dealers, Village Antiques Mall is a must- see attraction when you're in Fort Langley. Bob and Sandy Mauris have been running the Mall since 1984, and some of their employees have been with them for nearly that long. All their staff have wide-ranging backgrounds and knowledge of antiques. You can find anything there. Some of the specialties are home furnishings from the late 18th and 19th centuries, decorative china (many people come to the Mall to fill in gaps in their Royal Albert dinnerware collections), glass and rare advertising collectibles. Moviemakers often visit the mall looking for unusual props and furnishings to complete the set design for period films. With so many different dealers, unhurried browsing is the order of the day. Make sure you go early and allow plenty of time. In the highly unlikely event that none of the vendors has the specific item you want, you can sign up with the request registry. Sooner or later they will find it for you. 23331 Mavis Street, Fort Langley BC (604) 888 - 3700

Beach Basket Giftware

Diane MacDermott always has what her loyal shoppers are looking for. Gifts, collectables and cards to suite any occasion. Beach Basket Giftware is not just another gift shop. Diane and her longtime employee Tina Rattray have perfected the art of pleasing customers time and time again. Diane's shop has an unhurried, familiar atmosphere that invites you to take your time and truly enjoy the visually pleasing displays in every direction. There are many hard-to-find gift items, a wedding section and there is also a continual turnover of seasonal gifts. The ladies of The Red Hat Society are among some of her most loyal clientele, and for obvious reasons. Diane has an extensive retail background and she is committed to excellent customer service. Diane and Tina always go out of their way to help with any requests you may have, and they absolutely love what they do. Diane keeps very busy at Beach Basket Giftware, but she also has two other gift stores and a popular surf shop as well. As you can see, Diane truly loves working in retail. For a shopping experience you'll want to repeat, visit Beach Basket Giftware where Diane and Tina can show you why this shop is so loved by the locals. #11 13767 72nd Avenue, Surrey BC (604) 596 - 4299 www.beachbasketgifts@telus.net

And Everything Nice Children's Boutique

While visiting Whistler in the Blackcomb Mountains, you'll find not only sweeping views and world renowned skiing, but also a delightful village teeming with over two hundred shops and restaurants. Across from the Fairmont Chateau Whistler in the Upper Village you will find everything your little traveler needs at And Everything Nice Children's Boutique. Heather Aspden opened the store in 2003 offering several lines of clothing in sizes newborn thru 10, the majority of which are one-of-a-kind and made in Canada. She also stocks a full line of skiwear called Sport Obermeyer, exclusive to Whistler, as well as swimwear, sleepwear and accessories. Heather's daughter Nicola can be found in the shop each day, ready to lend a helping hand wherever it may be needed. Three-and-a-half-year old Nicola specializes in outfit coordination, acting as a mannequin for those shoppers who come without children, and as entertainment director for little shoppers who would rather visit the Kids Korner where they find television, books and toys to make their visit pleasant. This cozy store is open year round and provides not only friendly service but also a wide variety of beautiful, durable clothing that is sure to please everyone. #3-4573 Chateau Boulevard, Whistler BC (604) 938 - 6423 www.everythingniceboutique.com

Evolution

Jenine Bourbonnais lives in a mountain resort town and she has a passion for biking, boarding, art and fashion. Evolution is the perfect expression of those interests. Jenine is committed to helping people enjoy the Whistler lifestyle with high-quality products and service. The opportunity to be creative through product selection is a major element at

Photo by: David M. Di Biase

Evolution. An extensive denim collection, footwear, men's and women's fashions are all available there. No two items are alike. Open 364 days a year, Evolution offers sales, service, and rental of snowboards and mountain bikes plus all the accessories and clothing you could possibly ever need. Jenine is actively involved in her resort town. In her boutique you will listen to locals reporting on recent adventures, hear regional music and see the work of local artists on display. The name Evolution comes from revolution, as in the wheels of a bike moving forward. The store is a synthesis of Jenine's watchwords: style and technology, unity and respect, people and nature. #8-4122 Village Green, Whistler BC (604) 932 - 2967 www.evolutionwhistler.com

131

Kamloops Craft and Antique Mall

While visiting downtown Kamloops, you'll find four stores in one at the Kamloops Craft and Antique Mall. They are known not only for antiques, collectibles, dollhouses and miniatures, Kamloops souvenirs, postcards, stamps, film and local crafts made by local artisans, but also for model trains (they do a big mail order business in model trains and will ship them worldwide). Half the space is devoted to displays of model trains and they have an amazing variety of old toy trains, railway antiques and railway gifts. At Kamloops Craft and Antique Mall, you will enjoy an unhurried shopping experience. Every visitor benefits from the enthusiastic emphasis on customer service. They will happily stay open late for full tours. If you find the perfect gift but it won't fit in your suitcase, it's not a problem. They will ship your treasure so that it will arrive home when you do. The friendly staff at the Kamloops Craft and Antique Mall will cordially welcome your visit. 634 Victoria Street, Kamloops BC (250) 377 - 8510

The Horse Barn

At The Horse Barn you will find absolutely everything Western and more. This tack and ranch supply store has its own art gallery as well as cowboy clothing of every imaginable color, size and pattern and, well, everything else. It's not just a Western department store, they also carry English apparel and tack, but the art gallery sets it apart from any other. As a result of General Manager Tom Goode's interest in art, the gallery and gift store upstairs has grown to be the most comprehensive of any in British Columbia. The gallery displays a huge range of styles, from paintings, prints and jewelry to colorful handcrafted items and reproductions of bronzes. You will find it all in an inviting atmosphere where it's fun to shop. The Horse Barn's Western Wear Department was named Wrangler Canada's Retailer of the Year recently and the store just gets better over time. Go in, meet the friendly staff and go home with something uniquely Western from The Horse Barn. 517 Mount Paul Way, Kamloops BC (250) 374 - 3511 www.horsebarncanada.com

Kathy's Kloset Fashions

There are so many reasons why Kathy's Kloset has been dubbed Kamloops' unique boutique. This award-winning, home-based business offers much more than its wide range of designer clothing for every occasion and in every price range. There are also one-on-one fashion consultations, custom bra fitting, frequent-shopper cards, limousine shopping packages and personalized shopping service for men. You will enjoy the low-key, no-pressure atmosphere while you browse through beautiful fashions (most of which are Canadian made), custom foundations, scarves and accessories, or relax a while with tea or wine in their sitting area. Owners Kathy and Ian Roberts are firm believers in giving back to the community. After the tragic death of their son, they established the Brian Roberts Drug Awareness Fund and they pour their hearts and good works into the Street Services Safe House Program for kids. Annually, Kathy's Kloset puts on several fashion show fundraisers for various non-profit organizations. Among her many accolades, Kathy was honored with the YWCA's 2004 Woman of Distinction award. She was also nominated for the Business and Professional Women Association's 2004 Woman of the Year and 2004 Business Person of the Year awards. For expert fashion advice and a one-of-a-kind shopping experience, turn to Kathy's Kloset Fashions where the motto is "Pampering is our Pleasure."
5500 Kipp Road, Kamloops BC (250) 573 - 5739 www.kathysklosetfashions.com

Mallikka's Collection

If you can't get to India, Mallikka's Collection will bring a bit of India to you. Located right in the heart of downtown Kamloops, this family-based business is owned by Harpal Tate and her daughter Stephanie. Mallikka means "empress" and their designs are fit for royalty. They carry Indian products with a touch of North American flair. It is Harpal's desire to showcase the richness and texture of India in her British Columbian hometown. Her unique collection includes furniture, textiles, home décor items, clothing and jewellery. The selections of meticulously designed and manufactured products are exclusively done by Harpal. She deals directly with the craftsmen who make her products. She does not buy from factories but prefers to support the local people in India as she has a family-based business herself. Harpal oversees all aspects of the merchandise including manufacturing, quality control, packing and shipping. The details on her special designs are very important: even her tags on products are handmade with her specific design. It has been said that "there is a treasure in every corner" when you encounter India on Victoria Street at Mallikka's Collection. 367 Victoria Street, Kamloops BC (250) 372 - 5915

Bead Connections

At Bead Connections, it all started in 1995 when retail worker Brenda Tomlin found herself with extra time on her hands following a strike. She decided to make some earrings but she couldn't find what she needed. That's when it occurred to her there was a need for beads in Kamloops, so she created a store to provide them. Bead Connections started out in a small space at Thompson Park Mall. In its first year, it grew from a staff of one (Brenda herself) to five, and its inventory tripled. An expansion followed and Bead Connections moved into a 3,500 square foot retail space located in a downtown Heritage building. Now it offers hand-carved Native silver, clothing from acclaimed Canadian designer Dagoli, yarn, giftware, cross-stitching supplies, and lots of other merchandise in addition to the beautiful, high-end beads and crystals that it gets its name from. Bead Connections is also a place where crafters can get together. On Tuesday evenings, expert knitters and crocheters come to the store for "Needlemania" to share their skills with beginners. Cross-stitchers and beaders meet at the store on Thursday evenings. Classes are also a regular feature and helpful staff members are always available for consultation. 122 – 4th Avenue, Kamloops BC
(250) 372 - 1300 or (800) 260 - 9295 www.beadlady.net

The Golden Buddha

A WORLD IN ONE STORE... this certainly applies to The Golden Buddha. The Golden Buddha in downtown Kamloops provides unique products, imports, clothing and accessories from far away places such as India, China and even Africa. Exotic silks, tropical prints and casual cotton are all part of this one-of-a-kind collection that combines comfort with never ending style for all ages, including plus sizes and children's wear. You can find a dazzling variety of items ranging from imported giftware, to Mexican woven hammocks, to belly dancing accessories, to novelties, to tarot, crystals and metaphysical. It is similar to a mini emporium. Check out "The Bear Shed" for Kamloops and Canadian souvenirs. The Golden Buddha also offers costumes and costume accessories year-round, as well as costume rentals and fireworks. Karen and Brenda also believe in supporting the Kamloops community. They accept donations for their downtown Adopt-A-Grad program and they encourage people to bring in donations for the community food bank year round by offering 10% off any regular priced merchandise with donation. The Golden Buddha also puts together a relay team for the Cancer Society's annual Relay for Life and are an incentive prize donor for the event. The Golden Buddha is definitely a one-of-a-kind "World in One Store."
247 Victoria Street, Kamloops BC
(250) 374 - 1578
www.goldenbuddha.ca

Tulip Hill

On the busy and cheerful Main Street of Penticton, visitors will find a myriad of elegant and engaging shops to choose from. Among the most popular of these is Tulip Hill Inc. This charming shop specializes in stylish and contemporary clothing and accessories designed to make you feel and look your best. Owner Janice Ponce and her friendly staff are on hand to help you find exactly the right ensemble to fit your needs and personality. Tulip Hill carries the latest fashions, featuring Jennifer Lopez's chic urban line and known as the denim cult, Parasuco, from Italy. They also feature Canadian Designers, handbags with matching shoes and fabulous jewellery to compliment any outfit. The fun, relaxed atmosphere in the store puts shoppers at ease. While you shop, you can view stunning local artwork that acts as an intriguing backdrop to your shopping experience. Janice believes in listening to what the fashion community is looking for and providing it, along with consistent quality and service. As an active member of her community, she believes in giving back to the town that helps to support her and her shop. Tulip Hill sponsors the annual Miss Penticton Pageant and actively participates in other local events.

Janice is driven by her strong desire to help people find the specific item that is going to make them feel great about themselves and how they look. Whether you're looking for just the right thing to wear or you're in search of the perfect gift, Tulip Hill Inc., is the place to shop for fashion in the Southern Okanagan Valley. 326 Main Street, Penticton BC (250) 492 - 0662 www.tuliphill.com

Good Gracious Contemporary Gifts

Are you interested in an enjoyable shopping experience? If so, you'll want to visit Good Gracious Contemporary Gifts. Owner Judy Russell and her staff provide excellent customer service and enjoy their interactions with customers. You will be on a first name basis in no time! Good Gracious specializes in contemporary gifts, home accessories, and items to pamper yourself or friends. With an emphasis on Canadian-made art and gift items, Good Gracious has contemporary items like wall art, mirrors, glassware, wine racks and plaques, as well as paintings, pottery and jewellery. Products from Umbra, a major Canadian supplier of contemporary items for the home, can be found there. Among the many finds are a large selection of gift cards, candles, slippers, bath items and a charming baby section. If you don't see what you want, ask. Enjoy yourself!

3211 – 30th Avenue, Vernon BC (250) 545 - 2952

Terwilligers Gifts & We R Unique

The lively and cultured downtown area of Penticton offers a flourishing centre of commerce filled with interesting and memorable shops, restaurants and gathering places. Leading the way in a most prestigious group comes Terwilliger's Gifts & We R Unique, dual shops working together to provide you with a truly original and exciting shopping experience. The readers of *Okanagan Life Magazine* voted Terwilliger's as The Best Cool Gift Shop in the South Okanagan. Upon visiting, you are sure to agree. Terwilliger's features Canadian crafted items only and offer wonderful gifts of raku, kitchen collectibles, and gourmet goods, including handmade chocolates. We R Unique displays pieces found during the

owners', Cliff and Sharon Bristow's, extensive travels along with other desirable accoutrements such as 100% beeswax candles from Vancouver, hand-blown Polish glass and hand-hammered copper from Mexico. Both shops will provide you with interesting and exceptional pieces of work created by small-scale artisans who produce unique examples of functional and decorative art. Attaching the two shops is a roofed lane, which offers whimsical and practical garden décor during the spring and summer. During the winter this area features seasonal holiday vignettes. The weekend before Halloween in October finds the shop in especially high spirits while the Bristows host their annual, Christmas in the Lane open house. This special event draws visitors from Vancouver to the Prairies. Complimentary gift boxing is available for your convenience. Visit Terwilliger's and We R Unique to find special gifts that will help make lasting memories. 675 Main Street, Penticton BC
(250) 493 - 9221 & (250) 492 - 5990 www.terwilligersgifts.com or www.werunique.ca

Interior Gift Gallery

For 22 years, owner Lucy Glennon has been devoted to helping her customers find the perfect gift or hard-to-find treasure for their décor. Carol Owen has been her phenomenal manager for 18 years. Together they offer an amazing and ever-changing array of local pottery, collectibles, dinnerware, Italian bead and charm bracelets, and gift and home enhancement possibilities. Something new comes in every day. Customers are often heard asking if there has been a change in ownership because the

store takes on a new persona with its "always something new" merchandise. Gift wrapping and gift certificates are available too. Interior Gift Gallery generously donates part of its proceeds to the Hospice Foundation and Juvenile Diabetes. Stop by, meet Lucy and Carol, enjoy yourself and discover a special gift for you or a friend. 3204 30th Avenue, Vernon BC (250) 542 - 9216

Original Beach & Body Company

Looking for a shopping experience? The Original Beach & Body Company, X.10.sion 207 and Losers Ink., are "the" places to shop in the Okanagan! Promising a shopping experience you won't soon forget. Owners Rod Reinbold and Lori Mauro have gathered products that guarantee the purchaser an opportunity to express his or her distinctive style, as well as an opportunity to experiment. All three storefronts are adjacent to one another, each with their own flavor. Original Beach & Body Company features swim/surf fashion, footwear, sunglasses, jewellery, and in peak season, boasts over 5000 bikinis with only four that are similar. Next door at X.10.sion 207 you'll find casual fashion's biggest labels, along side the world's best premium denim brands, shoes, belts, bags and exciting, contemporary furniture. If you're looking for a great deal, just steps around the corner you'll find Losers Ink., Original Beach & Body Co. and X.10.sion 207's outlet store, where everything in the store is on sale all the time. Hard to believe but true. To see for yourself check out their website for the list of brands available.
207 Bernard Avenue, Kelowna BC (250) 979 - 0393
www.obbc.net

| Gifts | | Kootenays-Rockies |

Gold Yogi Imports

Thea Trussler has grown accustomed to hearing about the profound effect the energy flowing through her store has on her customers. Since opening Gold Yogi Imports in 2003, Thea has been working with international artisans, offering them an excellent opportunity to show their work in a venue that both honors creativity and beauty. Many patrons of Gold Yogi Imports say they feel energized and mysteriously healed the moment they walk through the door. Gold Yogi is one of those places that make an indelible impression on your memory. It's not just a place to buy gorgeous items for your home, Gold Yogi has a fantastic staff whom are always ready to help you with gift or decorating ideas. They truly love finding just the perfect item for each customer. Then there's also Beauregarde, the sweet-faced store mascot. It's worth a visit just to meet this lovable Great Dane who is well known by the locals as the keeper of smiles. With all of the visual delights and the shop's gentle giant, it's not surprising Gold Yogi customers come back time after time. If you like unique, yet reasonably priced items for your home then come and indulge your spirit in the intriguing aura of Gold Yogi Imports.
356 Baker Street, Nelson BC (250) 354 - 3938

Mary's Gifts

In the city of Quesnel, Mary's Gifts is the first choice of shoppers for unique, specialty items. Owner Lois Klotz and her excellent staff are committed to accommodating every wish for your special occasion. Wonderful scents and tranquil sounds add to the friendly atmosphere as you browse among the candles, pictures, ornaments and fine linens. All of the luxurious bath products are 100% Canadian-made. There are many collectibles including items from the Bradford Exchange. Once you have made your selection, you may have it beautifully gift-wrapped for that special someone at no cost to you. You will find what you are looking for and a great deal more at Mary's Gifts.

#102 – 246 St. Laurent Avenue, Quesnel BC

(250) 992 - 2959

Mason & Daly
General Merchants

Located in historic Barkerville and open only May to late December, during the Old Fashioned Christmas Celebration, Mason & Daly General Merchants consists of three businesses in one: The General Store, C. Strouss Dry Goods and A. MacPherson Watchmaker. The General Store is a unique 19th century style emporium carrying an extraordinary selection from sealing wax and stationary supplies to haberdashery,

straight razors and tonsorial supplies. Music boxes, traditional candies, and much more delightful merchandise that you may not have realized were still available can be found at The General Store. C. Strouss Dry Goods is a shop offering the best tea varieties available in Western Canada, including teas that are hand picked and hand rolled into tea pearls. In keeping with the traditional theme, C. Strouss also offers cheese cut from 30-pound wheels, steam pudding moulds, and other household goods evoking the best of bygone days. The prestigious A. MacPherson Watchmaker is a jewellery shop originally founded in the 1860s by the goldsmith whose tradition of exquisite craftwork is carried on by the modern-day jewellers. They proffer cameos, rings, amber and much more to the discriminating customer. As with jewellers' shops of old, A. MacPherson Watchmaker also offers watch repair, and you can even buy raw gold nuggets there. Step back in time at Mason & Daly General Merchants and rediscover the joy of shopping in a bygone era.

4301 Barkerville Highway, Barkerville BC (250) 994 - 3227

Santhi's Urban Boutique Co.

Santhi Thomas-Irvine wanted the people of the small city of Prince George to be able to have access to big-city style. With Santhi's Urban Boutique Co., she provides that and more. Fine men's and women's Canadian designers are featured in the beautiful clothing lines she offers. Santhi enjoys getting to know her customers and she has a real talent for helping them complement their own style or create a new look. Travellers and Prince George residents alike are

energized by Santhi's wide array of clothing and accessories. You will find designer dresses, jackets, robes, and ties. Just about everything you need to round out your wardrobe or provide the perfect gift for a friend or family member. Her accessory lines include body jewellery, handbags, sunglasses and ultra-cool hats in many styles and colors. Whether you are looking for business and casual attire or a perfect dress for a big night out, at Santhi's Urban Boutique Co., you are what's hot.

3093 Wallace Cres, Prince George BC (250) 614 - 2333

Health & Beauty

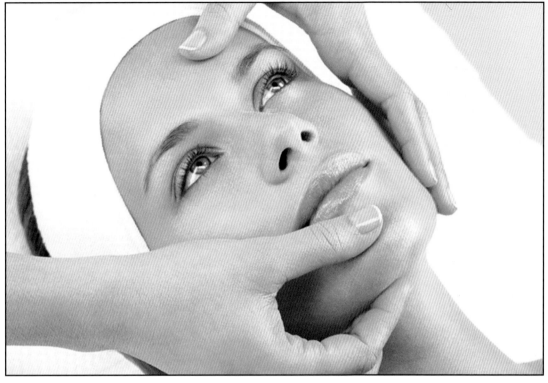

Tofino Massage Works

Tim Cariou of Tofino Massage Works has created his own massage style that evinces a distinctively Asian influence. In addition to his three years at the Canadian College of Massage and Hydrotherapy in Ontario, Tim trained for over 25 years with five master practitioners from China. In 1982, he became the Western Canadian Black Belt Champion of Tai Chi and Kung Fu, and he is an accomplished instructor in Chi Kung, also called Qigong, a centuries-old Taoist technique for improving health through a combination of physical postures, breathing techniques and mental focus. His signature massage combines five modalities into one for deeply effective and rewarding results. Tofino's rustic location enhances the healing qualities of the experience. Coming to this building that stands right on the beachfront, you begin to shed your tensions even before you enter. The soft, warm lighting and the foot massage devices in the waiting room further enhance the therapeutic experience. And you can even take the experience home with you through the information and charts provided for you on how to learn to become your own practitioner. 1180 B Pacific Rim Highway, Tofino BC (250) 266 - 4888 www.tofinomassage.ca

Solwood Healing Arts & Spa

Let the magic of Clayoquot Sound enter your soul. Solwood Healing Arts Retreat and Spa is an ever-evolving, one-of-a-kind sanctuary at the heart of Tofino's Chesterman Beach. Enjoy the powerful healing energy intrinsic to Clayoquot Sound while you relax and release tension through a full range of spa treatments. Owner Janine Wood's emphasis is on hospitality, health and healing. Located in the forest gardens of Chesterman beach, Solwood provides both inexpensive and luxury accommodations. If Bed and Breakfast is your preference, you may enjoy tranquility and rest at the main house where a delicious breakfast is prepared for you each morning. Also available are Solwood's West Coast cottages, complete with kitchenettes. Or stay in the salal berry cottage and listen to the surf as you sleep among the trees. The fully equipped forest den Cottage is cozy and rustic. You can revel in the forest setting as you watch the flames in your wood stove or walk to Chesterman beach. In addition to spa treatments such as Swedish/aromatherapy massage, Lomi Lomi, hot/cold stone therapy, crystal light therapy, Shiatsu, Thai massage and Reiki, Solwood offers yoga and dance classes and workshops. Rest, relaxation and tranquility in a beautiful setting, what more could you ask?
1298 Lynn Road, Tofino BC (866) 725 - 2112 www.solwood.ca

SpaEthos

When it first opened its doors in 2000, SpaEthos was called the Patina Spa & Salon. However it wasn't long before the owners, Dr. Peter Fransblow and his wife Ann, decided they needed to project a clearer message to their clients about what their scope of service represented. SpaEthos was the outcome. It wasn't just a cosmetic name change. The new name helped them to focus on the definition of the spa experience as part of a complete approach to healthy living. SpaEthos has been voted the Number One Spa in Vancouver by the *Vancouver Courier* as a result of its commitment to regarding each client as a guest deserving of exceptional treatment. Experienced, compassionate therapists and estheticians provide services in an environment that is contemplative and soothing. It is also kept at an unsurpassed level of cleanliness. The Fransblows offer educational seminars in the evenings, covering topics such as nutrition and personal career coaching, and they work with local fitness clubs doing personal fitness testing. Their holistic approach to spa therapy draws clients from around the world who, in turn, spread the word about the exceptional services at SpaEthos. 2200 West 4th Avenue, Vancouver BC (604) 733 - 5007 or (866) 826 - 3838 www.spaethos.com

BeautyMark

After only four years in business, BeautyMark has already acquired the reputation as an ultra-chic place to shop for cosmetics. Celebrities who've been spotted at BeautyMark are Bridget Fonda, Avril Lavigne, Jessica Alba and Selma Blair. Everyone on the BeautyMark staff is a makeup artist and is ready to provide services for weddings, photo shoots or other special occasions. A third of the staff have experience in the television industry, so they are fully capable and willing to give expert advice. Customer service at BeautyMark is incomparable. The staff all share a passion and commitment to educate their customers in the use of beauty products, even though regular clients are often already very knowledgeable about cosmetics. BeautyMark specializes in brands that aren't mass-marketed, and they are proud to be among the very first boutiques to launch lines like Cake, Principessa, Deserving Time and Safety Girl. Marc Brunet, owner of BeautyMark was the main buyer in the cosmetics division for his previous employer, so it was only natural for him to eventually establish his own cutting-edge beauty supply boutique. You can see this great treasure at any one of their three Vancouver locations. 991 Denman Street, Vancouver BC 1120 Hamilton Street, Vancouver BC 2830 West Broadway, Vancouver BC (877) 8BEAUTY www.beautymark.ca

TAP True Aromatherapy Products

This unique aromatherapy store and spa is nestled in the historic village of Fort Langley. TAP is more than just a store, it is an experience. As you step into the TAP Aromatherapy store, you will be welcomed by a variety of sensory delights. The aroma of the 100% natural, therapeutic grade essential oils will envelop you as you stroll through the store sipping on a cup of complimentary organic lavender tea. The holistic treatment rooms offer a variety of massage treatments such as Aromatherapy Massage, Hot Stone Massage, Shiatsu, Thai Massage, Reflexology and more! For those in a hurry, the chair massage in the front of the store will relax and ease muscular aches and pains in as little as 10 minutes. The TAP product line is manufactured in the lab located on the premises, ensuring the best quality control. 9183 Glover Road, Fort Langley BC (604) 888 - 6800 www.tapstore.ca

7th Heaven Day Spa

The focus is on esthetics at 7th Heaven Day Spa, with a full range of facials, pedicures, body waxes, and beauty services offered for both women and men. 7th Heaven features make-up artistry alongside more traditional spa treatments such as massage and body wraps. The soothing and luxurious hydrotherapy room features a hydro-massage tub with 250 water jets to rejuvenate your body while the fragrance of essential oils soothes your spirit. 7th Heaven takes a healthful approach to skin and body care, from hydrating manicure treatments to Decleor natural oil facial treatments. At 7th Heaven, you can select services à la carte or choose from a variety of packages, from "queen of the day" to the half-day revitalization package. Special offerings include the Merle Norman Teen Facial, a 90-minute treatment that includes education about proper skin care and make-up application lessons. There are five Grad packages, each a thoughtful gift for your high school or college graduate and special bridal packages. If you're looking for a place to enhance your beauty within and out, you've found it at 7th Heaven Day Spa. You can even get your ears pierced, or your nose if you wish. 2600 Guildford Town Centre, Surrey BC (604) 588 - 2711 www.7thheavendayspa.com

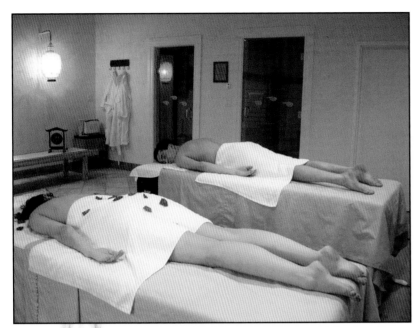

Sunmore Ginseng Spa

In a serene mountainside location, surrounded by evergreens, Sunmore Ginseng Spa helps the body and soul relax, revitalize and rejuvenate, Sunmore's "3 R" approach to total well-being. In 1991, Donna Chang, a master herbalist and chairwoman of Mintong Pharmaceutical Company of Taiwan, founded Sunmore Healthtech Ltd., the only professional ginseng production company in North America. Eight years later, Carrie Pan, the General Manager of Sunmore, brought her the idea of creating a spa that would employ the therapeutic properties of ginseng in a wide variety of treatments. In the fall of 2004, Sunmore Ginseng Spa opened for business. As you arrive, you'll see an inspiring waterfall fountain in the foyer, which also serves as an area where you can change from your street shoes into special slippers provided by the spa. Enter a world where you can select treatments a la carte or choose one of the special multiple-treatment packages. Sunmore offers a ginseng steam room, massages, aromatherapy, body wraps, facials and much more. The decor is simple but luxurious in the traditional Asian style. Most of the furnishings were shipped from Asia, including many antiques, to create this distinctive, healing environment. The next time you're in the Kamloops area, you owe it to yourself to make time for a visit to Sunmore Ginseng Spa.

925 McGill Place, Kamloops BC (250) 372 - 2814 www.sunmore.com

Endless Summer Beachwear & Tanning

Can't get to the beach? Then you'll want to visit Endless Summer Beachwear & Tanning, Doddie Hobbs' answer to time in the sun. With a reputation for the friendliest staff in Vernon, who provide the little things that count, Endless Summer is definitely worth a visit. The tanning section of the facility provides four levels of tanning featuring the King Cancun, a deluxe king size tanning bed. Of course you'll want spectacular swim gear to go with that fantastic tan. Endless Summer carries an extensive line of swimwear including Ripcurl, Groggy, Gossip and Maïa made by Baltex and featured in *Elle* magazine. You'll find a huge variety of mix and match swimwear, as well as men's beach wear and sandals. They also feature summer accessories, shoes and sunglasses. Doddie

makes every effort to keep her customers happy. She will custom-order lotions and clothing, and she changes promotions frequently. Also a travel agent, Doddie's vision is to make Endless Summer Beachwear & Tanning a one-stop shop to tan, purchase beachwear and accessories, and make that next trip to the beach a reality.

4412 – 27th Street #108, Vernon BC
(250) 542 - 3443

Amici's Hair & Body Spa & Group Day Spa

Coni Grande Lenza, owner of Amici's Hair & Body Spa & Group Day Spa, has created an oasis designed to soothe body and soul. She has used the ancient Eastern practice of Feng Shui to provide balance and harmony between the artisans who work in the spa, the guests who come to rejuvenate themselves, and the environment in which the transformation takes place. Amici's, which is Italian for friends, provides world-class service and was

voted Best Hair Salon & Spa in the Okanagan in 2004. Welcoming men and women, their friendly, knowledgeable staff is on hand to pamper you while providing body wraps, facials, massages and more. Staff members not only assist clients with their spa treatments, they also educate clients on follow-up care, products and treatments available. In the salon, guests will find multiple options available as well. Human hair extensions, full esthetics, tanning, skin and body care, and makeovers are just a few of the ways they can give you a new look. Many packages are available, including an hour long "Slumber Party" for four guests 12 and under, a three hour pre-teen package for those 16 and under, bridal or graduation bundles, and special getaways designed for couples. For those who wish to book a full day at the spa, a variety of sandwiches, salads and beverages can be added to any package. Your day in paradise awaits you at Amici's Hair & Body Spa & Group Day Spa.

595 Lawrence Avenue, Kelowna BC (250) 762 - 3000 www.amicishairandbodyspa.com

Carter & Company Salons

Imagine yourself in the sumptuous atmosphere of rich luxurious colors and comfortable furniture. Surrounded by charming antiques, you settle into a cozy chair. Music flows from a turn of the century baby grand piano and light from chandeliers twinkles above you. No need to rouse yourself, just surrender to the extra special salon care at Carter & Company Salons. Owners Sherry Carter and Larry Heck have created an oasis that invites you to treat yourself well. Sherry, winner of the 2002 BC Hairstylist of the Year award, will graciously assist you in determining your most flattering hairstyle. Carter & Company is a full-service hair salon. Talented hair color and technical specialists will expertly guide you from harried to haloed. The staff at Carter & Company work as a friendly and courteous team to bring you the best in personal care. It's no wonder that nearly 80% of Carter & Company Salons' clientele are returning regulars. Sherry and Larry have won numerous awards and look forward to exceeding your expectations. 122 – 1950 Harvey Avenue, Kelowna BC (250) 868 - 9669

Essential Elements Day Spa

Essential Elements Day Spa in stunning Vernon will transport you to paradise, if only for a few hours. Owner Candice Timm is a registered massage therapist and licensed spa technician who believes in both serving and educating her clients. Her state-of-the-art facility offers a relaxing and comfortable environment filled with warm, soothing scents and earthy tones. Candice and her staff pride themselves on attention to detail. Their mission is to provide the best quality of service, one hundred percent of the time to each and every client. Once a session has begun, no interruptions are allowed to disrupt the rhythm and flow of the experience. Services you can enjoy at the Spa include facials, massage, pedicures and manicures, body wraps, paraffin dips, waxing and artificial nail enhancements, to name a few. Essential Elements staff consists of a group of Registered Massage Therapists, licensed Estheticians, day spa Technicians and alternative healers. The staff is adaptable and makes every effort to accommodate the diverse needs of their guests. Candice urges guests to have a consultation with one of the Therapists if they have unique health concerns or if they are interested in a treatment that the spa does not currently provide. A variety of packages are available. After just one visit you too will see the happiness of its clients is truly the number one focus of Essential Elements Day Spa. 116-4411 32nd Street, Vernon BC (250) 275 - 7060 www.Vernondayspa.com

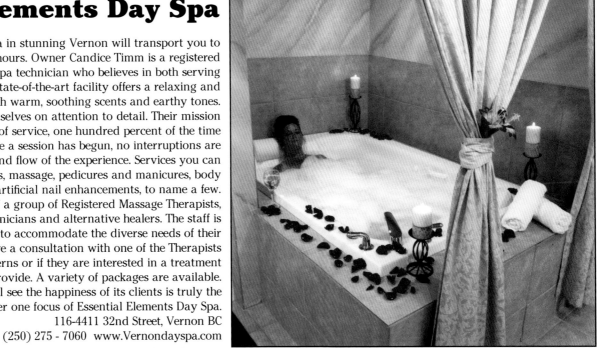

Euphoria Esthetics

Webster's Dictionary defines euphoria as a feeling of well-being or elation. The word is derived from the Greek euphoros meaning healthy. Euphoria Esthetics, in lovely Penticton, offers health, well-being, elation and more to its diverse guests. Owner Emily Baird brings more than 14 years of experience in esthetics to her fabulous spa. In 2003 Euphoria Esthetics was the recipient of the Best Day Spa award by *Okanagan Life*. Emily and her staff focus on providing the best care and service possible to their patrons, including sanitation that exceeds industry standards and expectations. The spa provides facials, massages, waxing, tinting for brows and eyelashes, foot and hand care, manicures and nail care, and treatments specifically designed for gentleman. Euphoria Esthetics also offers several packages such as the Especially Yours Package, which includes a pedicure, facial, and brow shaping, a perfect way to pamper yourself before a special night on the town. Several exclusive product lines are used at Euphoria Esthetics. Designed with your comfort and safety in mind, these include the formaldehyde free polishes and Gehwol, a medicated line of foot care items. The spa is open Tuesday through Saturday, welcomes walk-ins and has wheelchair accessibility. At Euphoria Esthetics you'll experience the difference and feel the euphoria. #112-2436 Skaha Lake Road, Penticton BC (250) 492 - 1065

Lattitude Salon & Day Spa

How would you like a place to go, a place away from home, where attendants want to provide soothing, head-to-toe relaxation and they want to do this at an affordable cost. Sound appealing? Michelle Connauton, owner of Lattitude Salon & Day Spa and licensed cosmetologist, wants you to relax your mind and let her staff help you feel your best ever. Inside the full-of-character building that houses Lattitude Salon, you will find a staff chosen for personality, pride, perfection and persistence. All are highly qualified professionals who make your well being their primary goal. Surrender your senses to any one of their personalized facial and skin care treatments. Luxuriate in the essences of Aromatherapy.

Experience relaxation and rejuvenation with personalized body treatments such as a Creamy Moor Mud Wrap, a purifying Seaweed Wrap or a Hot Stone Massage. These treatments are formulated using natural products for the benefit of your body, mind and spirit. For the "complete you," Latitude also offers nail, waxing, tinting, tanning and hair services. Gift certificates are available and Lattitude Salon & Day Spa is an ideal place to book your special events, from birthdays to bachelorette parties. Relax your way to a refreshed, vibrant you! 3609 32nd Street, Vernon BC (250) 549 - 3311

Koko Beach Tanning & Hair Salon

There is at least one place in Cranbrook "where the sun always shines." Koko Beach Tanning and Hair Salon, owned by Seana Lee and Jeffrey Coolbaugh, was winner of The Best of the Best business award for three consecutive years and was also voted Best in Service by the Chamber of Commerce.

Koko Beach is very involved in the community, too. A business with heart, the salon contributes to Minor Hockey Events, Muscular Dystrophy, Junior Chamber of Commerce, Slo-Pitch, Arthritis and various other organizations. The staff, including Cosmetologists Marla Smith and Andreja Scandland, are well-versed in their areas of expertise. Koko Beach features Kenra and AG products, and they intend to provide the most spectacular service and innovative products in East Kootenay, for the enjoyment of everyone. Koko Beach exists to help people look and feel their best all year, with special services for all of your important occasions. Whether it is Christmas, parties, graduation, ceremonies or a wedding, they know what to do and can arrange for the right package of services for your event. They offer the largest tanning salon in East Kootenays, with fair prices and fantastic color lines. Services are available for men and women, including all hair services imaginable. The salon also offers special occasion or every day makeup, updo, facials, and ear piercing. The nail, tanning and waxing processes round out the services. You can make an ordinary day special every time you visit Koko Beach. 20 B Seventh Avenue South, Cranbrook BC (250) 426 - 7098

Trendsetters Hair Studio & Day Spa

Rejuvenate, revitalize, renew and enjoy! Trendsetters Hair Studio & Day Spa will refresh and pamper you with a variety of services designed to stimulate your body and invigorate your soul. The staff at Trendsetters works as a team. Their hair stylists will help you create a look that meets your needs and suits your lifestyle. They carry a full line of products to give your hair control and help it stay healthy. Their Esthetics Services include laser technology, waxing, makeup, tinting and air brush tattooing. They offer nail services as well as rejuvenating body treatments, including soothing facials, oxygen aromatherapy, stone therapies, massage and more. Trendsetters also provides tanning. If body piercing is more your style, you will find the largest selection of body piercing jewellery in all of British Columbia and a guaranteed sterile environment. Owners Craig and Sonya Landon and their professional, friendly staff guarantee you won't be disappointed. Their desire is to exceed the expectations of their clients. They aim to build your self-esteem and make you feel and look beautiful. Be sure to ask about their spa packages. Then get away from it all and let Trendsetters Hair Studio & Day Spa take care of you.
6557 Hart Highway, Prince George BC (250) 962 - 9262 www.trendsetters.com

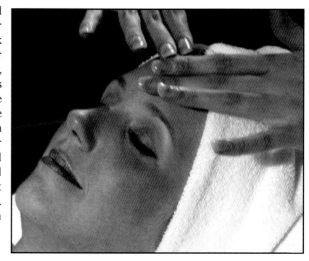

The Hills Health Ranch

Photos by
Don Weixl

Wrap yourself in the pure pleasure of a total well-being overhaul or simply a minor adjustment. You can be pampered by the caring staff, indulge in your love of the outdoor life or simply be allowed to quietly drink in British Columbia's beautiful rolling, forested Cariboo Wilderness. Owner Patrick Corbett operates the ranch with his wife, Juanita, Wellness Director Regula Wittmer and a staff that includes a fulltime kinesiologist, certified fitness instructors, nutritionists, lifestyle counselor, nurses and physiotherapists. An extensive menu of body treatments, wellness workshops, private consultations, exercise modalities, individualized meals, seasonal recreational activities and camaraderie, have been designed to help you focus your energy on building long-lasting habits which enable you to live a happier and more focused life. A Kids Kamp for children ages 4 to 12 provides educational, energetic activities for youngsters, with several activities centered around horses, their care and communication. In recognition of the ranch's dedication and patron satisfaction, The Hills Health Ranch has been acknowledged four times as Specialty Spa of the Year. Consider what your goals may be for your stay, which can be from one to 30 days. Once you are on your way, you will find the Ranch nestled in the serene mountains of the Southern Cariboo off Highway 97 North.
Box 26, 108 Mile Ranch BC
(250) 791 - 5225/6384 (FAX) www.spabc.com

Skin Sense Esthetics

The only Aveda spa in northern British Columbia, Skin Sense Esthetics offers one-on-one service that makes it possible for people to feel and look their best naturally. The fully licensed and certified technicians specialize in treatments that enhance natural beauty and help boost self-confidence. Made from pure flower and plant essences, Aveda products are in great demand worldwide. The Minnesota-based company was founded by environmentalist Horst Rechelbacher in 1978 to provide all-natural alternatives to chemical beauty and skin care products. Aveda is the exclusive supplier to Skin Sense Esthetics. The exceptional quality of treatments at Skin Sense Esthetics stems not only from Aveda products, but also from the time and attention devoted to each client. Whether new or quite knowledgeable, all clients are encouraged to talk with the staff both before and during their visits to let the practitioners know their individual expectations and needs. Each service is provided by an expert in that particular area, from electrolysis to aromatherapy. Rest assured, you'll be in great hands when you visit Skin Sense Esthetics.

1486 Second Avenue, Prince George BC
(250) 563 - 6808
www.skinsensesalonspa.com

TreSpa

TreSpa is a favorite destination in the Quesnel community. Owners Nellie Belbin and Melissa Sagar have created a warm and beautiful environment where earth tones and soothing sounds of the waterfall greet you at the entrance. Customers can truly relax and benefit from the best of personal service at TreSpa. "The power of touch is the essence of relaxation." You will receive personalized, professional spa treatments from the caring staff at TreSpa. The expert staff is made up of qualified technicians and skin-care specialists who are all licensed podologists. Their concern transcends external appearances with a whole-person approach to the client's well-being. There is an array of high-quality skincare products and makeup, as well as a lovely selection of jewellery. To visit TreSpa is to treat yourself to the finest in personal care.

310 St. Laurent Avenue, Quesnel BC
(250) 991 - 0916
www.trespa.ca

Photo by: Josephine Tan-Eber

Home Decor, Gardens, Flowers & Markets

Spinnakers Spirit Merchants

Spinnakers Spirit Merchants was founded in 2004 to fill a void in British Columbian beverage retailing, providing the hard-to-find wines, microbrewery beers, single-malt scotches and other interesting spirits unavailable from other retailers. The business is partly an offshoot of Spinnakers Brewpub, the first brewpub in Canada, Paul Hadfield, the Brewpub's founder, now acts as consumer and taster for Spinnakers Spirit Merchants, while Larry Arnold, well-known in British Columbia for his wine writing, holds the position of Manager. Through its relationship with an agency that represents many Vancouver Island and Okanagan Valley wineries, Spinnakers Spirit Merchants is able to provide wines that are otherwise available only at the wineries themselves. They also carry the largest local selection of craft beers, with an emphasis on the great American craft beers of the Pacific Northwest, and many intriguing brews from British Columbia as well. A wide assortment of imported beers and ales from around the world are also available, with well-known beers from Germany, Holland and England offered alongside unusual brews from Brazil, Denmark and elsewhere. Connoisseurs will be pleased to note Spinnakers offers Montecristo number four cigars and an assortment of fine crystal wine glasses to enhance enjoyment. In addition to store sales, Spinnakers Spirit Merchants also offers sales through its website, which shows the real-time store inventory amounts allowing you to order with confidence. 130 – 176 Wilson Street, Victoria BC (250) 360 - 1333 www.spiritmerchants.ca

Market on Yates

Market on Yates is an urban downtown shopping experience featuring healthy eating products. Owner Ernie Skinner's vision is to have a store that supplies a higher standard of food to people who genuinely want to eat better. This vision is abundantly clear as you roam around the different departments. Many of the Market products carried in the deli, bakery, meat and seafood departments are prepared from scratch. The Market is proud to have one of the largest selections of organic produce in Victoria. They offer Queen Charlotte salmon from an independent Sooke fisher and free-range and free-run poultry products. The full-service, fresh meat and seafood case offers butcher cuts to order. They also offer custom deli trays, bakery items and gift baskets. There are over 900 organic items in the grocery department. The bakery offers whole grain as well as carb-reduced baked goods. Don't forget to stop by and see the beautiful selection of cut flowers and plants. If you need to send flowers for a special occasion, the Market is registered with FTD and Teleflora for local and long distance service. Open seven days a week, Market on Yates is a truly rewarding shopping experience. 903 Yates Street, Victoria BC (250) 381 - 6000

Trilogy Fish Company LTD

John and Donna Fraser of Trilogy Fish Company Ltd., know most of their customers by name. John is a retired fisherman with over 30 years experience. His secret technique for smoking fish was taught to him by his friend and fellow fisherman John Sveboda. This amazing technique has been tested and refined over time to produce delicious cold smoked salmon unlike anything you've ever tasted before. John and Donna are hands-on store owners who personally cut the fresh alder used in the on-site smoking process, and they are always ready to share a story with a customer. It's reported they tell the best fish stories on the island. In addition to smoked fish, Trilogy offers fresh fish, big, fat, live crabs, food books, dinnerware and more. If you're a sport fisherman, you'll be interested in the custom smoking, hot or cold, and vacuum packing services available. Trilogy Fish has become a bit more famous since it was recently featured on Iron Chef, Rob Feeney's Christmas special, but John and Donna are not the type to let fame go to their heads. They continue to run the store in the same attentive manner that's already won them so many devoted customers. Visit Trilogy Fish Company LTD and find out for yourself why their loyal customers come back year after year. 630 Campbell Street, Tofino BC (250) 725 - 2233 www.trilogyfish.com

Photo by: Noriko Natsume

155

Cookworks

Vancouver's preeminent gourmet cookware source is Cookworks, where David Werner sells high-quality utensils for the everyday chef and the professional. He searches the world for the best-made products from silicone pastry brushes to Italian espresso machines. Cookworks is not to be confused with large impersonal chain stores. At both locations, individualized service with a commitment to the highest quality standards is apparent. The clean, comfortable and professional atmosphere is reinforced by knowledgeable staff providing insightful information. Their efforts have won awards for the stores including Retailer of the Year in Housewares from the Canadian Gift and Tableware Association. In the cookware category alone, there are steamers, stir fryers, chef's pans, French ovens, fondue pans, copper stockpots, sauté pans and iron woks to name just a few. A sample of small appliances includes rice cookers, juice fountains, panini presses, frozen dessert makers, pasta rollers, blenders and extractors. Other major categories are baking equipment, china and cutlery, knives and boards, tools and gadgets and wine and bar supplies. Cookworks ships worldwide.

1548 West Broadway, Vancouver BC
(604) 731 - 1148   377 Howe Street, Vancouver BC
(604) 662 - 4918   www.cookworks.ca

Still Life Interiors

Ellen Fairn and John Yamazaki, co-owners of Still Life Interiors, believe there is no compromise when it comes to quality and customer service is paramount. Still Life was born out of their love for hand-built, fine furniture and the realization that Vancouver was in need of a store where you can find it. Still Life is filled with beautiful handcrafted furniture created from natural solid hardwoods (i.e. Pennsylvania Cherry, Black Walnut) by local woodworkers. Traditional joinery techniques and classic designs are combined to make each custom piece of heirloom value. Every board is laid out by hand so the flow

of grain and color are seamless and pleasing to the eye. From custom beds to tables, dining chairs, and cabinetry, a Still Life hand-built piece will enhance any room. In addition, Still Life carries a spirited collection of upholstery, as well as lighting fixtures from Isamu Noguchi and Artemide. Ellen and John's commitment to customer service is the perfect complement to the merchandise. They will work with you to help find what best suits your needs. Each custom piece is designed and built to fit your space and reflect your style.

2349 Granville Street, Vancouver BC
(604) 730 - 5770
www.stilllifeinteriors.com

Salmon Village

All natural smoked salmon is the pride at Salmon Village in Vancouver. Started in 1988 by Yoshi and Akiko Gomyo, this store smokes, packages and sells its own products, offering the highest quality from sea to serving without using preservatives. Wild Sockeye salmon fillet is first delicately seasoned with salt and brown sugar, then gently smoked to its optimum flavor and texture using a hickory-based original blend. It is immediately vacuum-packed to lock in the flavors that make it a delicious Canadian treat. Among the popular items available at Salmon Village you will find, King and Sockeye Salmon cold-smoked with the Village's special blend of wood chips; various kinds of Cooked Smoked Salmon prepared and vacuum-sealed in its own delicious juices; and Salmon Jerky made from thinly sliced salmon that has been slowly smoked and dried. For a real treat try Indian Candy, smoked salmon marinated in pure Canadian maple syrup, then double-smoked and sprinkled with black pepper. Salmon Village also carries other Canadian specialty products like maple syrup from Quebec, maple sugar, butter and chocolates. Samples are plentiful at Salmon Village! Tours of the smokehouse can also be arranged.
779 Thurlow Street, Vancouver BC
(604) 685 - 3378
www.salmonvillage.com

Long Liner Seafoods

The bustling and colorful Granville Island Market is home to Long Liner Seafoods. As one of the original tenants of the market, Long Liner has a solid reputation and a loyal clientele. Just 40 meters from the ocean, Long Liner purveys only the freshest fruits of the sea to thousands of customers from around the globe and they can package your purchase for shipping anywhere in the world. Wild British Columbia salmon, Dungeness crab, halibut and prawns are among the favorites, as are the live clams, oysters and mussels. Long Liner also has the largest variety of smoked salmon in the province. The owners are Jim Scott and David Moorehead and together they make a walking encyclopedia of seafood and fishing information. They are happy to share their vast knowledge of all things seafood, from determining freshness and quality to great cooking ideas. For all you need and all you need to know, the most trusted fishmongers can be found at Longliner Seafoods.
P.O. Box 102, Vancouver BC (604) 681 - 9016

157

Westminster Quay Public Market

The First Nations people translate quay as gathering place, and the Westminster Quay Public Market has been a bustling place to gather since opening day in 1985. Situated next to the Fraser River, it is a quick walk to the Samson V Marine Museum. The only original paddlewheeler that still exists on the Fraser, Samson V takes you back through the history of New Westminster in stories and pictures. The Quay is the site of many fun festivals and community events. You can tour the boardwalk or visit Antique Alley just across the tracks. Shops, restaurants and services offer a little of everything. Ranging from traditional shops such as Cheese Please Plus, to specialty shops such as Made In BC and Touch of Africa, to fashion and accessory stores like C & E Silk and Personal Touch Silver, a wide variety of shops line the Quay. For food, Captain's Deck, the Paddlewheeler Pub and Top Gun Sushi restaurants, as well as the food court, provide a large variety of choices. Services include the Paddlewheeler Riverboat Tours, Q Garden Shop and Florists, Liquor World and so much more. The Visitor Information Centre makes it easy to find your way around the Quay. As they say at the Westminster Quay Pubic Market, "It all happens at the river's edge."

#235 – 810 Quayside Drive
New Westminster BC
(604) 520 - 3881
www.westminsterquay.com

Van Dusen Botanical Garden

A four-year transformation process changed a land that was once an isolated terrain of stumps and bush, and then an abandoned golf course, into an amazing array of botanical delight. It is now VanDusen Botanical Garden, opened to the public since 1975. The garden promotes biodiversity. They practice what they preach, with over 11,000 species on site. It also lends a strong educational voice to the cause of conservation. Plant-related courses are provided through the diverse garden curriculum.

A wealth of information is accessible in botany, horticulture, ecology and related topics for the public, from kindergarten age to adult. The garden has an enthusiastic Master Gardener program for anyone with a passion for growing plants. The program teaches environmentally responsible methods and brings the latest gardening news to members. The garden is 55 acres of awe-inspiring beauty, strewn with 11 sculptures created on the grounds in the summer of 1975. For two months, local and international sculptors worked from morning to night to fashion art works from the raw Turkish marble and travertine. Many other works have also been donated to or commissioned by the garden. After exploring the garden, try the onsite Shaughnessy restaurant. It is a tranquil retreat that utilizes the garden for a source of fresh ingredients. After the meal, don't forget to find a treasure to take home with you. The garden shop stocks many treasures, including seeds!
5251 Oak Street, Vancouver BC
(604) 878 - 9274 www.vandusengarden.org

Photo by: Dave Wright

Dundarave Fish Market

When Kim Hurford VanSickle and Frank Seabolt opened the Dundarave Fish Market in West Vancouver three years ago, it was just what its name suggests, a retail seafood market. Then they added a soup pot, panini maker and a few tables then started serving chowder and sandwiches. Business took off, encouraging them to expand to a full-service restaurant. Even though it now seats 80 customers at a time, there are usually lines to get in. Customers come for the wonderful food, the warm welcoming ambiance and special features like the ability to make their own choices of fresh fish from the cooler. Kim grew up in the fishing industry and Frank has a background hunting geoducks, the famous "gooey duck" clams, popular along the Pacific Northwest Coast, The two chefs, Shaun Spooner and Corbin Roger, work wonders with the seafood staples creating specialties like seafood chowder, made with 10 different types of fish. Fresh shucked oysters, smoked black cod risotto with crab butter and many more delights await the seafood lover here. Restaurant Manager Brook Parker makes his own contributions to the Market, including the Red Snapper martini, made with Absolut Currant, Chambord and cranberry juice. Wines and microbrewed beers on tap are also available. Dundarave Fish Market is open seven days a week for lunch and dinner.
2423 Marine Drive, Vancouver BC (604) 922 - 1155 www.dundaravefishmarket.com

Letto di Lusso

Letto di Lusso means bed of luxury in Italian. In the heart of Vancouver's prestigious South Granville shopping district you will find a store dedicated to making your dreams sweet and your bedroom a haven of sumptuous peace, Letto di Lusso. You will enjoy a remarkable, relaxed shopping experience at this long-established shopping mecca for those who desire the finest for their bedrooms. Their beautiful website showcases their outstanding lines of furniture, linens, draperies and accessories and describes the store's underlying principles. From the moment you enter the store, you will be aware of the philosophy espoused by owner Patricia Buckley and her partners. They believe that since people spend one-third of their life in bed, the bedroom should be a personal oasis, and that creating this oasis is an art form. A commitment to quality is one of the most obvious and abiding facets of Letto di Lusso. With a special emphasis on customer care and personal attention, their goal is your satisfaction. They offer the finest Egyptian cotton, down, jacquard weave and drapery fabrics. Their beds, from hand-carved mahogany sleighs to the faerie-tale cribs, are all of heirloom quality. If you wish to completely redo your bedroom, an interior designer will help you realize your dream.
3109 Granville Street, Vancouver BC (604) 732 - 6373
www.lettodilusso.com

The Gourmet Warehouse

Caren McSherry is a chef, cookbook author, radio and television host, newspaper columnist, and one of the first Canadians to become a Certified Culinary Professional. Since 1998, she's also been the owner and guiding spirit behind The Gourmet Warehouse, Vancouver's finest source for foodstuffs and cooking ware. A breathtaking assortment of products from around the world greets you as you enter The Gourmet Warehouse. You may find it hard to believe such high quality can be offered at such low prices, but it's true. The first store of its kind in Canada, Gourmet Warehouse provides cutting-edge gourmet products, hard to find ingredients, and unique housewares from renowned manufacturers such as Cuisinart, All-Clad, Peugot and Taylors of Harrogate. From Wasabi mayonnaise to mortar-and-pestle sets, Gourmet Warehouse takes a page from the big business model, buying large lots and selling them at wholesale prices. The idea has been so successful that Gourmet Warehouse has expanded to feature even more products. The custom gift baskets are an especially popular feature. You can get one designed to your exact specifications or choose from the selections already put together for events like weddings and birthdays. 1340 E Hastings Street, Vancouver BC (604) 253 - 3022 www.gourmetwarehouse.ca

Essential Kitchenware

Maria Fedyk has always loved creating in the kitchen, so it was perfectly natural she'd be inspired to open a shop called Essential Kitchenware. This exciting store has anything and everything you can imagine for chefs and amateur culinary geniuses alike. From the moment you enter, you'll appreciate the warm atmosphere and the knowledgeable service provided. Maria is passionate about finding attractive, yet functional pieces that compliment anyone's kitchen. Everything from pie birds, hand-picked specialty lines, international cookware, old fashioned mechanical apple peelers, and tabletop runners, to anything else your heart desires. You'll find fun, affordable and stylish items to fit every personality. Maria is originally from Mexico and gained her work experience though her family's retail business. She knows how to give the best in customer service and she'll stop at nothing to find the perfect item for a loyal shopper. For a look at what is probably the most popular kitchen store in North Vancouver, visit Essential Kitchenware, you're sure to find something you just can't live without.
Lonsdale Quey Market #107 123 Carrie Cates Court, Vancouver BC
(604) 983 - 2924

161

The Everyday Gourmet

The finest selection of culinary essentials is available at The Everyday Gourmet. From Tahitian vanilla and Valrhona chocolate, to balsamic vinegars and the best oils, you will find all you could ask for and more than you can imagine. Ann, Ben, and Graham Kilford are dedicated to providing

you with the best information too, whether you are new to the kitchen or an experienced cook. Ben is a journeyman chef at Vancouver's Four Seasons and is extremely knowledgeable about the various products. All three are able to assist you in choosing the right ingredients. They enjoy learning from their customers and are happiest when customers leave with a renewed confidence in their culinary abilities. The Kilfords offer herbs and spices, imported and local artisan cheeses, specialty coffee blends, fine teas and every gourmet ingredient and accoutrement you may need. There are exceptional gift boxes available that can be shipped worldwide and evening tasting parties you won't want to miss. You can relax in the book nook with a cup of coffee and any of the excellent cookbooks available. Whether you want a quick fix of chocolate-covered coffee beans, a leisurely stroll through a world of fine foods and accessories, or just a feast for the senses, visit The Everyday Gourmet, where your taste buds come to play.

102 – 2982 152nd Street, Surrey BC
(604) 541 - 3141 www.theeverydaygourmet.ca

Modern Accents by Design

Modern Accents by Design awakens memories of an era when personal service from helpful staff made shopping an experience to relish. Owner Susan Maloney and Assistant Manager Monique Rivard are committed to continually introducing contemporary fashions in dinnerware, crystal and silverware for the home, as well as distinctive gifts for every occasion. Popular items include Royal Selangor, Lord of the Rings pewter collectibles. Special Event Evenings are a trademark of the Modern Accents approach to customer service, with themes ranging from the art of table dressing to ideas for the perfect bridal shower. Modern Accents has been called, The Wedding Store due to its popularity as a supplier of wedding gifts. This store is the exclusive local supplier for Vera Wang housewares and features the work of many other popular and stylish designers such as Lynda Coroneille and Thomas Rosenthal. Check with Modern Accents to learn about their, Meet the Artist evenings, when designers come by and autograph their work.
910-15355 24th Avenue, Surrey BC (604) 536 - 3722 www.modernaccentsbydesign.com

My Kitchen Window

A part of the lovely downtown shopping district of Fort Langley, My Kitchen Window features a great supply of gadgets and utensils with a culinary theme. The array of implements and thingamabobs includes garlic presses, salad spinners, flaxseed grinders and avocado slicers, to highlight just a few. Dabblers in the kitchen and professional chefs alike love this store. Owner Ro-anne Johnstone, who was raised in Fort Langley and she traces her love of cooking to her childhood. If you're looking for cookware, she is happy to help you find every kitchen item you're ever going to need. She's constantly finding new sources and new wares to further your culinary adventures. In the unlikely event there's something you want and can't find there, at My Kitchen Window special orders are no problem at all.
102 - 23242 Mavis Avenue, Fort Langley BC
(604) 881 - 2061

Kept In Stitches

Gail Olson is a true yarn enthusiast and her shop, Kept in Stitches is distinguished by its truly impressive selection of gorgeous, high quality yarns from around the world, including such unusual variations as hemp yarn and alpaca from Peru. In addition to merchandise, the shop also houses a knitting and social area nestled in one corner where Gail hosts high energy, fun workshops. Besides yarn, Gail also sells beads and other decorative accessories, as well as patterns and knitting kits. One

of the most popular features of her shop is the range of one-of-a-kind gifts from local artisans, such as handcrafted knitting needles and purses. The focus here is on keeping the arts of knitting and needlework alive from generation to generation, and Gail's enthusiasm for the craft is infectious. Even non-knitters find the shop charming and fascinating. While you're there, don't miss the antique sock-knitting machine. Destination shoppers are never disappointed. Some say Kept in Stitches is the best kept secret in Fort Langley.
#110 - 23343 Mavis Avenue
Fort Langley BC (604) 882 - 8650

163

Minter Gardens

Cheam is a walk-up mountain rising 2107 metres into the sky. From the top, the Fraser River Valley can be viewed like a carpet of nature's rich bounty of beauty. At the foot of the mountain, Minter Gardens rests in an oasis of lush scenery. This area was the site of a massive rock landslide thousands of years ago, sculpting a topographically unique land filled with tall trees and a riot of colorful blooms. Wild bleeding hearts, geraniums, roses and columbine enliven the area. When Brian and Faye Minter found this site on Christmas Day, 1977, they conceived a dream to provide one of the premier show gardens of the world in this location. Less than three years later, Minter Gardens was ready to greet visitors with 11 thematic gardens reflecting Fraser Valley's seasons. A cornucopia of nearly 100,000 tulips arrives each year from Holland for the gardens. Floral beds are hosts to bold combinations of colors and species in eye-catching designs. A rhododendron garden surrounded by cedars, interspersed with delicate complimentary flowering shrubs and trees, blooms in breathtaking beauty. The sloping paths are wheelchair accessible. Impressive topiaries, such as the famous Victorian ladies and a giant peacock, amaze and delight guests. The Envision Conservatory and Garden Café and the Trillium Restaurant and Conservatory offer meals and refreshments in greenhouse-like buildings circumscribed by views of the spectacular setting. If you've been searching for Earth's Eden, come to Minter Gardens and you'll find it really exists.

52892 Bunker Road, Rosedale BC (888) - MINTERS www.mintergardens.com

Clearly Flowers

Brilliantly colored flowers, looking as fresh as the morning they were cut, in an elaborate vase or a simple bud jar. These are what Clearly Flowers provides for its happy customers, but with a big difference. These flowers will last for years with the bloom of fresh-cut perfection. The result of years of technological advances, they are made of silk. To add the final touch, Clearly Flowers' arrangements are designed to be set in acrylic "water." The effect is beautiful as well as realistic. You won't believe you're not looking at a bouquet that was just placed in a clear, sparkling vase of water. Clearly Flowers makes silk flower arrangements for every occasion, and gift certificates are a specialty. In addition to the eye-catching beauty and practicality of these flowers, they are hypoallergenic and, of course, no bugs or pollen come with them. For low maintenance beauty for homes or businesses, visit Clearly Flowers and see for yourself. It's a relaxed, pleasant place to shop. Owner Kim Morrell and Floral Designer Valray November welcome a chance to show you their creations. Along with their silk flower selection, they are a distributor for the Bearington Bear Collection.
1216D Battle Street, Kamloops BC (250) 372 - 3737 or (866) 377 - 9390 www.clearlyflowers.com

Horsting's Farm Market

Family-owned and operated, Horsting's Farm Market is a delightful place to visit any time of year. Plan to visit seasonally and you can appreciate the cycles of a working farm. Go in the morning and you will find air around the market stand wafting with the aromas of fresh-baked breads, cinnamon buns and homemade pies. The ice cream bar is a favorite stop for delicious frozen treats as well as soups and sandwiches, cookies and pies. They will even

pack you a lunch to take along when you stroll down to the picnic area to enjoy friendly donkeys, goats, chickens and rabbits or just soak up the beauty of the surroundings and the sounds of the Bonaparte River. The great variety of home grown and canned produce includes peppers and salsas, beans and berries, pickles and beets and jams. You can buy hand picked, fresh produce for eating fresh or for your own canning. In spring and summer the greenhouse offers thriving plants, shrubs, annuals, perennials and fruit trees. Parking is ample and tour groups are welcome. Donna and Ted Horsting are proud to provide the best of British Columbia produce and a relaxing, genuine farm experience to one and all. Horsting's Farm Market is located two kilometers north of Cache Creek on Highway 97 North
P.O. Box 716, Cache Creek BC
(250) 457 - 6546 www.horstingfarms.com

Castles and Cottages Antiques

Rosie Jonasson's pursuit for the most meaningful objects from the past and present becomes very obvious once one enters the alluring Castles & Cottages in downtown Kamploops. The unique floor plan lends to old and new with two separate spaces in perfect harmony for the best of both worlds. Uplift your spirits with calming aromatherapy candles and beauty products, inviting cozy quilts, garden ornaments, grandma's stoneware tureen and vintage jewellery are just a few of the treasures and fine period furniture that fills every corner. Castles & Cottages Antiques is sure to be the source of your next favorite thing. 263 - 265 Victoria Street, Kamloops BC (250) 374 - 6704

27th Street Florist

Welcome to a place where the sight and scents of vivid, fragrant blooms will inspire you. 27th Street Florist is a place where happy memories begin. Tucked into nooks and crannies, impressive in their assortment, are all the items you need to organize that special day, be it as standard as "Happy Birthday," or as impulsive as "It's Tuesday, and you deserve a present." Featuring an excellent assortment of fresh flowers, 27th Street Florist is an exceptional resource for any occasion and will happily customize even standard arrangements. They specialize in custom gift baskets, gift services, and made-to-order floral arrangements for any occasion or theme, from full wedding services to simple and heartfelt acknowledgements. Baskets are assembled according to individual specifications from a wide selection of gift and gourmet items. The knowledgeable and attentive staff takes an interest in you as an individual: a simple reminder that this lovely shop, voted the Best Florist in Okanagan, is beautiful in every sense of the word. At 27th Street Florist you're sure to find the perfect gift, whether shopping in person, by phone or online.

3803 27th Street, Vernon BC (250) 503 - 2262 www.27thstreetflorist.com

Planet Bee Honey Farm Tours & Gifts

What do you know about the World of the Honeybee? Planet Bee Honey Farms Tours & Gifts is Western Canada's premier honeybee attraction, outdoor honey bee observatory and interpretive center. It is perched at the top of the picturesque Okanagan Valley in Vernon. See live honeybees busily working behind glass in demonstration beehives and learn about these incredible insects and their intriguing social structure which has

survived for millions of years. Browse and shop in their "sweet" country store and discover the Treasures of the Hive some of the most beneficial natural health products on the planet. Owner and master beekeeper Ed Nowek began his beekeeping career in 1969 and within the past ten years began focusing his time teaching people, young and old, about the honeybee hive and its busy inhabitants. Ed encourages a positive approach to wellness and the use of honeybee health products for individuals who desire improved or optimum health. As an operating apiary, Planet Bee is able to offer pollination services to the agricultural industry of BC The honey farm attraction is open year round for tour bus groups and is a popular in season destination for school field trips. Children's play areas, picnic tables and washroom facilities are available for the public. Book early as they're busy bees. Please note: the Goal of Planet Bee is that when each visitor is ready to depart, they will have become more aware of, and more comfortable around honey bees!

5011 Bella Vista Road, Vernon BC
(250) 542 - 8088 www.planetbee.com

Washed Ashore Gifts

Washed Ashore Gifts on Front Street in historic Penticton offers an enticing array of pleasing gift and home décor items are sure to charm one and all. Owners Jenny and Molly Lewis take an active part in supporting the tightly-knit and convivial downtown business community. Washed Ashore Gifts not only strives to reflect the latest trends and tastes in the world of home décor; it also provides consistent, quality products and exemplary customer service. Washed Ashore features works of art by Canadian artisans

along with nautical design and beach inspired gifts and accessories. It also offers candles, bath amenities, organic cotton baby clothing, artisan jewellery and more. Seasonal themes are a standard of the store year round. Whatever the occasion, or for no reason at all, you can count on finding charming gift and home entertaining ideas from wine accessories to patio accoutrements. Washed Ashore Gifts is just the place to find those special touches you've been searching for, whether you're shopping for yourself or for a friend. 27A Front Street, Penticton BC (250) 493 - 3883

Z-Decor

Z Décor, a contemporary furniture and accessories shop, is located in downtown Kelowna, and gets a dash of flair from Canadian and Pacific Northwest artists. The show room is modest in scale, but huge in impact. A wide range of products to suit any budget is available. A major focus of Z Décor is the stunning resin and metal art from Martha Sturdy, a renowned British Columbia artist and designer. The colourful bowls, platters, and metal chargers add considerable punch to any décor. This is functional art at its best! Made-to-order metal tables and console bases have a simple yet attractive design with an unusual hand painted finish. Z Décor's high quality upholstered furniture, with clean contemporary lines, is also designed and manufactured in Canada. The unique accessories created by local artist Lonnie Zaitsoff, complement a large selection of contemporary glass and candles. Z Décor's vision for the urban lifestyle of minimal designs with maximum impact, makes for a special shopping experience. Owner's Johanna and Mike Howard look forward to your visit and will gladly help you ship your purchases home. Z décor is located at the corner of Water Street and Lawrence Avenue.
1615 Water Street, Kelowna BC (250) 860 - 4371

Wild Rose Cottage

In the Southern Okanagan Valley lies the hospitable town of Penticton. Pentiktan, from which the town derives its name, was one of the main villages of the Okanagan First Nations aboriginal tribes and translates to "a place to stay forever." After visiting this social town you may well wish to stay forever too. Consider the allure of Wild Rose Cottage on bustling Main Street. This inspiring shop is filled with home décor items that will have your imagination soaring. Established in 2002 by Rose and Ken Laidlaw, the shop offers incredible finds that will surprise and delight you. A few examples of the type of things you can find here are an 1896 Scandinavian day bed, a vintage pantry cupboard and a quaint old birdhouse. Wild Rose Cottage caters to a diverse clientele and offers a pleasing and eclectic variety of products to accommodate your home design needs. You will find classic country accessories, along with shabby chic, English garden and cottage-style accoutrements. Wild Rose Cottage continues to expand so that loyal customers can find an ever-widening selection of home décor items. Wild Rose Cottage is housed in an old hotel building that dates back more than one hundred years. The Laidlaws are considering future plans to add vintage accommodations such as a bed and breakfast, a parlor and an outdoor, cottage-style garden in back. Priding themselves not only on attention to detail but also on outstanding customer service, they go that extra mile to help with difficult decisions. Nothing is quite as rewarding as designing and decorating your own home to reflect your lifestyle and personality. At Wild Rose Cottage you can allow the ideas to flow. 218 Main Street, Penticton BC (250) 493 - 6776

Polka Dot Door Flowers & Gifts Boutique

One of the gems of British Columbia is the cheerful and thriving little town of Osoyoos, located in Canada's only living desert. This growing town offers natives and visitors a vast array of recreational, cultural, dining and shopping opportunities. Tucked in among the popular shops of the area, is a shining star called the Polka Dot Door Flowers & Gifts Boutique. Owner-Operator, Deborah Forlin, provides her community with the perfect place to find the right flowers and gifts for any occasion. Imported flowers from around the world are on display providing an inexhaustible selection of bouquet, corsage, wreath, posy or garland arrangements. Deborah strives for a browser-friendly place and succeeds beautifully. From her friendly, helpful staff to the elegant displays, this delightful shop invites you to come in, relax and enjoy your shopping experience. With so many incredible products and ideas available you may wish to set aside extra time for your visit. In conjunction with the amazing flowers, Deborah also offers an eclectic and desirable collection of gifts and souvenirs. Choose from specially made, custom cards, lovely gemstone and amber jewelry, interesting pottery, vases and flowerpots. Plus you'll also see a terrific selection of candles. There is something available for absolutely every taste and every occasion. Whether you require an executive business bouquet, a prom corsage, flowers for a wedding or just a little something to surprise that special person, you will find it at the Polka Dot Door Flowers & Gifts Boutique. 8141 Main Street, Osoyoos BC (888) 558 - 1511 www.myfsn.com/polkadotdoor

Gilded Goat

Globe trot through this warm, artistic shop discovering distinctive pieces for your home and garden. You can find unusual choices for all preferences at very affordable prices. The Gilded Goat has everything from hand-crafted gifts and home furnishings to interior design service. Owners Robin and Paul are always there to help you find exactly what you're searching for. No matter what your taste, you'll find the perfect home accent at The Gilded Goat. Open seven days a week, Robin, Paul and their caring staff will be there to help you find the perfect item or idea to make your home reflect your own personal style.

185 Deer Park Avenue, Kimberley BC
(250) 427 - 2333

Trends N' Treasures

Flowers and unique gifts have always played a part in the history of humanity. As far back as 2500 B.C., Egyptians were placing flowers in glazed vases. Designs were highly stylized, with the religious meanings of flowers influencing the choice of foliage and flower. In this culture, the lotus was sacred. The Chinese Han Dynasty revered the peony as the king of flowers, symbolic of good fortune, wealth, and high position. In the Greek and Roman Eras, wreaths, garlands and strewn petals were the style. The Byzantine Empire contributed cone-shaped arrangements with twining ribbons. Undoubtedly, gifts and flowers have been and still are an integral part of nearly all cultures. In 1993, Trends N' Treasures Gift & Flower Shoppe opened as a specialty gift store, featuring silk and dried flower arrangements. In 2003, they added fresh flowers. Owner Anne Simpson and her staff, have a master's touch when it comes to arranging. This treasure of British Columbia annually gives out some of their best flowers to regular clientele on Mother's Day, just to say, "thank you." Located on Baker Street, in downtown Cranbrook the shop's attentive atmosphere, aromas and music give it a tranquility usually reserved for visits to the spa. The staff at Trends N' Treasures truly appreciate their regular customers, and they look forward to meeting you. Anne and her incredible staff invite you to come in and browse to your heart's content. Help locating that unique gift is always at hand and they'll gladly design a breathtakingly rare arrangement for your special event. Come enjoy a leisurely stroll through this thoughtfully arranged shop. 1109 Baker Street, Cranbrook BC (250) 489 - 2611 www.trendsntreasures.ca

Museums

Quw'utsun' Cultural and Conference Centre

In 1986, the Cowichan Tribes, British Columbia's largest single First Nations group, began a project to disseminate information about traditional Cowichan knitting, carving and jewellery and to provide a center where visitors from around the world could learn about these and other aspects of the tribes' history and culture. Successfully outbidding 20 other organizations, the tribes acquired the Quw'utsun' Cultural Centre buildings that had been specially created for Expo '86 in Vancouver. They transferred them to a location just outside Duncan, in the tribes' ancestral home in Cowichan Valley Quw'utsun' is a more phonetically accurate rendering of the name Cowichan. In 1990 the Centre opened its doors. It is managed by the Khowutzun Development Corporation, a Cowichan economic development organization which oversees many successful businesses, such as Cherry Point Vineyards. The Cultural and Conference Centre offers live demonstrations of traditional crafts as well as singing and dancing, fascinating interpretive tours by indigenous guides and "great deeds," a dazzling multimedia presentation of the oral history tradition of the Cowichan people. Another feature of the complex is the dramatically different conference centre itself, which offers all the newest high tech equipment in a facility where the architecture and scenery combine to create an unmistakably Cowichan environment. 200 Cowichan Way, Duncan BC (250) 746 - 8119 or (877) 746 - 8119 www.quwutsun.ca

Royal London Wax Museum

Since 1961, the Royal London Wax Museum has been entertaining and educating visitors to Victoria, the capital city of British Columbia. It is North America's first museum to feature Josephine Tussaud wax figures from England, a connection that continues to this day. The museum's reopening in 1971 in the former steamships terminal building doubled the floor space available for exhibits. The inventory of wax figures has increased over the years from 50 to around 350. Victoria's "world of wax" offers lifelike insights into history, with an emphasis on notable personages of the United Kingdom and Canada. Figures include royalty, Henry VIII and his six

wives are all there, as is Queen Victoria, for whom the city is named, to writers such as William Shakespeare and Rudyard Kipling, to Canada's early explorers such as England's Captain Cook, Scotland's Alexander Mackenzie and France's Jacques Cartier. In addition to figures of royalty, exploration and literature, there are political leaders, religious leaders, astronauts and entertainers. Not all of this wax museum's offerings are wax. The replica Crown Jewels are an example. And then there is Captain George, the Official Greeter, resplendent in a British Royal Marines uniform of the 1790s. Now competing with him for the honor of greeting the most visitors is Selwyn, the Pembroke Welsh Corgi who joined the museum in 2004.

470 Belleville Street, Victoria BC

(250) 388 - 4461 or (877) 929 - 3228

www.waxmuseum.bc.ca

Burnaby Village Museum

Burnaby Village Museum faces a gurgling creek in the heart of the city of Burnaby. Designed as an authentic turn-of-the-century town, the shops and houses are attended by narrators in historically authentic costumes. Hands-on activities and demonstrations bring the past to life for guests at the museum village. Museum tours touch on different aspects of history, a walking tour with the romantic title, Ladies of the Lake celebrates four women with histories of influence over the local landscape: Ethel Moore, Violet Eagles, Harriet Woodard and Grace Ceperley. Places of Worship takes visitors on a fascinating journey through the architecture, history and cultural affinities of the many churches on Canada Way. Haunted Deer Lake, site of unexplained mysteries and hauntings, is the location for the tour of five scary buildings. This one is for teens and adults only. A cemetery tour takes a full day to explore all facets of Forest Lawn and Ocean View cemeteries. Listen to music playing from

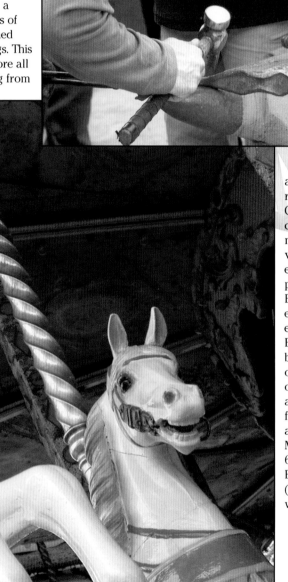

a 1925 Wurlitzer as you ride on a fully restored C.W. Parker 1912 carousel steed. This museum provides a vibrant way to experience and to be a part of the history of Burnaby. For those who enjoy a more hands-on experience, there are Beginning and advanced blacksmithing classes offered once a month on Saturdays. There is always something of fascination for all ages at Burnaby Village Museum.
6501 Deer Lake Avenue, Burnaby BC
(604) 293 - 6500
www.burnaby.ca

The Canadian Museum of Rail Travel

The Canadian Museum of Rail Travel is a social history museum. Visit the Museum and enjoy an extraordinary excursion into the era of the great trains. You will step back into the lifestyle of railway travel of yesteryear. Tour packages are available and are designed to give you an in-depth experience depending on your available time and your level of interest. All tours provide access to viewing corridors, audio-visual and model railway. On the 1907 Soo-Spokane Train Deluxe tour, you will see a first-class Edwardian train that ran from 1907 to 1914 on an international line between Minneapolis

and Spokane. The cars contain all the original walnut and mahogany panels, Art Nouveau style inlays, stained glass, wicker and wood furniture, beveled mirrors and plush mohair upholstery. Cars of this era are extremely rare. The Museum has been collecting and restoring railway cars since 1977. They exhibit the only set (7 cars) of the Trans-Canada Limited from 1929. This service was deluxe transcontinental travel from Montreal to

Vancouver and was first-class sleeping only. There were no day coaches, no mail or express cars and no tourist cars were provided. Due to the stock market collapse of 1929 and the Depression, the Trans-Canada's were discontinued, having run for only two years. All of the cars were heated by steam engine. The Argyle Dining Car was the foundation of the Museum and you can still enjoy refreshments served in this beautifully restored train car.

57 Van Horne Street South, Cranbrook BC (250) 489 - 3918 www.crowsnest.bc.ca

Photo by: Jason Weimer

Restaurants

Royal Dar Restaurant & Take-Out Deli

Kam and Gurb Gill are involved in the charming and picturesque Edwardian community of Ladysmith. They have completely renovated a house which is 90 years old, added a new addition, a deck and a patio, then opened for business as the Royal Dar Restaurant (Dar means "doorway" in their native language). The restaurant features unique ethnic Mediterranean, Indian and West Coast cuisine. Everyone at the Royal Dar welcomes to you experience great fine dining. You will enjoy exceptional food and wine in a serene atmosphere and beautiful surroundings. Whether you visit for lunch, dinner or the Sunday brunch buffet, you are sure to be satisfied. Delicious take-out meals are also available from the Deli. For your next special meal, visit the Royal Dar, your doorway to exotic flavours and aromas.
120 Roberts Street, Ladysmith BC (250) 245 - 0168

The Wheatsheaf Inn

Established in 1885, The Wheatsheaf Inn was once a stagecoach stop on the Island Highway. It was also a bar with a restaurant added until Prohibition closed the bar. Shortly after the repeal of Prohibition, the original building burned to the ground. The owner hauled two houses to the site, added connecting doors, and was back in business in short order. Since 1978, The Wheatsheaf has been owned and operated by the Hutt family. Today the pub is a cozy place where locals gather and visitors are always welcome. They serve terrific food including homemade pizzas and pirogies. The beer, wine and liquor stock conveys a large selection with lots of regional offerings. To honour the memory of Marion Hutt, the family planned and built the large, private ball field complex just across the highway. It's a popular spot for tournaments throughout the season. At The Wheatsheaf Inn, you'll enjoy a brew, a meal and a taste of history.
1866 Cedar Road, Nanaimo BC (250) 722 - 3141

Long Beach Lodge Resort's Dining Room

One of the highlights of Long Beach Lodge Resort is the restaurant. Open to the public as well as guests of the lodge, the dining room of Long Beach Lodge celebrates the unparalleled environment of Vancouver Island's Pacific coast in its colours and furnishings, as well as the windows affording magnificent views over Cox Bay. The food also celebrates the best of the Pacific coast, featuring many kinds of local seafood including Dungeness crab, oysters from Clayoquot Sound and Quadra Island mussels. Head Chef Rob Wheaton, who joined the Long Beach Lodge team in May 2004, hails from Ontario. He made his way to Tofino by a circuitous route that took him through the South Pacific and Australia. He has many years of experience in area restaurants, including the Water Street Café, where his culinary talents first came to the attention of Lodge Owner Tim Hackett. The restaurant completes its tribute to the surroundings with a wine list offering an extensive selection of British Columbia vintages.
1441 Pacific Rim Highway, Tofino BC
(250) 725 - 2442 or (877) 844 - 7873
www.longbeachlodgeresort.com

Servus on Creekside

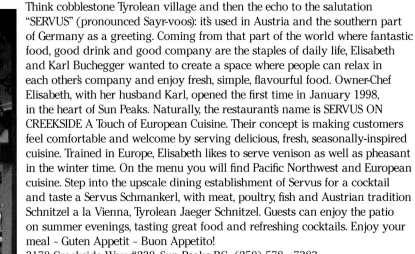

Think cobblestone Tyrolean village and then the echo to the salutation "SERVUS" (pronounced Sayr-voos): it's used in Austria and the southern part of Germany as a greeting. Coming from that part of the world where fantastic food, good drink and good company are the staples of daily life, Elisabeth and Karl Buchegger wanted to create a space where people can relax in each other's company and enjoy fresh, simple, flavourful food. Owner-Chef Elisabeth, with her husband Karl, opened the first time in January 1998, in the heart of Sun Peaks. Naturally, the restaurant's name is SERVUS ON CREEKSIDE A Touch of European Cuisine. Their concept is making customers feel comfortable and welcome by serving delicious, fresh, seasonally-inspired cuisine. Trained in Europe, Elisabeth likes to serve venison as well as pheasant in the winter time. On the menu you will find Pacific Northwest and European cuisine. Step into the upscale dining establishment of Servus for a cocktail and taste a Servus Schmankerl, with meat, poultry, fish and Austrian tradition Schnitzel a la Vienna, Tyrolean Jaeger Schnitzel. Guests can enjoy the patio on summer evenings, tasting great food and refreshing cocktails. Enjoy your meal ~ Guten Appetit ~ Buon Appetito!
3170 Creekside Way #230, Sun Peaks BC (250) 578 - 7383

Steamers Pub

Steamers Pub is an unpretentious Pub that has been in the same brick Victorian building for over 100 years. It offers a fully stocked bar with a nice selection of brews and a menu that features appetizers, soups, salads, flatbreads, burgers, pasta dishes and daily specials. Live music and friendly staff are additional reasons why Steamers is so popular with locals and out-of-towners. During the day, you can enjoy a friendly game of pool. In the evening, a younger crowd, in their 20s and 30s, turns out to enjoy the great music and party atmosphere. A variety of bands play there, the common thread being lively, danceable and up beat-music. It can range from funk to rock, jazz, ska, reggae, hip-hop and Celtic on any given day. Steamers is open seven days a week. Steamers' Manager Andrew will tell you, "Steamers is an age-friendly environment, a place to have fun. If you are fun at heart, you will fit in." Victoria's home of food, music and dance, Steamers Pub. 570 Yates Street, Victoria BC (250) 381 - 4340 www.steamerspub.ca

The Japanese Village Restaurant

Voted the Best Japanese Restaurant in Victoria since 1995, and the 2002 People's Choice Award Restaurant of the Year, The Japanese Village Restaurant is everything you could want and more. The beautiful, authentic décor is complemented by a relaxed family atmosphere. The Teppan Grill Dining Room is true to the tradition of food prepared at the teppan, or iron table, as part of the dining experience. A chef at each table performs a dazzling sleight of hand. They "chop, season, and sizzle" the choicest meat, poultry and seafood, along with the freshest produce. Complete dinners include appetizers, soup, salad and dessert. For further adventures in the art of food, master chefs create exquisite masterpieces of sushi and sashimi in the Sushi Dining Room. The restaurant also has a fully licensed bar featuring excellent Japanese beer and wine as well as local selections. A visit to The Japanese Village Restaurant is truly an extraordinary dining experience.
734 Broughton Street, Victoria BC
(250) 382 - 5165
www.japanesevillage.bc.ca

Gina's Mexican Cafe

Owner Don Corfield calls it a "tacky but friendly place." The long lines of customers call it the place to go for Mexican food in Nanaimo. Gina's is pink and blue and purple and has window boxes spilling over with bright flowers.

Perched on a cliff top and a block from the harbour, you really can't miss it. Out on the pleasant patio, there are beautiful views of Mount Benson and sunsets over the water. This is a festive restaurant with consistently delicious Mexican food, and lots of it. The ingredients are fresh and local and the seafood selections are very popular. The mole and chipotle sauces are exceptional and the fiery creamy smoked jalapeno sauce is fantastic, it is said to be an effective labor inducer for pregnant women! All of the entrees are very, very good, but be sure to save a little room for the Kahlua cheesecake. Gina's has been there for over 20 years and is now into its second generation of staff and patrons. For sumptuous food, fun and friendly service, and a delightful family atmosphere, Gina's Mexican Cafe is the perfect choice.

47 Skinner Street, Nanaimo BC

(250) 753 - 5411

Calico Cat Teahouse

In a lovely Edwardian-era house on a quiet street just off Island Highway, Heather Frank welcomes visitors to the Calico Cat Teahouse. She opened her popular business in 1994. Since then the Calico Cat has quietly built a reputation as one of Nanaimo's most delightful eateries. It's open for breakfast and lunch, but high tea in the traditional English style is the hallmark there. Sitting at one of the tables that look out on the beautiful British garden, sipping tea and eating home-baked trifle, is an experience to be cherished. And if you wish, you can set up an appointment with Calico Cat's resident tea-leaf reader. Customers say she's uncannily accurate. In fact, she is so popular that reservations are recommended for a reading. Calico Cat Teahouse also features a unique selection of gifts for purchase.

1081 Haliburton Street, Nanaimo BC

(250) 754 - 3865

Ribs N Bones

Ribs N Bones Restaurant does it the old fashioned way no compromises. Business Owner Petter Lam is a third generation restaurateur who believes whole-heartedly in the best ingredients with the best value. In the same location for 30 years, only the Ribs N Bones' name has changed. It started as Al's Rib House in the early 1970s and was Isabel's Ribs in the mid 1980s. When Petter took over in 2004, he vowed to continue the tradition, serving the best ribs in Victoria for generations to come. You will be welcomed to this small restaurant by long-term, experienced waitstaff. The wine selection is tailored to the menu because they personally choose what they sell. For those who prefer spirits, they also feature an excellent scotch selection. Everything is made from scratch and local suppliers are used whenever possible. Ribs aren't the only thing on the menu, they also offer steak, chicken, seafood and pasta. There is a memorable atmosphere that is sure to make Ribs N Bones the last rib house standing in Victoria.

1813 Douglas Street, Victoria BC

(250) 995 - 2992 www.ribsnbones.ca

Barb's Place Fish & Ships

Barb's Place Fish & Ships is open and making hungry customers happy from spring through mid-October, and has been ever since Barb's opened in 1984. It is a floating restaurant where you can sit in the sunshine and enjoy the meal that has been voted #1 Best Fish and Chips in Victoria for the past 18 years. Try their burgers, chowder, fresh steamed mussels, or cod and halibut burgers. Whatever you pick, it will be fresh and delicious. And if you want a peek into the inner workings of the restaurant, the Barb's Place pages on their website feature pictures of the impressive behind-the-scenes prep areas. Barb says they have remodeled many times to keep up with the growth of the restaurant over the years. Look for the bright blue roof and the sign that says Barb's Place Fish & Ships. You'll have found the place where "Treating customers well is simply treating them like welcome guests." Erie Street Fisherman's Wharf, Victoria BC (250) 384 - 6515 www.bcexplore.com/barbs

The Bay Pub

Built in 1859 as the John Bull Inn, this location has witnessed a lot of living. The original building was not only a hotel and pub, it was also a jail. For a brief time it even housed a church. The current building was erected in 1973 and the site still echoes with 150 years of history. The Bay Pub is owned by Chris and Irwin Killam. With their wonderful long-term staff, they provide a friendly neighborhood atmosphere that locals and tourists alike enjoy. The pub is right on the water with unobstructed views of Cowichan Bay, fishing boats, and gorgeous sunsets. Boaters have easy access from the breakwater dock and public marina. The food is great, from pub snacks to the Eggs Benny or full meals such as prime rib with Yorkshire pudding. The popular burger special is available every day and people flock to Wing Night Wednesdays. The Bay Pub rocks to live music on weekends and is available for special events and charity functions as well. You can enjoy relaxed ambiance, surrounding beauty and excellent food and service at The Bay Pub. 1695 Cowichan Bay Road, Cowichan Bay BC (250) 748 - 2330 www.baypub.ca

India Curry House

India Curry House in Victoria has great credentials. It has been named Best of the City – Best Indian Restaurant on the Island for seven years in a row. You will find it a charming family restaurant with authentic décor and music. It is also centrally located within walking distance of major hotels and the tourist information centre. As well as receiving awards for first-rate food, the restaurant is proud the government has certified it for "Food Safe Excellence." You'll find a variety menu at lunch, a wide range of vegetarian main courses, and many house specialties and combinations offering many

enticing dishes, such as the Chicken Tikka Masala or Lamb Vindaloo. Of course, you'll also find delicious clay oven-baked breads and Indian desserts. Ashok and Rakesh Dhaul and their family will give you a warm welcome as well as host a wonderful eating experience at India Curry House.

102 - 506 Fort Street, Victoria BC
(250) 361 - 9000
www.indiacurryhousejr.com

Miller's Pub

Miller's Pub has been serving simply good pub fare for nearly 20 years. A favorite of locals and tourists from 19 to 90, Miller's makes folks feel welcome from the first visit. Located right in the marina, Miller's has a quintessentially West Coast atmosphere. It is a comfortable place to enjoy an ice cold beer on the patio and watch the activity of boats and seaplanes in the busy harbour. With the best appetizers in town, plentiful pub meals such as the fresh halibut and chips, and great personal service, Miller's Pub is a delightful place to spend time. The Pub also features nighttime entertainment, and acoustic jam sessions have been known to pop up spontaneously. Owner Rob Parker and his staff invite you to join the fun.

102 – 1840 Stewart Avenue, Nanaimo BC (250) 753 - 4833

Spinnakers Gastro Brewpub & GuestHouses

Canada's oldest brewpub, Spinnakers, is a business with a mission: to take people back to the farm days to enjoy the bounty that southern Vancouver Island has to offer. The restaurant offers artisanal cuisine using the purest, freshest ingredients such as organic local produce, wild Pacific salmon, free-range eggs, Metchosin turkey and much more. Spinnakers makes its own malt vinegar, brewed from Jameson's Scottish Ale. You can buy it and other specialty food products at the Brewpub's deli, Provisions. Of course, Spinnakers brews a lot more than vinegar. Under the guidance of Publican and Innkeeper Paul Hadfield, it brews a wide range of styles of beer, from a Bavarian-style Hefeweizen (wheat beer) through English standards and their legendary India Pale Ale. Their exemplary Tsarist Imperial Stout and Fog Fighter is a big, rich 8½ percent Belgian seasonal ale that's just the thing to ward off the damp of a long winter night on the coast. The GuestHouses at Spinnakers are four-star accommodations in a variety of styles, ranging from the 1884 Heritage House cottage, a fully-modernized five-room historical building, to the four contemporary Garden Suites tucked away behind the pub. The Garden Suites feature amenities such as in-suite Jacuzzis and open harbor views. Spinnakers Gastro Brewpub & GuestHouses offer you a thoroughly good time, whether you're coming in for a drink, a leisurely meal or planning to spend the night in a beautiful setting.

308 Catherine Street, Victoria BC (250) 386 - 2739 or (877) 838 - 2739 www.spinnakers.com

Masthead Restaurant & Ocean Deck

Built in 1863, the building housing the Masthead Restaurant is the oldest wooden structure in the Cowichan Valley. It was originally a roadhouse serving weary travelers on the wagon road north from Victoria and in the mid 20th century it was a favourite fishing haunt for Bob Hope, Bing Crosby and John Wayne. A beautiful deck overlooks the village and harbour with views out to Saltspring Island and Mt. Tzouhalem, sacred to the First Nations. International clientele goes there for the fresh local fish, fowl, meats and produce. Chef Andrew Stevens and his culinary team prepare a sophisticated cuisine with a focus on organic, free-range and sustainable ingredients. The atmosphere is elegantly understated and the service is second to none. The thorough and well-chosen wine list showcases the very best of the Cowichan Valley's growing wine industry and includes many exclusive varitials and vintages. For fine West Coast dining in a beautiful setting, visit the Masthead Restaurant & Ocean Deck.

1705 Cowichan Bay Road, Cowichan Bay BC
(250) 748 - 3714 www.themastheadrestaurant.com

Lighthouse Bistro & Pub

Lighthouse Bistro & Pub are two separate venues; the restaurant and patio on the lower level and the pub upstairs. Centrally located on the waterfront at the foot of Anchor Way, this unique building also houses the seaplane terminal. With views of the harbour, the bistro and pub are lively and inviting spaces that cater to small or large parties. Young and old, singles and families are welcome. There is also a boardroom that can be reserved for meetings. The pub and lunch menus are refreshingly varied and the dinner fare is sophisticated and delicious.

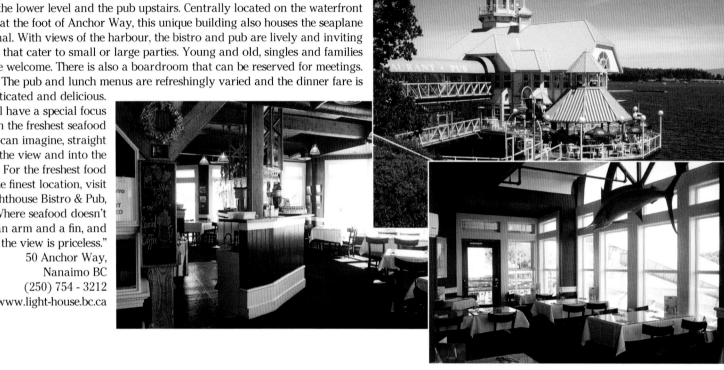

All have a special focus on the freshest seafood you can imagine, straight from the view and into the pan. For the freshest food in the finest location, visit Lighthouse Bistro & Pub, "Where seafood doesn't cost an arm and a fin, and the view is priceless."
50 Anchor Way,
Nanaimo BC
(250) 754 - 3212
www.light-house.bc.ca

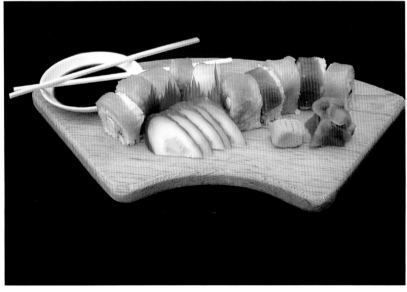

Blue Ginger

From the outside, Blue Ginger is deceptively modest and a little bit out of the way, but you will find it's well worth the trip. For the past seven years, Eric and Larry Lim and Doreen Lee have made it their mission to provide customers with an exciting and imaginative Asian fusion menu featuring Thai, Malaysian, Japanese, Chinese and Indian specialties. Locals have acclaimed Blue Ginger as "the best sushi bar and satay grill on Vancouver Island." But Eric, Larry and Doreen are not content with the fine reputation they've already achieved. They continue to challenge themselves in their quest to evolve the best tasting, most exceptional menu items. Every detail receives personal attention. Unwilling to rely on the quality of prepackaged products, the creative owners even prepare all their own sauces from the beginning. A new addition at Blue Ginger is the Zen Lounge, which features an eclectic mixture of drinks, including "bubble tea," a Taiwanese specialty made with tapioca. Blue Ginger is located at Longwood Station on Turner Road, just a little way off the Island Highway.
Unit #1 5769 Turner Road, Nanaimo BC
(250) 751 - 8238 www.blue-ginger.net

Huong Lan Restaurant

Huong Lan Restaurant serves wonderful Vietnamese cuisine. Its authenticity is ensured by Manager Tom Vuu and Head Chef Lan Huynh. One of the increasing numbers of restaurants created following the arrival of Vietnamese emigrants to Canada in the late 1970s and early 1980s, Huong Lan, meaning sweet orchid, has found favor among a wide variety of diners, many of whom have found it to be a delightful introduction to an unfamiliar world of cuisine. Among the specialties is pho, the soup that is virtually the national dish of Vietnam: noodles and sliced beef served steaming hot at the table, where the diner mixes in items such as lemon and hot peppers. The extensive menu also offers lemon grass chicken, salad roll appetizers and more. Iced coffee made with sweetened condensed milk is a traditional treat that will cool down the spiciest dish. Tom and Lan invite you to enjoy an authentic taste of Vietnam at the newly renovated Huong Lan Restaurant in Bowen Centre.

19 – 1925 Bowen Road, Nanaimo BC (250) 756 - 7943

Glow World Cuisine

A seasonal and international menu with everything made from scratch: this winning combination draws a nice mix of guests from their teens to their 90s. Glow World Cuisine is a handsomely decorated restaurant housed in a historic brick fire station at the foot of Nicol Street in Nanaimo. The signature dish there is tapas, an amazing array of tapas! There are tapas with fish or shellfish, tapas with escargots, tapas with crisp tofu and grilled veggies, and a host of other innovative and delicious options. There is also a full dinner menu which features fresh, local produce, plus free-range and organic meats. From the chef's five-course tasting menu to 20 items under $20, the food is fabulous. There's a big Sunday brunch and Glow is open for weekday lunches too. On Friday and Saturday, there is live music for your enjoyment. For great food from a varied and creative menu and excellent service in an exciting atmosphere, Glow World Cuisine is the scene.

7 Victoria Avenue, Nanaimo BC (250) 741 - 8858
www.gloworldcuisine.com

The Cranberry Arms Hotel and Beer & Wine Store

The Cranberry Hotel was erected in 1878 on a site above the Nanaimo River. It was built to last and still lives up to its original promise supplying the table with the best the market affords. Wendi Aldcroft bought "The Crannie" in 1982 and it lives on as a popular neighborhood pub, with the addition of a Beer, Wine & Liquor Store. The menu is extensive and the ingredients are fresh. The Cranberry Arms Pub menu is known island wide for its substantial breakfasts served all day, lunches, pizza and exceptional house specials. The chicken wings, cranny bites and veal cutlets are some of the favourite offerings. The Beer & Wine Store is stocked with all of your favourites, with a large selection of wines. If there is a product you don't see, let the staff know and it's sure to be on the shelf during your next visit. Wendi and her staff also host many annual fundraising events including the Father's Day Duck Race in June, Tricycle Race in August and a turkey barbecue every December with all proceeds going to Nanaimo Special Olympics. Well into its second century, The Cranberry Arms Hotel and Beer & Wine Store continues its tradition of excellent food and warm hospitality.

1604 Cedar Road, Nanaimo BC (250) 722 - 3112

Hugo's Grill and Brewhouse

Planning an evening on the town? Hugo's Grill and Brewhouse is the place to be any night of the week. Located just footsteps from the Parliament Buildings and Empress Hotel in downtown Victoria, it is the most notable brewhouse in town. Hugo's Brewmaster, Benjamin Schottle has been perfecting his craft for over eight years. For beer connoisseurs, Benjamin has created an exclusive selection of true non-pasteurized traditional beers, based on Eastern European recipes. And don't forget the food. Chef Andrew Dickinson believes "good food is not just based on the chef; it's about a good team that trusts his judgement." There is something on the menu for everyone, from seafood and chicken to steaks, pizza and more. The huge windows of the upper mezzanine are perfect for watching downtown activity anytime of the day. The rich textiles and woodwork in the Grill lend a warm, relaxing feel to the atmosphere. You can enjoy cocktails before dinner or stay to dance the night away, with a different DJ every night. Hugo's Grill and Brewhouse is open seven days a week, with a diverse menu that is sure to please. Stop in for great food and brew, stay for a while to enjoy the excellent entertainment! 625 Courtney Street, Victoria BC (250) 920 - HUGO
www.hugoslounge.com

Photo by: Frank van den Berg

Longwood Brew Pub & Restaurant

Renowned for its on-site brewery and ever-changing menu, Nanaimo's Longwood Brew Pub and Restaurant is the creation of Barry Ladell, an enthusiastic home brewer who was also one of the guiding forces behind the creation of Spinnakers Brewpub in Victoria, one of the pioneers of the movement. The brewery at Longwood, which offers tours on Saturdays, uses barley imported from the original Guinness Malt House in England as the starting point for the eclectic variety of beers and ales offered at the pub. With over 40 recipes to choose from, Longwood's brewers have created an array of rich brews with a truly international feel, from the raspberry-accented Framboise to Scottish Oatmeal Stout and a classic German Weizenbock. Taster packs are available if you have trouble making up your mind. The restaurant features a varied bill of fare. No matter what brew you choose, there's something that suits it perfectly, from light appetizers and hamburgers to sumptuous entrees like chicken filo, chicken stuffed with smoked salmon and cream cheese and wrapped in filo pastry. For those new to the brewpub scene, the menu at Nanaimo's Longwood Brew Pub & Restaurant also provides helpful suggestions for accompanying beers.
5775 Turner Road, Nanaimo BC
(250) 729 - 8225
www.longwoodbrewpub.com

Mahle House Restaurant

Cozy, romantic Mahle House Restaurant is located in the farming community of Cedar, 10 minutes south of Nanaimo. Built in 1904, the house is a lovingly restored, architectural delight with a bank of windows overlooking an enclosed English style garden. Family- owned, the restaurant has been in business for 20 years. The menu, which changes weekly, takes advantage of the freshest possible products from the local area. Rabbit, free-range chicken and venison are all locally raised. They take great pride in serving their herbs and produce fresh from their garden, produce from the earth to their table. The Mahle House is open for dinner five days a week, Wednesday through Sunday. On Wednesday nights they feature "Adventure Wednesdays" with a five-course, Surprise Dinner. They offer up to four different dinners, a selection that ensures every diner will have a memorable meal. It's no wonder Mahle's has a large contingent of regular patrons who appreciate the relaxed atmosphere, superb food and extensive wine list. Reservations are appreciated. 2104 Hemer Road, Nanaimo BC (250) 722 - 3621 www.mahlehouse.ca

New York Style Pizza & Pasta

Per and Vivian Maltesen made Old New York the theme of their award winning restaurant, New York Style Pizza & Pasta. The cuisine is Italian and features gourmet pizzas, pasta dishes and excellent barbecued ribs. Their world-famous Manhattan salad includes artichoke hearts and their proprietary dressing. Nominated to the top five for Provincial Restaurant of the Year and a five-time Service Award winner of Restaurateur of the Year, it is a very popular casual dining destination. Take-and-bake pizzas are offered and there are off-premise breakfast, lunch and dinner menus for groups of 10 or more. A private dining room is available. Additionally you can plan your next big event to be catered by Maltesen's Big Apple Catering company, also onsite. Be sure to catch live music on the weekends. And there is Jakeob's, an old-fashioned ice cream bar with shakes, floats and sundaes made from special local Island ice cream. For great Italian food and excellent service, New York Style Pizza & Pasta can't be beat. 299 Wallace Street, Nanaimo BC (250) 754 - 0111 www.newyorkstylepizza.ca

Photo by: Liany Cavalaro

191

The Schooner on Second

Owner Mare' Dewar has created an elegant gem in this world famous destination resort community. The staff at the Schooner on Second promises to exceed all of your expectations. Originally built as a hospital then moved to its present location on the west side of Vancouver Island, The Schooner on Second has been in Tofino for over 55 years. One reviewer commented "the food was sublime and beautifully presented." The desserts were irresistible and the dinner experience was so exceptional that he and his guest changed their plans and returned the next morning for breakfast. The Schooner with its cozy, yet elegant atmosphere is so popular that only four reservations are taken every half hour. A standard that ensures the Schooner staff are able to accommodate their clients dining experience in every possible way. This one-of-a-kind treasure is not without a sense of humor. Whenever there is a quirky mishap in the kitchen, the staff affectionately blames it on "Morris", a one-time chowder chef who worked in the restaurant some 35 years ago. Present day Chef, Nigel Davidson is a brilliant young talent who will prepare a meal for you that is beyond your expectations. Visit Mare' and the exceptional staff at The Schooner on Second for a dining experience you're sure to love.

331 Campbell Street, Tofino BC (250) 725 - 3444

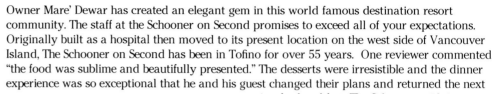

Dinghy Dock Pub & Family Restaurant

Great seafood and delightful maritime decor await you at John Logan's Dinghy Dock Pub & Family Restaurant, the only floating pub in North America. It is one of Nanaimo's preferred destinations. To get there, you can take the 10-minute ferry ride to Protection Island, the "Protection Connection" for a small fee or, you can bring your own boat and dock anywhere around the door. If you've been on the water for a while, there's a free laundry and showers so you can freshen up before dinner. Bring your camera; Dinghy Dock gets celebrity visitors from all over the world, you might even see local celebrity Diana Krall and her husband, Elvis Costello, Dinghy Dock is open year-round, with live entertainment on weekends. When you're at Dinghy Dock, observe the other diners when a boat approaches; the ones who lift their glasses off the table are the regulars, following a tradition that began many years ago after a yachtsman, who shall remain unnamed, accidentally brought his boat in a little too close, impaling a table with his bowsprit. Nothing like that has happened recently, but there's no sense in risking your drink. # 8 Pirates Lane, Nanaimo BC (250) 753 - 2373 www.dinghydockpub.com

192

Pioneer House

A warm welcome awaits you at Pioneer House Restaurant. This popular local family eatery serves hearty helpings of breakfast, specialty sandwiches and burgers, prime rib, fresh fish and homemade desserts. Located at Whippletree Junction, Pioneer House is home to a majestic, timeless beauty: "the Bar from Butte." Built into the north wall of the restaurant, the bar originally hails from Butte, Montana, where it stood in the St. Francis Saloon from 1890 to 1971. It is constructed of solid oak and mahogany with handcarved accents, and has been witness to many a quarrelsome card game, dancing cancan girls and, perhaps, a few gunfights. In the 1970s, Whippletree Junction founder, Randy Streit, found the bar in the deserted mining town of St. Francis. He bought it, dismantled it, and then realized he didn't have a place to put it. So he sold a plot of land and attached a promissory note requesting the buyer to build a structure specifically designed to accommodate the bar. Plans for Pioneer House came to life and today its log house style serves to complement the bar perfectly. Owners, Shelagh and Gerald John are proud to share this historic treasure and an excellent dining experience with you and your family.
4675 Trans Canada Highway, Duncan BC (250) 746 - 5848 www.emenus.ca/pioneerhouse

Sake House Japanese Restaurant

Eric and Larry Lim attribute the success of their restaurants to the fact they give people great healthy alternatives to fast food. The fact that they're devoted to customer service and share a passion for wowing their guests helps too. Sake House is perfect for people with special dietary needs and that includes a special need for adventurous dining. Vegetarians will find plenty to enjoy here, even vegetarian sushi. And naturally there's plenty of the best imported sake at Sake House. The Lims consider Sake House the mothership to their stable of restaurants, which includes Nanaimo's Blue Ginger. Unlike that restaurant's pan-Asian menu, Sake House specializes in Japanese food, both traditional and innovative. Seafood is extraordinarily popular there. On Monday and Tuesday nights you can feast on their all you can eat sushi special. You'll also want to try their Japanese tapas bar. And if you enjoy music while you dine, visit Sake House on Fridays for live entertainment.
#55 - 650 S Terminal Avenue, Nanaimo BC (250) 741 - 8833 www.sakehouse.net

Blackfish Café

The Blackfish Cafe is Victoria's only fully-licensed floating restaurant. Located in the heart of Victoria's Inner Harbour, in the Inner Harbour Centre, the staff at the Blackfish are proud to serve quality food in a relaxed, family-friendly setting. On its beautiful ocean-side patio you can enjoy fresh salads, calamari, salmon burgers or some of the best halibut and chips in Victoria. With a host of activities including whale watching, sportfishing charters, kayak tours and rentals as well as flight-seeing tours all departing from the Inner Harbour Centre, the Blackfish Cafe is the ideal jump-off point for your Victoria adventure. Come in and enjoy breakfast, lunch or dinner while you plan an afternoon that you and your family are sure to remember. Open year round for breakfast and lunch, the Blackfish Cafe is also open for dinners from mid-April through mid-November. Featuring an extensive menu including local, wild fish and many house-made specialties the Blackfish Cafe is sure to offer something for everyone. 950 Wharf Street, Victoria BC (250) 385 - 9996
www.victoria.com/restaurantsandpubs/blackfish.htm

Pescatore's Seafood & Grill

The freshest seafood and the best local oysters are the specialty of this locally loved seafood house. Pescatore's has built its stellar reputation on what makes west coast dining exquisite. It's fresh seafood and the hedonistic enjoyment

of it. Chef Ben Cram sets a high standard for his seafood, buying it from local purveyors to ensure the best quality and flavour. The comprehensive menu offers tasting notes on the dozen varieties of oysters always available. The menu, on view at their website, is an inventive testament to Chef Cram's love for seafood featuring everything from cedar plank roasted salmon to the most exquisite Dungeness crab cakes on the Island. The casually elegant atmosphere of this beautifully remodeled heritage building is accentuated by its stunning mahogany bar which serves a decadent selection of cocktails and a connoisseur's selection of scotch. The extensive wine cellar pays homage to the Pacific Northwest with a respectful nod to the great wine making regions of Europe, Australia and California. Situated beside the Empress Hotel, Pescatore's offers delicious food and the means to stroll it off afterwards around the beauty of Victoria's Inner Harbour. Open for lunch and dinner until midnight, Pescatore's is a west coast dining experience well worth visiting. 614 Humbolt Street, Victoria BC (250) 385 - 4512 www.pescatores.com

Korean Gardens

If you are in the mood for authentic Korean food, Korean Gardens is the place to satisfy your craving. When Arnold Lim decided to open the first Korean restaurant in Saanich, Victoria he did his homework. As a teenager he was a sushi chef, studying under David Nakayama and Kozo Kawada. He has carried the techniques he learned into the kitchen of Korean Gardens. He is also very familiar with the various nuances of running a great restaurant. By the time Mr. Lim turned 20 years old, his dream had become a reality. Keeping strong ties to the community is the focus of this restaurant as a part of the city of gardens. In addition to a full Korean menu, Korean Gardens also offers a full Japanese menu and full sushi bar. No matter what menu you order from, you can accompany it with a Japanese beer or saki. Korean Gardens was named the Best Korean Restaurant by the Victoria News group, as voted by the citizens of Victoria. Korean Gardens is only a 10 minute drive from downtown Victoria, so come meet the experienced staff and enjoy a one-of-a-kind Korean dining experience. 3945C Quadra Street, Victoria BC
(250) 744 - 3311 www.koreangardens.com

Pablo's Dining Lounge

Pablo's Dining Lounge is in a restored Victorian mansion designated as a Heritage Building by the city of Victoria. Owner Pablo Hernandez started in the restaurant business at the tender age of 19. Since then he has spent his entire life perfecting the nuances and services that define what a fine dining establishment should be. Pablo believes he's found the recipe for success in his field: "You do what you do, you do it right, that's it." That's the philosophy which has made Pablo's Dining Lounge a treasure for nearly 30 years. Pablo's has been hailed as the best restaurant in Victoria by the L.A. Times and is recommended as one of the best restaurants in Canada. The menu lists fine French cuisine prepared

Photo courtesy of Tourism BC

with inimitable flair and presented with impeccable service. Frequently requested dishes are the de-boned rack of lamb or the Dover sole. Trademark Caesar salad is prepared at your table while tableside desserts for two are highly popular. Add strolling musician, singer and classical guitarist Keith Cooper and you'll find the perfect atmosphere for dining. Pablo's also features an extensive wine list, and if your interest runs to spirits of a less earthly nature, please note that the restaurant is a popular stop during the annual Ghosts of Victoria Festival held the last two weeks of October. For an unforgettable evening, visit Pablo's Dining Lounge.

225 Quebec Street, Victoria BC
(250) 388 - 4255
www.pablos.com

195

Kerkis

Bobby Bonofas was born and raised on the Greek isle of Samos. Near his home was Mount Kerkis, the highest peak of the Aegean islands. It is this majestic peak which bequeathed its name to the restaurant he and his wife Julie opened in Vancouver in 2004. Prior to opening Kerkis, Bobby and Julie ran the Spiros Taverna in Port Coquitlam for 11 years. They decided to return to Kitsilano to be closer to Julie's family. Family is important to the Bonofases, whose children Rania and George can also often be found working at Kerkis. Like the Spiros Taverna, Kerkis is a restaurant devoted to authentic Greek cuisine. Familiar dishes such as moussaka and souvlaki share space with specialties such as the roasted lamb dish arni psito and appetizers such as aginares, breaded artichoke hearts. The wine selection includes the monastery-produced Greek white Agioritikos and Rapsani, a red wine from Thessaly. The menu also features superb vegetarian specialties and ekmek, a custard cake dessert. Kerkis is the home of wonderful Greek food and a warm welcome always awaits you there. 3605 W 4th Avenue, Vancouver BC (604) 731 - 2712

Chambar

Nico Schuermans and his wife Karri have created a restaurant to embody their philosophy which is, "the focus of a restaurant should be incredible food, not status." Chambar offers an unusual menu of modern Belgian cuisine with North African and Asian influences, drawing on Nico's extensive knowledge of international cuisine. He trained at the CREPAC, a school of culinary arts in Belgium, and has worked in restaurants around the world, including the Savoy in London, where as the Chef de Partie he oversaw dinners for as many as 1000 people per sitting. Now Nico brings his outstanding skills to British Columbia. For example, appetizers include the Carpaccio de Chevreuille: a venison carpaccio with Asian pear, truffle oil, gin, and warm brioche. Among Chambar's signature entrees is Tajine d'Aziz Â L'Agneau: lamb shank cooked with honey, cinnamon, figs and cilantro for six hours, served with cous cous and zalouk, a Moroccan eggplant salad. Dessert offerings include the Gaufre Liégoise – a Belgian waffle with warm chocolate fondant, raspberry coulis, and homemade ice cream. Nico and Karri's desire to provide a carefree, informal dining experience is embodied in the name Chambar, which derives from chambard, a French word used to describe the situation when the teacher leaves the classroom and all the students start having fun. Come relax and partake in the incredible food at Chambar. Reservations are always recommended. 562 Beatty Street, Vancouver BC (604) 879 - 7119 www.chambar.com

Café de Paris

The oldest traditional French eatery in Vancouver, the Café de Paris has reveled in countless accolades from loyal diners and various critics since 1977. All the warmth and casual elegance of a French bistro is evident here in vintage posters, wine bottles and bibelots along the walls, dark wood sideboards, parquet floors, red leather banquettes and brass railings. Trained in Europe at Cordon Bleu, Executive Chef Scott Kidd offers a menu featuring classic French cuisine incorporating local seasonal ingredients. Café de Paris is especially well known for its fabulous steaks and the best pommes frites in Vancouver. It also features an excellent cassoulet, a mouth-watering selection of wild seafood dishes and classic desserts made fresh daily. The selection of French and British Columbian wines has won praise from *Wine Spectator*, and the judges at the Critics Choice Awards have voted Café de Paris among the top three French restaurants in Vancouver. Friendly, unobtrusive service and traditional French music add to the ambience. 751 Denman Street, Vancouver BC (604) 687 - 1418

Nat's New York Pizzeria

Nat's New York Pizzeria is well-known for its thin-crust pizzas, with familiar toppings or unusual specialties such as hot capicollo and bocconcini. The menu also offers other classic Italian-New York fare such as foot-long hero sandwiches. The success of Nat's is very gratifying to Natalino and Franco Bastone, cousins who graduated from Kitsilano Secondary High School. They feel honored that their community has embraced their family's prized traditional recipes. They created Nat's New York Pizzeria in Vancouver in 1992, but the pizza they serve originated with their great-great-great-grandmother in Naples. From there it made its way to New York City, and in 1991 Nat and Franco went back to Yonkers, New York to learn the century-old family secret. Their authentic New York-style pizza became an immediate hit in Kitsilano. In January 2000, they opened a second location in downtown Vancouver. Nat and Franco still run the Kitsilano pizzeria, and the downtown store is in the capable hands of John Sofikitis. The Bastones believe in giving back to the community, and they contribute to causes such as childhood cancer research and local community agencies like the Big Sisters of BC Lower Mainland, which in 2004 recognized their contributions with its Big Heart Award. Drop in to enjoy great pizza and great atmosphere at Nat's New York Pizzeria.
Kitsilano: 2684 W Broadway Avenue, Vancouver BC (604) 737 - 0707
Downtown: 1080 Denman Street, Vancouver BC (604) 642 - 0777
www.natspizza.com

Ouzeri

The Phillis family, Chris and Anna and their children Angelo and Vivian, are the key to the authentic Greek flavours and atmosphere of Kitsilano's most popular Mediterranean restaurant, Ouzeri. As you might expect, lamb chops are a signature dish at Ouzeri; people come from far and wide for these chops, made from imported New Zealand lamb. Calamari is another favorite, whether served grilled or marinated with olive oil. Ouzeri is also known for its mezethes, the Greek equivalent of tapas, delightful dips served with pita bread. In Greece, an ouzeri is a cafe that serves mezethes and ouzo, and patrons traditionally sit, sip ouzo, eat mezethes, and converse for hours. Try it and you'll see why it's such a popular pastime. Anna makes the desserts from scratch every day. If you're not lucky enough to get there on a day when she's made her celebrated bougatsa, keep trying, it's worth it. The restaurant is comfortable in a cozy yet open-air atmosphere with seating at two separate patios, one of them known for the longest lasting daily sun on Broadway West. You'll overhear a lot of Greek conversation at Ouzeri. The authentic atmosphere is irresistible to Vancouver's substantial population of Greek immigrants. 3189 Broadway West, Vancouver BC (604) 739 - 9378
www.ouzeri.ca

Aurora Bistro

A neighborhood restaurant with a fresh modern approach, Aurora Bistro is the creation of Jeff Van Geest. The year after it opened, *enRoute* named it one of the 10 best new restaurants in Canada. Aurora features creative modern bistro cuisine using fresh local seasonal ingredients. Jeff buys his produce from local organic farmers. He puts the wine list (featuring exclusively British Columbian vintages) in the capable hands of Wine Director and General Manager Kurtis Kolt, who also has years of experience in Vancouver restaurants, plus certification from the Wine & Spirit Education Trust of London. Sous Chef and Pastry Chef Dan Tighchelaar, longtime friend of Jeff's, left his position as chef at the award-winning Tangerine Restaurant to come and work at Aurora. His special contribution is mouth-watering delicacies like spiced callebaut chocolate or roast pineapple ice cream sandwich, which superbly complements Jeff's signature dishes like pork tenderloin with maple and mustard seed glaze. Aurora serves dinner Tuesday through Sunday, brunch on Sundays, and reservations (telephone only) are a must.

2420 Main Street, Vancouver BC (604) 873 - 9944
www.aurorabistro.ca

Afghan Horsemen Restaurant

Opened in 1974, Afghan Horsemen Restaurant was the very first Afghan restaurant in Canada. The menu at this family owned and operated restaurant is a sampling of the many fine foods of Afghanistan, and every item is prepared as if it was home cooked in an Afghan kitchen. If you wish, you can eat in the traditional Afghan manner at low tables and seated on Afghan teahouse cushions. Recently WHERE *Vancouver Magazine's* Most Memorable Meal awards for Best Ambiance, Most Romantic, and Best Ethnic Cuisine categories went to Afghan Horsemen Restaurant. Perhaps you'd like to try the Horsemen's Special Platter which serves two. Begin with an appetizer of humus or sabzi mast, salata with feta cheese and whole wheat pita bread. Then enjoy boneless chicken and lamb shish kebabs, lamb shoulder, baked rice, baked eggplant, dolmah (cabbage rolls), pakawra (batter-fried potatoes), and chaka (sour cream and yogurt). If you prefer the Vegetarian's Platter Delight, your main dish will include baked rice with kabuli topping (sautéed carrots, raisins and almonds), served with aushak (Afghan ravioli), baked eggplant, dahl (lentil stew), pakawra, and chaka. The complete menu includes a variety of kebabs from the charcoal grill, traditional specialties and many vegetarian dishes. Complement your meal with wine from their well-stocked bar.

445 W Broadway, Vancouver BC (604) 873 - 5923 www.afghanhorsemen.com

The Cellar Restaurant and Jazz Club

For the best live jazz in Vancouver presented in a listener-friendly environment, you can't do better than The Cellar. Owner Cory Weeds is a jazz saxophonist who performs at the club with his band, Night Crawlers. He established The Cellar in 2000, realizing his dream to create a venue where both musicians and aficionados can feel at home. The Cellar's popularity testifies to how well he has succeeded. As you can see on the lively website, The Cellar is a showcase for the rich local talent scene, with a rotating schedule: Contemporary Jazz Mondays, Latin Tuesdays, Funk Night on Wednesdays, and Thursday through Sunday it's all jazz all the time. Cory's commitment to music led him to found his own CD label, Cellar Live, and the CD release parties at The Cellar are eagerly anticipated events. The Cellar also features occasional touring acts from around the world. Every month brings an exciting variety of new acts and returning favorites. Music is the heart of The Cellar, but food is more than an afterthought. Chef Elizabeth Reid offers a menu of delights to enhance your enjoyment, from bruschetta to pan-seared tiger prawns and scallops in garlic butter. The Cellar is open seven nights a week. On Mondays, Tuesdays and Wednesdays, the cover charge is waived.

3611 West Broadway, Vancouver BC (604) 738 - 1959 w.cellarjazz.com

Habibi's Lebanese Restaurant

Habibi's Lebanese Restaurant is a delightful Vancouver eatery dedicated to providing the best in traditional Lebanese food in a friendly, intimate setting. Habibi's is a family-run business, created by husband-and-wife team Richard Zeinoun and Lisa Gibson, who previously worked at Vancouver's celebrated Star Anise Restaurant. Appropriately, their new venture takes its name from habibi, an Arabic term of endearment equivalent to "darling." Marco Stevens, the current manager, has a success story that mirrors the restaurant's. He started as a dishwasher in 2002 and worked his way up to the top spot in just three years. At Habibi's, food is served in the traditional Lebanese manner. Bread is used in place of silverware and meals are accompanied by an assortment of condiments, known as meza. If you are unfamiliar with Lebanese food, you might try the Tasting Menu, which lets you sample a wide variety of dishes. Habibi's makes three different kinds of homous, which have proven so popular they are now packaged and sold. You'll also want to try specialties such as the delicious Warak Anab, stuffed grape leaves marinated in lemon juice. Open every day but Sunday, Habibi's Lebanese Restaurant offers full lunch and dinner menus as well as food to go.

7-1178 W Broadway, Vancouver BC (604) 732 - 7489
www.habibis.com

The Naam Restaurant

In Kitsilano, close to the beach, you'll find a restaurant that has won Best Vegetarian awards year after year. The warm, woodsy atmosphere and inspiring menu have also made The Naam Restaurant a winner of the Best Organic Meal Award. Bob Woodsworth and Peter Keith have owned the restaurant since 1980. Their philosophy is not to follow trends, and that's the way they have created an enduring one-of-a-kind restaurant. They say, "Years ago we had to decide whether to get bigger – or better. We decided to just get better." The atmosphere is lively and funky, with a wood-burning stove to heat up the winter and a garden patio for the summer. They are open 24 hours, seven days a week and have live music every night. Award-winning salads, Thai stir frys, Dragon Bowls with hot peanut sauce, apple crisp and organic blueberry pies are just a few of the culinary delights at The Naam. There are lots of vegan items, and a full breakfast with range-free eggs and real maple syrup. The Naam Restaurant really is without equal.
2724 West 4th Avenue, Vancouver BC
(604) 738 -7151

Don Francesco Ristorante

Fine food, music and people are Francesco's passion. It all started with his grandfather back in Italy, and has continued with his father and his brothers, as well as himself. Francesco Alongi was one of the first Italian immigrants to settle in Vancouver. In 1975, he opened Francesco Alongi Ristorante Italiano, the city's first truly authentic Italian restaurant, and it was a smash hit. The restaurant attracted gourmets from around the world, as well as celebrities as diverse as Luciano Pavarotti, Charlton Heston and Canadian Prime Minister Pierre Trudeau. In 2002, Francesco brought his special touch to Burrard Street with the opening of Don Francesco Ristorante. As with his first restaurant, Don Francesco Ristorante features the signature slow roasted duck a la Vignarola, a recipe originally created by Mussolini's head chef and perfected by Francesco. Don Francesco Ristorante also boasts the largest menu of wild game dishes in Western Canada and many more tempting treats. They are all served in an atmosphere so warm and inviting, it's earned the restaurant a reputation as one of the most romantic in the city. It's also one of the most popular, so reservations are recommended. A legendary host, Francesco once studied to be an opera singer. He is still in very fine voice and serenades diners on occasion at Don Francesco Ristorante.
860 Burrard Street, Vancouver BC (604) 685 - 7770 www.donfrancesco.ca

Boua Thai Restaurant

Boua Thai is a family-owned restaurant that features true Thai cuisine. Owner Phak Pratoomsima and Head Chef Pidapa Warokron pride themselves on an extensive and authentic menu of fine Thai offerings, prepared using the freshest ingredients available. The service is friendly, attentive and fast, and the food presentation is beautiful. You can pop in for a quick and delicious lunch or linger over an exceptional dinner. Boua Thai is beautifully appointed with bistro-style furnishings, lush green plants and plenty of natural light. Customers return frequently and word of mouth has made this a very popular place to dine. The restaurant also provides catering and take-out service.
7090 Kingsway, Burnaby BC (604) 526 - 3712
www.bouathai.com

Frankie G's Boilerhouse Pub

Frankie G's Boilerhouse Pub is worth a visit just to appreciate the architecture. When it was built in 1999, it received New Westminster's coveted Commercial Building Award. The post-and-beam construction aptly shelters the rustic, nautical boilerhouse theme that is effectively stated throughout. Fireplaces, cedar pillars and hardwood floors contribute to the warmth and dynamism of the room. There are many historical photographs and artifacts including part of an actual boiler that recall 100 years of the rich heritage of this region. But apart from the visual feast, this is one great pub. The menu far surpasses the usual fare, thanks to Chef Colin McGlinn, whose work has won raves at several of the area's finest eateries. About four times a year, he puts on wine and food tastings focusing on different regions of the world. And every day there is a great selection available, from seafood and burgers to pizza, pastas, steaks and homemade desserts. The large bar offers daily specials and a vast array of wine, beer and liquor. Frankie G's has won New Westminster's Annual Reader's Choice awards for Best Pub and Best Service. Close to a variety of shopping and just minutes off the main highway, it's open seven days a week. For great food and excellent service in an extraordinary setting, Frankie G's Boilerhouse Pub is the place to go.
305 Ewen Avenue, New Westminster BC (604) 515 - 1678 www.frankiegspub.com

Kingston Taphouse & Grille

A self-proclaimed "urban oasis" in the heart of downtown Vancouver, the Kingston Taphouse & Grille offers rich and enjoyable experiences. This leader in the urban pub scene has been described as five restaurants in one, with a selection of settings that are sure to please. The food is top-notch Northwest, and in a recent newspaper review the writer described the Kingston's portions as "stacked higher than the rooftop terrace." With all this to offer, Kingston Taphouse & Grille is an ideal location for special dining events, from intimate sit-down dinners in The Wine Library to sparkling cocktail and appetizer receptions. The contemporary 300-seat restaurant has comfortable private booths, an inviting fireplace, exposed brick walls and display kitchen. The downstairs Wrec Room is perfect for large groups; guests can enjoy one of the Kingston's signature drinks over a game of pool or enjoy a classic cocktail outside on either the Lido deck or Oasis patio, finished with a heritage water fountain and palm trees. Menus at the Taphouse are an eclectic delight, starting with appetizers like Kingston Kettle Chips, made in-house and served with salsa. From salads like Seared Ahi Caesar to entrees like the Kingston Seafood Hot Pot, you'll enjoy wonderful food and warm service. Kingston Taphouse & Grille is open seven days a week.
755 Richards Street, Vancouver BC
(604) 681 - 7011 www.kingstontaphouse.com

The Vineyard Restaurant Ltd

Gelly Gnissios took over management of The Vineyard Restaurant from his father Nick seven years ago, and has been proud to maintain the tradition of serving the absolute best in Italian and Greek dishes. Since it opened in 1977, The Vineyard has been a unique find among Vancouver's restaurants: great food, late hours, and a wine list that *Wine Spectator* has recognized with its Award of Excellence. The Vineyard is open for breakfast, lunch, dinner and brunch on weekends. Whether you're looking for a dish of eggs Florentine to start the day or a piece of spanacopita late at night, it is the place to go. Try one of the many pasta dishes, perhaps a vegetarian specialty like the butternut, portobello and spinach farfalle or a classic dish like the moussaka. Whatever you select, you'll be delighted! Accompany the meal with a wine from the extensive selection of domestic, French and Italian vintages. There are wines for all budgets, but if you feel like splurging, try one of the limited quantity reserve selections. It isn't every day you'll have the opportunity to pair a '94 Caymus Special Selection Cabernet Sauvignon with a homemade hamburger or AAA angus sirloin.
2296 West 4th Avenue, Vancouver BC (604) 733 - 2420 www.thevine-yard.com

Las Margaritas

In the heart of the Kitsilano neighborhood, Las Margaritas serves the finest Mexican food and drink you could ever hope to find. Stepping into this beautiful cantina will transport you to the other BC, Baja California. Baja, northern Mexico and southern California are defining influences on the menu. Owner Daniel Rodriguez visits those areas frequently, scouting new directions in the cuisine and bringing both innovation and authenticity to his menu. Committed to the well-being of his customers, Daniel ensures that cooking methods are health-conscious with grilling, broiling and baking preferred. Ingredients are unadulterated by additives, preservatives or lard. You won't miss them. The food is fantastic! Only white-meat chicken, the best Angus beef, and the freshest local seafood are used. There are fine vegetarian selections as well. Fajitas and grilled wild-salmon burritos are signature dishes. The skilled and loyal staff is like family. In fact, entire families have been with Daniel from the beginning. Las Margaritas is a consistent winner of awards including the Readers Choice Award for Best Restaurant and the Gold Winner for Best Mexican Restaurant for four years running. It is also the winner of Vancouver's coveted Best Margarita Award, confirming its reputation for the most sophisticated tequila selection in the province. Daniel has owned cafes in London, Paris, Amsterdam, Milan and Cologne. We are just very lucky that he and his family chose to settle in Vancouver. 1999 West 4th Avenue, Vancouver BC (604) 734 - 7117 www.lasmargaritas.com

The Cannery Seafood House

Located in the Port of Vancouver, The Cannery Seafood House restaurant has been a prime lunch and dinner destination since 1971. Amidst the surrounding fisheries, The Cannery exemplifies a simple, rustic style of traditional West Coast fish cannery with a mix of nautical artifacts and breathtaking views of the harbour and North Shore mountains. While The Cannery has always been recognized for serving the freshest seafood available, the menu has evolved over the past three decades. Today, The Cannery offers one of the largest selections of fresh fish and shellfish with refined presentation and cooking techniques. The natural waterfront beauty perfectly complements Chef Frederic Couton's vibrant cuisine. Born in the French Alps, Couton trained in France at Michelin Star restaurants, honing his culinary skills at the Hilton Paris and Geneva, then in Montreal, Bangkok and Vancouver. "Integrating my French heritage and innovative cooking techniques, I combine international flavours with the freshest local and exotic produce…to entice a new generation of diners…to come and rediscover The Cannery," says Couton. Staff and management's philosophy is to offer guests more than they expect. This commitment is reflected in the extensive wine list which has won more than 35 Awards of Excellence. Two exciting additions have been launched: a 60-foot private dock making The Cannery accessible by boat, and a "Picnic Basket" for anyone planning a relaxing day in a park or at sea. The Cannery is recognized as a Vancouver landmark and a restaurant of distinction. With its solid roots, innovation and continued commitment to excellence, The Cannery Seafood House is guaranteed to be successful for decades to come. 2205 Commissioner Street, Vancouver BC (604) 254 - 9606 or (877) 254 - 9606 www.canneryseafood.com

La Rustica La Lorraine

Whether you are looking for a romantic atmosphere for an intimate dinner for two, or a charming and cozy place for friends and family to gather for a festive celebration, La Rustica La Lorraine is always the perfect choice. Owner Robert Tang has been with the restaurant for over 25 years and ensures exquisite food and impeccable service are what you receive, whether it is your first visit or your 20th. The elegant charm of the lovely old home built in 1894 will draw you in, but the delectable food will bring you back. The chef has been creating dishes that delight the eye as well as the palate for over 10 years, never tiring of finding new ways to bring happiness to his guests. Enjoy a glass of your favorite wine with a tantalizing appetizer. Take your time selecting from an extensive menu of fine Italian and French cuisine, as well as mouth-watering seafood dishes, steaks and vegetarian delights. Whatever your selection, the experienced staff will make sure your dining experience is a memorable one and that you will want to return again. They look forward to your visit!
228 Sixth Street, New Westminster BC (604) 525 - 6355 www.larustica.ca

Thai House

The Thai House Restaurant group has evolved as one of Vancouver's most recognizable and reputable restaurant chains by offering award-winning authentic Thai cuisine, exciting Thai atmosphere, and innovative and signature Thai fusion entrees and tapas. In 1986, the first Thai House Restaurant opened its doors on Robson Street, becoming one of the first Thai restaurants in Vancouver. Additional locations soon followed, each featuring different décor and a loyal serving staff. These award-winning restaurants now include Thai House (4 locations), Urban Thai, Chilli House and Samba Brazilian Steak House. They all consistently strive to set the highest standard by offering the best quality food through creative and careful attention to detail and impeccable service. You can call or visit the website for further information and locations.

Robson: (604) 683 - 3383
Kitsilano: (604) 737 - 0088
Richmond: (604) 278 - 7373
North Vancouver: (604) 987 - 9911
Yaletown: (604) 408 - 7788
Chilli House: (604) 685 - 8989
Samba Brazilian Steakhouse:
(604) 696 - 9888
www.thaihouse.com

Le Gavroche Restaurant

For lovers of food, wine and romance, Le Gavroche Restaurant is the first choice for dining in Vancouver. Owner/Sommelier Manuel Ferreira has been in the restaurant business for over 20 years. Internationally recognized for his expertise in fine wines, he takes special pride in Le Gavroche's award-winning wine cellar. A menu of delightful global French cuisine awaits you. From hors d'oeuvres like filet of ahi tuna with herbed couscous salad to entrees like the venison chop with spiced lentils and the fresh lamb rack with Dijon mustard, you will find choices to excite and delight the palate. Vegetarians need not feel left out. The wild mushroom ragout or the eggplant lasagna with tomato confit are both superb. Desserts include the house specialty, Madame's Lili Cake, is a triumph of patisserie you will find unequalled.

Professional service and a lovely setting enhance the restaurant's charm. Situated in a two-story Victorian house with a fireplace, upstairs terrace and magnificent view of the Coast Mountains and Vancouver harbour, Le Gavroche also has a private room available on the main floor for small parties and business groups. Awards aplenty have been bestowed on this restaurant. *Gourmet Magazine* has honored it with the Top Tables Award, Wine Spectator has recognized its excellent selection of French wines, and the *Vancouver Sun* says Le Gavroche Restaurant is the Most Romantic Restaurant in Vancouver.
1616 Alberni Street, Vancouver BC
(604) 685 - 3924
www.legavroche.com

Minerva's

Noda Pavlakis came to Vancouver from Greece in 1967 and worked at a variety of jobs before friends suggested that he should open a restaurant. What a good suggestion that turned out to be. Minerva's opened in 1975 and is still going strong 30 years later. Minerva's is a restaurant that attracts loyal customers and devoted employees. Six of the staff members have been there for over 20 years and Noda, himself, as well as his son John are there seven days a week. Though Noda, John and Executive Chef Stalios Anayioutou are all Greek, and Minerva's offers traditional Greek specialities like souvlaki and roast lamb, there is an emphasis on pizza, a staple of the restaurant since it opened. The menu features five gourmet pizzas and 29 other varieties. Pasta is also a hallmark of Minerva's and they are famous for their Caesar salads, baby back spareribs and delicious steaks. You really can't leave without trying the chocolate mousse cake. Noda and his team look forward to spending many more years serving fresh, wholesome and delicious food to the Kerrisdale community.
2411 West 41st Avenue, Vancouver BC
(604) 263 - 1774 www.emenus.ca/minervas

Wild Garlic

Would you like to treat your taste buds to a menu with garlic as a major focus? Then Wild Garlic in Vancouver is for you. In the beginning, Wild Garlic was just the restaurant's name, but it soon became its raison d'etre. Chef Alfred Fan was taken with the medicinal qualities of garlic, and its ability to transform a dish from ordinary to extraordinary. A child prodigy who learned the culinary craft from his master chef father, Fan creates French-Asian fusion. For example, you might order Szechuan asparagus with chili and preserved black bean sauce as a vegetable course, or fresh horseradish crusted wild salmon with garlic cream, persimmon, green beans and garlic mashed yams as an entree. For the serious garlic lover, there's caramelized garlic, roasted garlic and camembert cheese fondue, slowly roasted candied garlic with crostini, and a dessert terrine of white chocolate, candied garlic and hazelnuts. The generous wine menu includes over 150 selections and the service is superb. Alfred Fan also takes time to teach others about his cooking and is a frequent guest on local cooking channels. Wild Garlic on Broadway, near the Kitsilano area, has a vibrant, modern atmosphere while Wild Garlic Bistro in downtown Vancouver is more intimate. Private functions can be arranged for up to 30 people at the downtown location, and up to 55 people in Kitsilano.
792 Denman Street, Vancouver BC (604) 687 - 1663
2120 W Broadway, Vancouver BC (604) 730 - 0880
www.wildgarlic.com

Tamarind

Opened in 2004, Tamarind is the newest venture by the Jamal family of Vancouver restaurateurs and long time associate Satvinder Sandhu. In 1983, they opened Rubina Tandoori on the city's East Side and almost immediately began to get requests for a restaurant on the West Side. Chef Krishna Jamal has a unique gift for creating new and intriguing recipes that have made Rubina Tandoori such a hit. What can you expect at Tamarind? Dishes with strong West Coast influences that are still unmistakably Indian, served with a sense of whimsy that makes the dining experience delightful. The dishes sometimes bear comical names, such as Tamarind's signature dish, pondicherry popsicle lamb, but this dish is no joke: the minted cream tamarind curry sauce is a serious treat. Tamarind also invites you to indulge yourself with their Tantalizing Tapatizers, Indian variations on Spanish tapas, such as chicken frankie, inspired by the chaat snacks sold by street vendors in Mumbai. Or the simla panir, described by Robin Mines of the *Vancouver Westender* as "absolutely the best Indian starter I've ever eaten in my entire life." And don't miss the mystic martinis or the incredible desserts, either. If there's a more perfect example of a fusion dish than the chocolate and tamarind truffles, it's hard to imagine. After dining at Tamarind, you'll see why Vancouver's food critics have been lavishing praise on it from the beginning.

1626 W Broadway, Vancouver BC
(604) 733 - 5335
www.bistrotamarind.ca

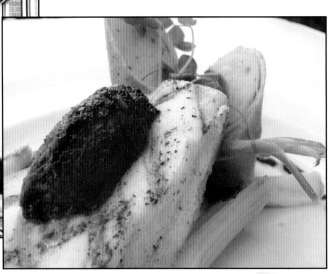

Coast Restaurant

Coast is more than a family business; it's a true extended-family business. Emad Yacoub and Shannon Bosa Yacoub state, "We have a committed management team that shares our genuine passion of food, wine and memorable experiences with each and every guest." Emad, with a wealth of knowledge as an executive chef, along with his wife Shannon Bosa Yacoub, who has years of marketing and public relations experience, owned several Toronto restaurants before venturing back to Vancouver. Partnering in this venture is long-time friend Jack Lamont who came on board as director of operations, Sean Riley as executive chef, and John-Paul Lamb as general manager. Coast is a culmination of all their dreams as one of Vancouver's most highly acclaimed restaurants. Coast Restaurant, located in the heart of trendy Yaletown, serves up some of Vancouver's finest seafood in a contemporary and up-scale setting. As its name suggests, Coast Restaurant features seafood from famous coastal regions throughout the world. A menu boasting of the freshest seafood the world has to offer is cooked to perfection and served with your choice of an accompaniment from an award-winning 350 bottle wine list. The service meets the same high standards as the culinary execution and a warm ambiance is nothing but complementing. Coast Restaurant offers a unique dining experience at Vancouver's only true Chefs Community Table: groups of two to 16 people can enjoy Chefs Tasting Menus prepared center stage. In keeping with the theme of the restaurant, Chefs Community Table offers a menu with seafood tastefully inspired from various coasts.
1257 Hamilton Street, Vancouver BC (604) 685 - 5010 www.coastrestaurant.ca

The Fish House in Stanley Park

Reminiscent of a lush country estate, The Fish House in Stanley Park is an urban gem. This tranquil oasis in the city is surrounded by vibrant gardens and trees, with the shimmering backdrop of English Bay. Dark wood paneling, terra-cotta walls, crisp table linens and sunshine spilling through the oversized windows and French doors provide an elegant yet warm atmosphere. Enjoy a plate of freshly shucked oysters with house sauces, to accompany your favourite beverage. The "seafresh" fish and seafood menu has earned consistent praise from both patrons and media. Executive chef and acclaimed cookbook author Karen Barnaby changes the menus seasonally so you can enjoy what is local, fresh and at its best. The dedication to regional cuisine is reinforced by Barnaby's innovative, uncomplicated approach. A favourite worth noting: Grilled wild salmon with maple glaze. Desserts include decadent crème brûlée and chocolate lava cake. Brunch is the focus on Sunday, and Afternoon Tea is served daily. Wine Director Barb Philip's list has been recognized by *Wine Spectator* magazine since 1999 as one of the world's finest. It offers a wide selection of half bottles and wines by the glass. Few Vancouver restaurants offer award-winning cuisine and wines amid such a natural and beautiful setting as the Fish House in Stanley Park.
8901 Stanley Park Drive, Vancouver BC (604) 681 - 7275 www.fishhousestanleypark.com

Bistro Pastis

Bistro Pastis is elegant and unpretentious, intimate and cosmopolitan. A deft blend that perfectly expresses John Blakeley's vision of the small neighbourhood bistro he always dreamed of owning. Open since May of 1999, Bistro Pastis is a warm and lovely place for relaxing with friends and enjoying simple, classic fare at uncommonly reasonable prices. Since that time, it has won many accolades including Best New Restaurant of the Year and Best French Bistro for the past five years. Blakeley's own design, the Bistro has an expanse of windows reflected in large mirrors and is warmed by a welcoming fireplace. Cozy seating, crisp white linens and the beautiful bar ground the room in quiet luxury. The menu is a synthesis of Blakeley's training in Strasbourg, his long experience in fine restaurants from Paris to Vancouver, and his intuitive mix of honest "cuisine ordinaire" expertly served in an atmosphere of comfort and camaraderie. Steak tartar, Coq au Vin, and rack of lamb are mainstays and a different classical dish is featured every night. There is a contemporary West Coast note to the menu, with fresh local produce and seafood. The delectable desserts include homemade Madeleines and Valrhona chocolate cake. The wine list shows great depth of knowledge and makes a good 50 selections available by the glass. For a memorable meal in a friendly and relaxed atmosphere, you must visit Bistro Pastis. 2153 West 4th Avenue, Vancouver BC (604) 731 - 5020 www.bistropastis.com

A Kettle of Fish

In the highly competitive restaurant industry, longevity speaks for itself. For more than 25 years, A Kettle of Fish has consistently given Vancouver diners what they want. The freshest ingredients, imaginatively prepared, exceptional service, and comfortable, elegant surroundings. The Kettle is where Vancouverites take their out-of-town guests for fresh seafood. Established in 1979 by Glenn and Gwen Anderson along with Glenn's son Riley, who runs the restaurant today, A Kettle of Fish has earned a worldwide reputation. A Kettle of Fish is a welcome oasis on a rain-soaked Vancouver day. The décor is classic with a stunning indoor garden with skylights, flagstone floors and candlelit tables, creating an atmosphere of casual, upscale elegance. Executive Chef Morgan Lechner apprenticed at the famous Banff Springs Hotel in Alberta. He creates his menus to reflect the seasonal availability of fresh seafood and produce. Daily additions

to his menu are featured on chalkboards throughout the restaurant. Featured entrees include wild B.C. Salmon, seared rare Ahi tuna with wok-fried edamame, spring rolls, spicy cucumber and citrus ginger soy vinaigrette, seared golden crispy pacific halibut served with a sweet sour onion peach confit, with cumin drizzle, Nova Scotia Lobster, Dungeness Crab, Cioppino, and their famous Kettle fish soup…just to name a few. Steaks, pastas and chicken are alternatives for the non-seafood lovers. The well-balanced wine list is another statement of excellence and value, with a focus on the quality and depth of wines from British Columbia and California. The knowledgeable staff will help you match the perfect wine to your food selection. The highly competitive nature of today's restaurant industry has created a very demanding, discerning customer. A Kettle of Fish has gone to great lengths to ensure an excellent, overall dining experience providing quality food, creatively prepared and presented, a friendly, efficient and knowledgeable staff, and a warm, inviting ambiance of casual elegance. Come in and see what makes A Kettle of Fish an enduring Vancouver tradition.
900 Pacific Street, Vancouver BC
(604) 682 - 6853 www.akettleoffish.net

Kalamata Greek Taverna

Efstathios Rallis, "Stathi" to his friends, came to Canada when he was 17. He was born and raised in Messini, just five miles from the olive-growing center of Kalamata. You might say cooking is in his blood. When he was a boy, his family grew olives and eggplants and he and his brother gathered wild oregano and sold it to local chefs. No wonder he styles himself a traditional taverniari, a term usually translated as tavern-keeper, but which Stathi translates as a Greek who likes to cook. With the help of his Scottish wife Laura, Stathi has created an award-winning restaurant in Kalamata, consistently winning raves not only for the outstanding food but for the service. Stathi and Laura adhere to the old Greek tradition of being hospitable to strangers because they might be gods in disguise. You'll find any dish you try here to be food fit for the gods, but the special signature dishes include Kleftiko, a lamb dish that takes its name from the Greek word for "steal." The slow-roasted dish was invented by Greek freedom fighters during World War II, who would steal their own sheep back from the occupying German troops. For a dining experience like no other, come to Kalamata Greek Taverna and you'll be treated like a god.
478 Broadway W, Vancouver BC (604) 872 - 7050

La Piazza Dario Ristorante

La Piazza Dario Ristorante is owned by Lidia and Claudio Ranallo. Claudio is the Executive Chef and brings a wealth of experience from across the world. His cooking career began in Sorrento at culinary school, and included cooking for all the generals while he was in the Carabinieri. From there he became the executive chef at one of Switzerland's famous hotels. Then he came to British Columbia where for more than 30 years he has provided Vancouver

with the finest in Italian food. The authentic Italian menu doesn't permit shortcuts. It's all homemade and all delicious. One of La Piazza's intriguing features is its ever-changing dessert specials. To complement the fine cuisine, La Piazza has a wine list that's six full pages long. Attention to detail is one of the most endearing characteristics at La Piazza where customer service is supreme. Every need is met. Fittingly, you will find La Piazza Dario Ristorante in the Italian Culture Centre. 3075 Slocan Street, Vancouver BC (604) 430 - 2195/6
www.lapiazzadario.bc.ca

Lucy Mae Brown

The original Lucy Mae Brown was a widow from the United States who ran a combination opium den-bordello in Vancouver some 50 years ago. After a number of run-ins with the law, she mysteriously vanished in 1959. Under the guidance of Owners Mike Mitton and Sean Sherwood, Lucy's place of business has been transformed into a restaurant named for her. Though it stays on the right side of the law, it's still proud to advertise itself as Vancouver's most decadent dining location. Decadent, perhaps, but not to be missed. *Conde Nast* magazine named it one of the 50 hottest restaurants in the world. Now the good times offered there are culinary, but under the care of Executive Chef Michael Saville, you'll enjoy yourself so much you just might wonder if it's a sin. Social dining is encouraged there, and the menu includes sampler platters perfect for sharing. Michael's signature dish is duck breast served with plum compote, but you'll want to try a little bit of everything. If you're in the mood for lively entertainment, the Opium Den is downstairs. You'll find tasty tapas, exclusive cocktails and live DJs who keep the party going into the wee hours. Visit Lucy Mae Brown for a great meal, friendly service and a memorable setting.

862 Richards Street, Vancouver BC (604) 899 - 9199 www.lucymaebrown.ca

Moose's Down Under

If life is a party, why not celebrate it at Moose's Down Under Restaurant in Vancouver, British Columbia? Owner Corina Aquino and her staff will provide you with everything you need from the four major food groups: breakfast, lunch, dinner and appetizers! Enjoy them all in an atmosphere that is relaxed and casual. Known for their Australian meat pies and Australian brews, Moose's serves mouth-watering homemade pub style food and wines from around the world. A mere sampling of the Moose's favorites follows: two thick slices of homemade meatloaf, served with mashed potatoes and topped with a generous serving of gravy; generous portions of Moose's famous chicken strips served with Moose's honey mustard sauce; veggie, chicken shrimp or steak tortillas with salsa, melted cheese and sour cream; Aussie Meat Pie filled with just-ground beef, onions and gravy, served with a side of gravy and generous portion of chips; and a "Real Men Do Eat Quiche" chef's creation served hot or cold. The menu is extensive, and Moose's offers take out and delivery too. Moose's Down Under is located in the basement at 830 W. Pender Street, Vancouver, British Columbia. Call (604) 683 - 3300 You can visit their whimsical website at www.moosesdownunder.com

Photo by: Lucía Pizarro

Saveur

Stephane Meyer, Co-Owner and Executive Chef of Saveur, brings true continental style to this popular Vancouver dining destination. Before coming to British Columbia, he cooked for highly esteemed restaurants in the south of France. After he and his wife Nathalie, who has 26 years of restaurant experience in her own right, emigrated to Canada, Stephane cooked for Vancouver's Piccolo Mondo Ristorante until owners Michèle Geris and George Baugh decided to leave the restaurant business to devote more time to wine importing. Michele and George offered Stephane and Nathalie the chance to take over, and after just three weeks of remodeling, Piccolo Mondo was rechristened Saveur and opened for business. Haute cuisine is the order of the day at Saveur, where Stephane's signature dishes include Arctic Char in a ginger-and-tomato glaze and Braised Lamb Shank with orange. A prix fixe dinner includes an appetizer, don't miss the Mediterranean fish soup if it's available, entree, and dessert, perhaps the honey-lemon creme brulee? Nathalie and Stephane are passionate about food and wine, as you will easily appreciate when you dine at Saveur. If you are dining alone, you may be invited to join others for communal dining at Saveur's Harvest Table. 850 Thurlow Street, Vancouver BC (604) 688 - 1633 www.saveurrestaurant.com

Rodney's Oyster House

Rodney's Oyster House Owners Stafford Lumley and Todd Atkinson have put together a restaurant with a casual ambiance and a serious attitude towards food. So don't worry about the dress code, just come prepared for fine dining. Praised by Jimmy Buffett as the best seafood dive in Vancouver, Rodney's is decorated to look like a ship's interior, and the authentic Cape Breton music will make you feel as though you're out on the open sea enjoying the best of its bounty. For the freshest oysters in Vancouver, bought directly from British Columbian ocean fishermen every day, Rodney's Oyster House is the place to go. Everything, from oysters to clams, mussels and homemade chowder, is prepared on site from traditional recipes. Founder Rodney Clark, the Oysterman, opened his first oyster house in Toronto in 1988. The Yaletown Rodney's was opened 10 years later, and quickly developed a reputation for excellence that matches and even rivals the original. You'll want to arrive early to be sure you get a parking place, but you'll want to do that anyway, so you can have a long, leisurely meal. A meal at Rodney's Oyster House isn't an experience to be rushed. 1228 Hamilton Street, Vancouver BC (604) 609 - 0080

Anton's Pasta

Antonio Mauro came to Vancouver when he was 14 and worked at a number of different jobs before he discovered his love of cooking. In 1983 he opened Anton's Pasta. At first it was a modest establishment with only one four-burner stove, nine tables, and three different sauces. But it also had Tony's unflagging dedication to make his underlying vision of good food, good value and genuine hospitality a reality. As the good word of mouth spread and business increased, Anton's Pasta expanded. In order to accommodate the ever-growing list of regulars and delighted newcomers, Anton's Pasta moved to its present location in 1989. These days, Vancouver's original pasta bar offers over 70 pasta dishes, ranging from traditional Italian favorites like penne alla calabrese to West Coast-fusion dishes such as linguine con salmone affumicato, smoked Pacific salmon. Other dishes are inspired by Indian and Cajun cooking, and Anton's also has an outstanding selection of vegetarian dishes. Whatever your preferences are, there's something at Anton's for you. If you'd rather not have pasta, try one of the delicious risottos. To accompany your meal at Anton's Pasta you can choose wine from the eclectic international assortment available, including selections from some of British Columbia's finest vineyards. 4260 E Hastings Street, Burnaby BC (604) 299 - 6636 www.vancouverrestaurantguide.net/burnaby/antons

Photo by: Klaus Post

La Terraza Restaurant

Gleaming white linen on spaciously arranged tables under swathes of silk fabric. This distinctive, luxurious atmosphere is La Terraza's trademark. It's a Yaletown restaurant treasure where you can find luxury along with a wonderful meal, a relaxed atmosphere and 1,600 wine labels. The restaurant has won a long list of awards, including many from *Vancouver Magazine* (Most Memorable Meal) and Wine Spectator (Best Metropolitan Wine List). The Vancouver Playhouse Wine Festival says, "La Terraza is the best large metropolitan restaurant." Visit their website to see the beautiful setting, two private dining rooms and their menu. Renowned Chef Gennaro Iorio features his specialty dishes from classic pasta, to fresh local seafood and game, finished with exquisite desserts. Treat yourself to La Terraza Restaurant and Lounge where you can experience the best of both worlds. Enjoy a beautiful dining experience or a special martini in their luxurious and plush lounge. At La Terraza Restaurant you will feel the warm ambiance, receive fine service and enjoy excellent cuisine. 1088 Cambie Street, Vancouver BC (604) 899 - 4449 www.laterrazza.ca

Nirvana

Davinder Dahni opened his renowned Nirvana restaurant in 1972. It is the longest-running Indian restaurant in Vancouver, and there is no better place to go for authentic, consistently delicious Indian cuisine. Dahni and Executive Chef Fatima Hasan have won numerous awards and are sought-after caterers for prestigious events. Nirvana has catered Hollywood and Bollywood productions, The International Film Festival, and private parties for the Consul General and Prime Minister of India and members of Parliament. You will find some very famous autographs in the Guest Comment book, yet the restaurant, with its truly Indian atmosphere, is nearly a home away from home for regular customers who dine here as often as five days a week. The friendly staff provides excellent service which ensures you'll enjoy every aspect of your meal. From tantalizing appetizers to signature chicken dishes, seafood, lamb, beef and an extensive selection of vegetarian fare, you will experience a nirvana of dining pleasure with: curries, tandooris, kormas and vindaloo. The preparations are authentic expressions of the Mughal cuisine of Northern India. There is a fine wine list and a number of Indian beers are available. Top it all off with homemade mango ice cream or fresh carrot pudding with cashews and cardamom. One thing is certain, at Nirvana you will come away deeply satisfied and looking forward to your next visit.

2313 Main Street, Vancouver BC
(604) 872 - 8779 www.nirvanarestaurant.ca

Steveston Seafood House

You would think after being voted Best Seafood Restaurant seven years in a row, and winning Best Fine Dining in 2004, that Steveston Seafood House would be happy to rest on their reputation and relax a bit. Not so! Owner Dino Arsens and Chef Sushila Narain share a passion for making sure every one of their guests receives the finest, freshest, most delicious food possible, and the highest level of graciously provided expert service. Steveston Seafood House is located in the heart of the historic fishing port of Steveston Village and the seafood is as fresh as if you caught it yourself. In addition to the extensive dinner selections there's an impressive wine list and fabulous appetizers. The setting, the wines and the tantalizing foods all combine to make this a most memorable place to plan for a special evening out or a memorable gathering with family or friends. Come and see for yourself why Steveston Seafood House has maintained its reputation as the finest restaurant in Richmond for so many years.

3951 Moncton Street, Richmond BC
(604) 271 - 5252 www.stevestonseafoodhouse.com

Bouzyos

Bouzyos is all about authentic Greek food served in a fun environment. Owner Johnny Georgopoulos, who grew up in Athens, daughter and General Manager Natalie, and Chef Casey Aheer have created a restaurant that offers traditional dishes like souvlaki along with less familiar treats like lamb stamnas, lamb and vegetables baked in an unglazed pot and papoutzaki, baked zucchini stuffed with crab and cream cheese. Customers return again and again, lured back by entrees like those above and seafood specialties like the stuffed calamari and the Mediterranean prawn and scallop platter. The entrees, like the desserts include superb renditions of traditional favorites like baklava and crème caramel. Usually thought of as a French dessert, the Greek version served there will open a new world of eating pleasure. Bouzyos also features an extensive selection of wines and a bar that specializes in martinis. As you enter Bouzyos, you'll notice a dance floor across from the dining area. On weekends, diners can dance the night away to live band music, and an outdoor patio allows delightful open-air dining when the weather's nice. Open seven days a week for lunch and dinner, Bouzyos is the perfect location for parties and receptions. 1815 Commercial Drive, Vancouver BC (604) 254-2533

Hy's Encore Steakhouse

Now managed by his son David, Hy's Restaurants have been going strong since 1956. The first Hy's in Calgary was the brainchild of businessman Hy Aisenstat, who spent 10 years searching for success in various fields before finding it in the restaurant business. Fine dining was almost unknown in western Canada at the time, and Hy's Restaurant caught on quickly. He soon opened another in Winnipeg. Hy's Encore Steakhouse was the second of two locations opened in Vancouver and remains one of the most popular links in the successful chain. Steak has been a mainstay of Hy's restaurants from the beginning, and Hy's Encore serves the trademark cuts. The New York Strip comes with Hy's steak sauce for just a little extra; it is a treat you will find nowhere else. Start your meal with a succulent appetizer like, smoked sockeye salmon or enjoy a bowl of the baked onion soup. Make sure you ask to see the wine list with its superb selection of reds. If you still have room, try some pecan pie or bananas foster for dessert, Hy's is known for superb service too; six members of the staff share two hundred years worth of combined restaurant experience! 637 Hornby Street, Vancouver BC (604) 683 - 7671 www.hyssteakhouse.com

Hell's Kitchen

Mark Durland, founder of Hell's Kitchen, came to Vancouver from New York, where Hell's Kitchen is the name of a legendary West Side neighborhood. So it was a natural name for a restaurant that specializes in New York-style thin crust pizza. The "Pizzas from Hell" come with innovative and exotic toppings such as smoked bacon and Thai peanut sauce, and there are also extra-spicy varieties, appropriately named "El Diablo" and "Ring of Fire." There are other devilish delights besides pizza here: Hell's Kitchen serves brunch, lunch and dinner, with an eclectic international menu including curry, fajitas, pad Thai and more. Signature martinis such as the Fallen Angel attract night owls to the lounge, where low lighting and soft leather couches create a sinfully comfortable atmosphere. In addition to Hell's Kitchen, Mark owns the restaurant/bar Nevermind, located just down the street, in Kitsilano. James Iranzad acts as General Manager of both businesses, and during the summer they're equally "hot" places to be. Nevermind also features an eclectic menu, though with less emphasis on spicy fare and more emphasis on tapas. The staff at Hell's Kitchen is just waiting to dish up something hot for you.
2041 W 4th Avenue, Vancouver BC (604) 736 - HELL (4355)

The Five Point

In September 2003, Matt Thompson and Graig Jensen opened Vancouver's hippest new restaurant, The Five Point, in Vancouver's hottest neighborhood, Main Street. Housed in a former Russian restaurant, The Five Point's interior is distinguished by cherry-red walls and a glowing chandelier. If you prefer outdoor dining, the restaurant boasts the largest patio on the block. Chef Jonathan Bose's menu is highlighted by a West Coast spin on traditional Spanish tapas, with uncommon offerings such as vegetarian sushi rolls and their signature blackened tuna bites. The Five Point also offers a full dinner menu and an exciting selection of wines, martinis and beer on tap. Being hip doesn't keep The Five Point from having a casual, welcoming ambiance, thanks in large part to the exceptionally friendly General Manager, Tanya Ravensgarden. If you enjoy live entertainment, be sure to come by for open mike night on Mondays. Unlike many trendy restaurants, The Five Point has surprisingly reasonable prices. The fact of the matter is there's no downside to The Five Point. Whether for weekend brunch or a midnight snack, you will always find a warm welcome and a comfortable seat at The Five Point, a joint with lots of style.
124 Main Street, Vancouver BC (604) 876 - 5810 www.thefivepoint.com

Stamps Landing Pub

Established in 1977, Stamps Landing Pub was the first real neighborhood pub to open in Vancouver, British Columbia. Regulars insist that the pub, located on beautiful False Creek near the world-famous Stamps Landing Yacht Club, is one of the most inviting and comfortable neighborhood pubs anywhere. Menu mainstays like halibut and chips, ribeye steaks and steak and kidney pie are made from scratch using fresh ingredients. Stamps Landing Pub offers 10 different drafts of beer from around the world, as well as an extensive array of wines due to the recent addition of Pacific Spirits, the pub's own wine store. Relax on the outdoor patio overlooking the marina while you enjoy the great food and beverages. Or schedule a party; private parties are always welcome and you can even have your own room with private catering. Stamps Landing Pub is the place to go for a great evening of food, drink and friends.
610 Stamps Landing, Vancouver BC (604) 879 - 0821

Photo by: Arnout Van Scherpenzeel

Brix Restaurant & Wine Bar

Partners, David Hannay and Patrick Mercer are the dedicated team behind Brix Restaurant & Wine Bar. Their name alludes to the winemaking term "brix" (used for the measurement of sugar content in grapes). It also punningly refers to the exposed brick walls you see as soon as you step inside from the beautifully arranged courtyard. In the summer, the courtyard is one of Vancouver's most romantic places to dine and Brix lets you linger for as long as you want. With the completion of plans to add a glass ceiling above the patio, the courtyard will be available for dining rain or shine. There are plenty of attractions inside the restaurant as well, such as the local art exhibits adorning the exposed brick. Whether you dine inside or out, you'll be delighted by the dishes created by Chef Jason Wilson, a man of few words and many talents. He has crafted a menu that's balanced between comfort food and haute cuisine, including locally-themed specialties like the Fraser valley chicken and duck duo. The wine bar at Brix offers 60 different wines by the glass. David Hannay is the sommelier as well as co-owner. Most days and evenings he is available for consultation on wine-related matters. David and Patrick are convivial hosts who always do their best to ensure your visit to Brix Restaurant & Wine Bar is an experience you'll want to repeat.
1138 Homer Street, Vancouver BC
(604) 915 - 9463
www.brixvancouver.com

winebar@fiction

Comfortable and inviting is a good description of winebar@fiction, a neighborhood restaurant on West Broadway in the Kitsilano district. Fiction's focus on customer care and satisfaction makes it a wonderful place for quality, high-end dining without pretension or stuffiness. Chef Nick Gain uses his European trained background to create small plates with a French wine country influence. *Vancouver Magazine* has described Fiction's dishes as "punctuated with flavour, nicely detailed, with a whiff of whimsy." To complement the attractive menu of contemporary small plates, fiction offers 65 single malt Scotches, a 50 import bottled beer cellar and a wine list boasting over 200 selections from around the world. Owner Sean Sherwood has created a pleasing ambiance with great music. DJs spin nightly after 10:00 pm. A recent Vancouver Weekly review stated, "It all sounded good; we just didn't expect it would be that good, or that creative." If you are looking for a wine bar/lounge with style, terrific food, and a highly knowledgeable friendly staff, winebar@fiction is the place.
3162 W Broadway Street, Vancouver BC
(604) 736 - 7576
www.fictiontapas.ca

216

WaaZuBee Café

Benny Deis's WaaZuBee Café originally opened 12 years ago and quickly acquired a reputation for being what Georgia Straight calls a "hipster magnet." Located in a former Italian restaurant, WaaZuBee's casual ambiance is set off by oversized murals depicting life in rural Italy. These charming relics of the former business compete for attention with the bicycle-wheel sculptures hanging from the ceiling. Chef Andre Tremblay and General Manager/Sommelier Stephen Bonner make sure that you'll remember more than the decor. The menu features tasty treats like the chipotle-marinated three fish entree, with a changing medley of fish selected personally by Chef Andre. Appetizers include WaaZuBee's locally-famous garlic mayo fries, and there are 30 different wines available by the glass, as well as draught beers and specialty martinis. WaaZuBee is the first restaurant in Vancouver to offer a wine club, the WWWC (Wicked WaaZuBee Wine Club), featuring monthly tasting, wine dinners and other events. Eclectic, energetic, and friendly; you are sure to enjoy a visit and a meal at WaaZuBee.

1622 Commercial Drive, Vancouver BC

(604) 253 - 5299

217

Riverside Restaurant

The site of Riverside Restaurant has seen nearly a century and a half of rough and tumble history since its beginnings as the Fort Langley Hotel. Surviving numerous proprietors, a couple of Prohibitions, remodelings, renamings and total devastation by arson in 1974, this site almost continuously provided food, liquor and hospitality to visitors and residents of Fort Langley. Today, Jim and Drew Thompson are pleased to maintain that tradition, offering an unpretentious atmosphere for fine dining. Known for their home-style dinners, the Thompsons offer roast beef and chicken as well as outstanding seafood entrees such as coconut shrimp. The friendly and knowledgeable staff can assist you in choosing a wine to accompany your meal with local selections from the fine Domaine de Chaberton or the all-organic varieties of Glenugie. And you can round out your meal with any of the homemade cheesecakes or pies for dessert. Every month there is featured entertainment such as tribute bands and the popular Neil Diamond impersonator, Nearly Neil. At the north end of the current complex, the restaurant overlooks the Fraser River and has a fantastic patio with wonderful views. The Thompsons invite you to join them for delicious fine dining in comfortable style.
9275 Glover Road, Fort Langley BC (604) 513 - 1456

Fork N' Chopstix

Fork N' Chopstix is one of Langley's exceptional restaurants, a Chinese and Western bistro dedicated to providing the healthiest and tastiest food possible. John Xue, who emigrated from China in 1995, created the business with Tina An, who came to Canada from Taiwan in 1992. In addition to being business partners, John and Tina are also newly married. John has more than 10 years' experience as a chef, and Tina has a degree in hotel and restaurant management. Together they make a formidable team. Specialties at Fork N' Chopstix include traditional Chinese dishes such as the House Special Chow Mein, available with either soft or crisp noodles; Western favorites like the lobster melt, and fusion dishes such as crispy ginger beef. In keeping with John and Tina's commitment to healthy food, there's also an excellent assortment of vegetarian and seafood dishes. Everyone is welcome at Fork N' Chopstix. There's an extensive children's menu, and there are some desserts that are so good you'll have a hard time believing they're good for you, but they are.
#102 - 9292 200th Street, Langley BC
(604) 881 - 1333

Stella's Restaurant and Lounge

Sandra Papageorgiou and Ward Richards, the owners of Stella's Restaurant and Lounge, want you to come by and make yourself at home. Relax and enjoy the "Stella's Mix": one part great food, such as Triple-A rated prime rib from Alberta; one part phenomenal service from the dedicated staff; and one part fun, with special events such as Mardi Gras Evening. More than just a fun night of music and dancing, it raised thousands of dollars for the victims of the 2004 tsunami disaster. Sandra and Ward's sense of commitment has earned them the Mission Chamber of Commerce's Business of the Year Award. "Tender steaks and stiff drinks" are on the menu at Stella's, which offers classic dishes like the aforementioned prime rib and innovative specialties like the Heat Wave Pizza, made with banana peppers and crushed chilies. The lounge offers daily drink specials, an unsurpassed selection of wines and cocktails, and multiple television screens for watching sporting events, including a giant 100" screen that'll make you feel like you're actually in the stands at the big game. Drop by in the summertime and enjoy drinks and dinner on the luxurious patio. There's no end to the enjoyment you can experience at Stella's Restaurant and Lounge.

7230 Horne Street, Mission BC (604) 826 - 4444

Vasilio's Seafood and Steak House

With 25 years of experience in the kitchens of five-star hotels, Executive Chef Sanjeev Khanna brings vast expertise to Vasilio's, the premier destination for seafood and beef in Langley. Born in New Delhi, Sanjeev began his culinary career at the Hyatt Regency there. After emigrating to Canada in 1991, he worked at the Vancouver Hyatt and the Four Seasons Hotel before coming to Vasilio's. At Vasilio's, prime rib is served every night and you can be sure it's good: all cuts served here are Canadian AAA grade or higher. Vasilio's takes advantage of its proximity to the Pacific to bring you the freshest seafood, and it also offers the best pizza and lasagna in the area. Don't hesitate to bring your children along as there's a special menu just for them. If you're not traveling with children, you can take advantage of the separate bar area, which includes televisions for watching the Vancouver Canucks and other local teams. Whether you're traveling or local, part of a group or by yourself, you'll love the comfortable atmosphere and wonderful food at Vasilio's Seafood and Steak House.

20270 Fraser Highway, Langley BC
(604) 530 - 3515

Lampliter Gallery Café

Lampliter Gallery Café is located in Fort Langley, about one hour east of Vancouver. This village blends restaurants and shopping with pictorial views of rolling hills, farmland and parks. Highly recommended, Lampliter Gallery Café is cozy and reminiscent of an old European inn. It is owned and operated by Swiss trained Chef Paul Buckley and his wife Nicoletta. Chef Paul has developed his refined country cooking over a period of years to offer "the kind of food a five star chef would cook if he invited you into his home." Lampliter is known as a local "peoples favourite" restaurant. The menu is a veritable bounty of innovative offerings. Informal lunches encompass homemade soups, cooked to order sandwiches, fresh fish and gourmet salads. Dinners feature multi-course meals of free-range game and meats, fresh local produce and seafood. Enticing offerings like crispy duck salads, Tuscan steak, garlic roasted rack of lamb and sesame-crusted Ahi are among the favorites. There is even a prix fixe gourmet menu that includes appetizer, entree and dessert. This charming restaurant is open seven days a week for lunch and dinner.
9213 Glover Road, Fort Langley BC (604) 888 - 6464

Eleni's Restaurant

Named for the beautiful Helen of Troy, Eleni's is truly a great Greek restaurant. It was founded in 1990 by Nikos and Vicky Apostolopoulos, who both came from Kalamata, Greece. They are fixtures at Eleni's. Dimitri and Litsa Apostolopoulos and the entire kitchen staff have been here since the beginning. Along with the friendly and able servers they maintain a cozy, family-oriented dining atmosphere. With olive oil straight from Greece and the freshest local products, fine ingredients are at the heart of their cuisine. Their signature dishes are Greek and seafood platters and roast lamb. But the schnitzels, barbeque, pastas, burgers, and stir fry items are also consistently delicious. The featured wine is from Domaine de Chaberton, the first winery in British Columbia, and a superlative choice. Beer drinkers will enjoy Coquitlam's excellent Warsteiner Draft on tap. Top off your meal with baclava or the flambe ekmek and you too will be a satisfied, repeat customer. For wonderful food and pleasing service, Nikos and Vicky invite you to enjoy Eleni's Restaurant. 33262 1st Avenue, Mission BC (604) 826 - 4430

Greek Nights

All the delights of Greek cooking await you at Greek Nights. This is an exceptional restaurant with an extensive menu of wonderful food. The souvlakis, moussaka, keftede meatballs and calamari are among the favourite choices of locals and visitors alike. The seafood, fowl and meat dishes are all exquisitely prepared, as are the pastas and stir fry choices. They offer share plates for sampling and you can order platters for two to four people that provide beautifully balanced selections. Wines from around the world are featured and the house wine is the very good Wycliff Chablis.

The desserts are equally enticing, particularly the tiramisu or New York cheesecake topped with strawberries or chocolate. This family business is dedicated to ensuring that each and every guest feels completely at home. Mature diners, families and the hip young crowd all congregate here for an unparalleled dining experience, as well as to enjoy the belly dancing that is presented each week. For Greek food at its finest in a warm and welcoming setting, don't miss Greek Nights.

2607 Ware Street,
Abbotsford BC
(604) 556 - 0055

Chilie's Thai Cuisine

Lynn Chen's Thai restaurant, Chilies Thai Cuisine, offers an imposing menu of authentic Asian cuisine, conveniently categorized and coded to let you know which dishes are the spiciest. Featuring dishes prepared by both Lynn and her mother Sue, this is a restaurant where you'll hear the common Thai phrase, "Khin ped dai mai?" ("Can you eat spicy food?"). If you can, you're in for a real treat. There's more than heat to chilies; they're also a fine source of vitamins A and C, and many patrons swear by their therapeutic properties. At Chilies, patrons are welcome to ask for the amount of chili in their food to be increased or decreased according to taste; Lynn's guide ranges from a single pepper to a five-pepper maximum, which she advises is only for addicts and Thai nationals. Fortunately there's plenty of cold Singha beer on hand, and you may need it. But don't be intimidated, because there's also a wide assortment of chili-free foods for those who prefer to enjoy the milder but no less savory flavors of Thai cooking at Chilies Thai Cuisine.

46212 Yale Road, Chilliwack BC (604) 795 - 3693

Photo by: Nathalie Dulex

La Belle Auberge

The four-star La Belle Auberge was one of the first restaurants to be inducted into the British Columbia Restaurant Hall of Fame. The renowned and award-winning Chef Bruno Marti is President of the Canadian Culinary Federation. He is also a teacher and mentor, and his restaurant is an extraordinary training ground for young chefs. Marti sited La Belle Auberge in a 100-year old heritage house. The leaded-glass windows, antique brass fixtures and period architecture contribute to the warm and elegant atmosphere. Working with Chef and Manager Tobias MacDonald, Marti presents classic yet innovative French cuisine. Whether choosing from the Table d'Hote or à la Carte menu, prepare yourself for an epicurean delight. From l'Amuse Bouche (the opening "bites that delight") through brilliant entrees, to delectable desserts, every care is taken to provide a memorable meal. The fine and knowledgeable staff gives discreetly attentive service in this intimate setting. Reserve your table at La Belle Auberge for a dining experience par excellence. 4856 48th Avenue, Ladner BC (604) 946 - 7717 www.labelleauberge.com

Seh-Mi Japanese Restaurant

Tea-Woon Yoon of Seh-Mi Japanese Restaurant has been a sushi expert for 42 years. He took his first job in the restaurant business when he was 16 years old. By the time he had emigrated to Canada, he'd worked as head chef at the Ambassador Hotel in Seoul. His international experiences are reflected in the restaurant's name, which means "world taste," and the menu, which offers Japanese specialties with a distinct Korean influence. Seh-Mi is a family business: Tea-Woon's wife, Jung-Soo, son Ki Young, and daughter Mia all work here, as well as Mia's husband, Sean Park. Seh-Mi features a broad selection of entrees, from familiar favourites such as tempura to intriguing specialties like sunomono, a dish made of sliced vegetables and yam noodles with sweet vinegar sauce. The sushi bar offers a wide variety of tasty selections, and if you need assistance Tea-Woon will be on hand to guide you with his expertise. Seh-Mi also offers an excellent selection of beverages, from premium local microbrews to sake and jinro soju, a special charcoal-filtered liquor made in Korea. Seh-Mi Japanese Restaurant is perfect for a dinner for one or a party; they can seat up to 30 people in their Tatami room, and the locals say the She-Mi Japanese Restaurant has the best sushi in town.
2443 McCallum Road, Abbotsford BC (604) 850 - 1242

Rendezvous Restaurant

Toni Kelly is knowledgeable in the restaurant industry and her husband Dave has extensive training in the preparation of Greek food. So it's hardly surprising that when they took over the management of Rendezvous Restaurant in Chilliwack, Dave added a superb selection of Greek dishes to a menu that also embraces several other international cuisines. At the Rendezvous, you can enjoy a menu with such diverse offerings as stir fry, schnitzel, and even Southern U.S. style barbeque. As the name suggests, Rendezvous is truly a place for people to meet. The atmosphere is casual and friendly; families are welcome, and private parties of up to 60 can easily be accommodated. In addition to a menu that offers something to suit every taste, Rendezvous encourages conviviality with its assortment of special cocktails and a select array of fine wines from around the world. 9360 Young Road, Chilliwack BC (604) 792 - 9033
www.rendezvousrestaurant.com

Photo by: Christopher Woods

Capital Restaurant

For over 20 years, Paul Lo and his son Ken have been preparing the best Asian food in Chilliwack at Capital Restaurant. Natives of Hong Kong, the Lo family emigrated to Canada in 1977 and opened Capital Restaurant five years later. Paul, the gregarious host at Capital, and Ken have built up a clientele of devoted customers who sit down for dinner and don't even bother with the menu because of their confidence in Paul and Ken's knowledge of their preferences and ability to create exactly what they prefer. People drive great distances to dine here, and if you're lucky enough to be visiting here for the first time, you'll soon understand why. If you are ordering from the menu, be sure to try the signature dish, Singapore prawns, named not because the recipe originated there, but because the first person to whom it was served happened to be a CEO from Singapore. Capital Restaurant's reputation continues to grow as it was voted Favourite Asian Restaurant by the readers of the Chilliwack Times in 2004. If you love Chinese food, you owe it to yourself to visit Capital Restaurant.
45766 Kipp Avenue, Chilliwack BC (604) 795 -7805

Photo by: Khin Yee Teoh

Assini's Greek Restaurant

After learning about cooking at his mother's knee, Vic Sergiannidis followed his father into the restaurant business so he could make other people happy by providing them with food like mama used to make. Open since 1991, Assini's offers traditional Greek cooking, almost 40 different kinds of pizza, pasta dishes and North American favourites such as top sirloin (made with Canada AAA beef) and barbecued chicken. From the pizza dough to the fresh-cut souvlaki, everything is made fresh each day. When you are enjoying an evening at Assini's, be sure to try Vic's signature roast lamb, accompanied by a glass of wine imported from the famous Greek winemaking region of Naoussa. Assini's Greek Restaurant also offers both take out and free delivery to your home, with special family packs that provide a sumptuous meal at a remarkably reasonable price. Whether dining in the restaurant or your home, you will find that Assini's is dedicated to preparing incredible food at reasonable prices. Be sure to order dessert at Assini's Greek Restaurant or you'll miss the amazing, homemade strawberry cheesecake.
#109-15551 Fraser Highway,
Surrey BC (604) 589 - 7203

Pasta Lupino Gourmet

Skiing, hiking and biking, oh my! But when do visitors to Whistler's Blackcomb Resort area have time to eat? Pasta Lupino Gourmet makes it easy and delicious. Located at the Market Pavilion, this innovative Italian deli offers up a feast of homemade pastas, soups and breads ready to be enjoyed in-house or as takeout. Five years ago when Owners Kendra and Kevin noticed a lack of fresh pasta around the Whistler area, they decided to remedy the situation and Pasta Lupino Gourmet was born. Lupino (Italian for Lupine) is a wildflower prevalent in and around the town. Lupine is most recognized for its dense spire of deep-blue petals. Kendra and Kevin have designed their deli with an open kitchen where guests can watch fresh batches of pasta being made on the imported Italian pasta machines. Folks have traveled great distances for Pasta Lupino Gourmet's Italian sausage. Locals also say they have the best coffee in the village: a rich brew which goes nicely with a serving of their signature tiramisu. Those who are dining in can select from a wine list that includes British Columbia, Australia and California vintages. The staff is further known for friendliness and willingness to impart local knowledge and stories to out-of-area visitors. When you're done with your last trail of the day, you'll want to head to Pasta Lupino Gourmet. 121 – 4368 Main Street, Whistler BC (604) 905 - 0400 www.pastalupino.com

Ingrid's Village Café

Ingrid Morgan was an integral part of the Whistler community as it changed from the tiny town of Alta Lake to one of the world's fastest growing vacation destinations. She opened her café/deli in 1986 with a commitment to providing the best in home cooking. That tradition continues to this day through the dedication of sisters-in-law Fiona Minton and Nancy MacConnachie. They and the rest of "Ingrid's girls" prepare and serve wholesome home-cooked fare popular with locals and visitors alike. Fresh bread and produce are delivered daily and prepared to order. From soups, salads, and schnitzels to its world-famous veggie burgers, Ingrid's turns out delicious, hearty fare that will stoke your engines for mountain biking, skiing, gallery-browsing or any of the activities Whistler is famous for. You can dine indoors or enjoy the outdoor seating on the heated patio. Always a family-run café, Ingrid's will make you feel right at home. Located in the heart of Whistler Village, Ingrid's Village Café is a tradition you're sure to enjoy. 4305 Skiers Approach, Whistler BC (604) 932 - 7000 www.ingridswhistler.com

Bavaria Restaurant

Angela Ruffer and her late husband Joel Thibault met in 1984. Angela was writing restaurant editorials for a national magazine and Joel was a French-trained, award-winning chef. They met again in Whistler in 1989 and together opened Bavaria Restaurant in 1999. Their concept was European alpine cuisine and it is beautifully realized here. The warmly elegant dining room and semi-private dining room have old-world charm. In summer, the outdoor patio is a popular gathering place and includes the newly developed petanque court. Visitors are able to borrow a set of petanque balls and play as many games as desired. Fondue is the restaurant's signature dish and here it is second to none. There is the traditional Swiss cheese, as well as dessert and savoury fondues. The hearty fare includes raclettes, veal or pork schnitzel with spaetzle, steaks, roasts and game meats, as well as poultry and fresh Pacific Coast fish. A favourite dish is Black Forest-style pan-seared Jaeger Schnitzel in wild-mushroom sauce. The desserts are extraordinary. The wine list is international and features selections from the Alsace. There are also German, Bavarian and other European beers. Bavaria Restaurant is family-friendly fine dining of the highest order; a fitting legacy for Joel Thibault.

101 – 4369 Main Street, Whistler BC

(604) 932 - 7518 www.bavaria-restaurant.com

Black's Original Ristorante & Black's Pub

Photo by: David Quiring

Many places will satisfy your hunger, but perhaps it is time to feed your sight and soul as well as your appetite. Cradled at the scenic base of Whistler and Blackcomb mountains is an award-winning design concept that invites history into the room with you in a far more tactile and memorable fashion than simple photos on the wall. Incorporated objects, such as the very tables themselves fashioned out of wood forms used in the construction of the Lion's Gate Bridge, bring you a solid reminder of strength and perseverance. The patio is formed of volcanic rock, an echo of the rugged beauty of your surroundings. Whether you're sipping beer, wine or scotch upstairs or relaxing in the family friendly environment downstairs while enjoying a summer barbeque or a warming winter stew, Black's will always stand out as a local favourite.

Of course, if you have the opportunity and a thirst for a good story, take the time to ask for Lawrence. Perhaps he'll tell you how he once discovered a simple cold slab of concrete while skiing and immediately envisioned what is now one of Whistler's most popular destinations.

4270 Mountain Square, Whistler BC
(604) 932 - 6945
www.whistlerblackspub.com

The Wildwood Pacific Bistro

In 2002, The Wildwood Pacific Bistro at Whistler Racquet Club opened for breakfast, lunch and dinner. A delightful menu of nouvelle cuisine was developed using flavourful Pacific Northwest ingredients with an emphasis on seafood. Breakfasts feature classics plus eight varieties of eggs benedict and numerous other dishes. Lunches feature a variety of soups and salads, sandwiches, pasta, pizza and more. For dinner there are wonderful seafood, meat, chicken and stir-fry entrees as well as an excellent selection of desserts. Wildwood has a friendly relaxed environment. It's the perfect place to meet before or after lessons, matches and tournaments. Whether athletes or spectators, diners can appreciate the beautiful Whistler and Blackcomb mountains from their tables, or dine on the patio during the summer months. The restaurant is also available for private functions or as part of corporate tennis tournament events.

4500 Northlands Boulevard, Whistler BC (604) 935 - 4077

Zen Whistler Japanese Restaurant

Eastern mastery meets Pacific Northwest flair at Zen Whistler Japanese Restaurant in the Creekside Village at the base of the Creekside gondola in spectacular Whistler. Old World magic and contemporary style blend in this 4,500 square foot, multi-level eatery. Guests can feast on breathtaking mountain views while Master Sushi Chef Nobu Ochi and Chef Charlie Cho prepare and serve a bountiful selection of Japanese delights. Owners Chef Jun Pak and Master Sushi Chef Nobu Ochi strive to offer their guests a meal that they themselves would enjoy. Along with traditional favourites, you will find delicious originals such as Seafood Butteryaki, Zen's signature teppan-grilled prawns and scallops; San Francisco roll made with Dungeness crab, cocktail shrimp, and cucumber wrapped in egg crepe; or refreshing green tea ice cream. If you're not sure what to order, allow your hosts to arrange your dining experience for you with six courses of gastronomic temptations. Zen Whistler Japanese Restaurant serves 15 different premium sakes, a variety of signature desserts and daily chef specials. The waitstaff is friendly, knowledgeable, and more than happy to take the time to explain the ingredients and preparation of each dish. Zen Whistler Japanese Restaurant is open for dinner hours only and reservations are recommended during the ski season.

101 – 2202 Gondola Way,
Whistler Creekside BC
(604) 932 - 3667   www.zensushi.ca

Southside Diner

Les Ecker, John Henry and Doug Lundgren sought to re-create the popularity of a Whistler landmark formerly known as the Southside Deli. Now the Southside Diner, this eatery has captured a magic that attracts long-time locals and visitors alike. The Southside is the pick-up point for Powder Mountain Catskiing, a destination for skiers and boarders from all over the world. Maintaining the tradition of hearty fare, the signature breakfast is eggs benedict, and breakfast is served all day at the Southside. Lunch boasts the famous sandwich selections, along with a tempting array of generous ingredients. For dinner, lasagna and pork schnitzel top the list. There is a full bar, beer on tap and a wine list that features fine British Columbia selections. The décor, reminiscent of diners past, is fresh and welcoming. Bring your family and enjoy a Whistler classic.

2102 Lake Placid Road, Whistler BC (604) 938 - 6477

Photo courtesy of Tourism BC

Kamloops Inn

The Kamloops Inn has been a true, old-style neighborhood pub since 1935. The interesting building was built in 1905 as Kamloops' first fire hall. At that time the wood frame, two story building was one of the many wooden buildings, sidewalks and roofs to dominate the downtown. A team of fire horses and a wagon were kept at the hall and fire call boxes were located all over town. A series of coded sirens told the firefighters the general location of the fire, and they were expected to attend the fire no matter where they were or what they were doing. In subsequent years the exterior of the building was stuccoed to cover up the old fashioned wood. It is likely that the original siding is protected beneath the stucco, waiting to be revealed. The fire hall was replaced in 1935 and the building became a pub, featuring a friendly atmosphere and lively entertainment on weekends. The interior of this quaint little pub still houses antique fire paraphernalia. There's no cuisine, just an endless supply of popcorn that you can scoop for yourself and share with friends while you enjoy draft beer. You will find two pool tables, two televisions, a jukebox, and a whole lot of live music of every description. There are scheduled acts as well as rollicking open-mike nights and Saturday afternoon jam sessions. Manager Bob Slater and the friendly staff maintain a genuinely fun and wholesome gathering place in the heart of town. Whether you bring your friends or go alone, you can count on making some new ones at the Kamloops Inn; it's that kind of place. 354 Victoria Street, Kamloops BC (250) 374 - 1127

Ric's Grill

"Welcome to the place where the traditional meets the original." That's the promise of Ric's Grill in Kamloops. The self-proclaimed steakhouse of the 21st century works hard to deliver the best quality, wonderful service and atmosphere, and reasonable prices. All this is yours to enjoy in a lively but intimate setting. Ric's may be known for great steak, Sterling Silver Beef, but Executive Chef Reid Hanna also turns out marvelous tapas and the wild salmon is truly memorable. With fresh seafood and tasty pasta too, everyone is happy after sitting down to eat at Ric's. And you can get whatever you like to drink with your meal or in their cozy lounge, where "You name it. We'll pour it!" Operations Manager Rob Fryer makes it his personal goal to put customer service first. Ric's Grill is found in the Four Points by Sheraton complex. 1175 Rogers Way, Kamloops BC (250) 377 - 3113 www.ricsgrill.com

This Old Steak & Fish House

Quiet streets and stunning gardens are what enclose This Old Steak & Fish House. Located in the historic residential district of Kamloops and within walking distance of the city's centre, this turn-of-the-century home provides an unexpected dining experience. During warm summer evenings, patio dining is an enjoyable alternative for those wanting a more relaxed atmosphere. Inside is the unique ambiance of a fine dining restaurant within a heritage home. A reputation for quality ensures a memorable meal with the freshest fish available, tender juicy premium steaks, crisp organic salads and vegetables. Traditions tracing back to the Southwest inspire perfectly seasoned dishes prepared with chile pods imported from the Rio Grande Valley. To complement these offerings, an extensive wine list and ever-changing selection of desserts is available, from light and refreshing lemon dacquoise to decadent chocolate creations. A visit to This Old Steak & Fish House will graciously take you to the best Kamloops has to offer.
172 Battle Street, Kamloops BC (250) 374 - 3227 www.steakhouse.kamloops.com

Goldie's Gourmet Flavours of India

Nandi and Sumita Spolia provide an extensive menu of authentic East Indian food at Goldie's Gourmet Flavours of India. What began as a take-out stand, built a strong customer base and expanded into a

restaurant that seats 30. Even though Goldie's Gourmet is busy it is a favourite with locals and orders to go are always welcomed. Catering is also available for special occasions such as birthdays, weddings and parties.

When Nandi first came to Goldie's in 1998 it was as a customer. He ended up liking the business so much he eventually bought it. Goldie's continues to thrive and Nandi looks forward to expanding in the near future. Goldie's signature dishes include butter chicken, which is marinated overnight and simmered in spices with a touch of cream. Then there's Bhartha, a dish which begins with a whole eggplant and then is pan fried with tomatoes, peppers, onions and Indian spices. During your visit be sure you try the specialty desserts Kheer, Rasmalai and Gulab Jamun. Goldie's is also a popular stop for vegetarians because of the fine selection of meatless dishes. The Spolia's are frequently involved in fund-raising events and they have a deep commitment for participating in community oriented projects. Goldie's is located in the heart of downtown Kamloops right behind the RCMP office on Seymour Street. 563 Seymour Street, Kamloops BC (250) 374 - 0340

Roma's Italian and Continental Cuisine

Leave everything to Roma's Italian and Continental Cuisine! For the past 25 years Roma's has been serving the people of Kamloops great food from their location on Tranquille Road. Owners Mike and Tammi Rose have kept their successful menu as is. "Why change it when it works?" is what they believe about their menu, atmosphere and location. Their customer base consistently comes back for Roma's pizzas, pastas and Caesar salad. They know they will enjoy the usual friendly, comfortable and casual dining atmosphere. Roma's supports fundraising in the community and presents jazz sessions monthly. Mike and Tammi have added catering for social events to their successful repertoire. Give them the opportunity to bid on the catering for your activity. They provide a wide range of extra services so you can one-stop-shop. Liquor services and licensing, audiovisual services, linen supplies, added tableware, flower arrangements, staffing and midnight snacks are just a few of the services they can provide for you. Choose from an outdoor barbecue for any number of people, an Italian buffet, a seafood buffet or an imposing selection of appetizers for a reception! Roma's can do it all!
311 Tranquille Road, Kamloops BC (250) 554 - 2022

G's Pot

Fondue is always the order of the day at Gord Van and Angie Jackson's Kamloops restaurant, G's Pot. You'll find it served in a casual, relaxing atmosphere. Chef Luc Dufort prepares lots of interesting variations on traditional fondue recipes, such as Spanish-style tapas. The menu changes seasonally, but the emphasis is always on fun. In fact, Gord and Angie call their new twist on the old dish a fun-do. The tables at G's Pot are outfitted with state-of-the-art induction burners that stay cool to the touch even while they're keeping the fondue piping hot. This is a world away from fast food. It's an interactive event where you can relax and enjoy and never feel rushed. Try a martini or make a selection from the wine list, which features plenty of homegrown British Columbia vintages, especially during the summer. For dessert, naturally there's chocolate fondue. The next time you're in Kamloops and you need a fun place to dine, think of G's Pot, where Gord and Angie invite you to, Dip in and hit the spot.
369 Victoria Street, Kamloops BC (250) 851 - 3100

Westsyde Pump

Amy Cooper, Scott Smith, and Garth Butcher opened Westsyde Pump in 2005 and their success has been amazing. With the welcoming atmosphere of a comfortable neighborhood pub, Westsyde Pump offers nine beers on tap, including their own original pump genuine draft. The ambitious menu is impressive in its range. House specialties such as pumphouse sliders, chicken supreme Caesar salad and their "world famous" wings are the favourites among neighbourhood clientele. For a taste of home, don't forget the all-you-can-eat ribs, triple Black Angus steak, and Westsyde Pump's award-winning chilli. It's all homemade from original recipes and served by an efficient and friendly waitstaff. Westsyde Pump: good food, good friends, good times. 3020 Westsyde Road, Kamloops BC
(250) 579 - 8221

East Side Mario's

East Side Mario's is renowned for providing real New York-style Italian-American cuisine at over 90 locations across Canada. In Kamloops, Nick DiMambro and his wife Pam bring an especially authentic touch to the restaurant. Nick has an extensive restaurant management background and loves to cook, too. Though the restaurant has a full-time executive chef, Nick can often be found in the kitchen preparing dishes and putting his personal touch on signature favourites like Lasagna al Forno and other oven-baked pastas that East Side Mario's specializes in. Dishes are made from authentic Little Italy recipes, and you can order off the menu or build your own pasta meal. East Side Mario's features a variety of sauces, including the red-hot arrabbiata that puts a little extra zing in your meal. The restaurant also features décor evocative of New York's Lower East Side. A scaled-down Statue of Liberty welcomes you inside, street signs for Mulberry and Canal Streets hang on the walls and another sign directs you to the Scalero Brothers' backroom. In a little more than a year, East Side Mario's has become a dining destination so popular that reservations are recommended, especially on weekends. Unit 117 – 1320 W Trans Canada Highway, Kamloops BC (250) 374 - 7174
www.eastsidemarios.com

Photo courtesy of Valerio Lo Bello

The Barley Mill Brew Pub & Bistro

Settle in for a pint at the bar or throw a game of darts with your mates at The Barley Mill Brew Pub & Sports Bistro in Penticton. This authentically-designed Olde-English style pub is said to be one of the finest watering holes in North America by travelers. 30 foot-high, angled ceilings with sparkling skylights blend harmoniously with vibrant green plants and richly patterned carpets to create a relaxed and comforting atmosphere. Authentic English pub signs dot the walls and a majestic moose head dominates the area above the stone fireplace. An extensive menu gives patrons an impressive selection of dining options. There is definitely something for everyone, including a menu for young diners. A local favourite is the barley burger, which was voted #1 in the Okanagan Valley. You will also find cooked-to-perfection steaks, a daily buffet and an assortment of homemade soups and salads. A wide selection of local wines is on hand to accompany your meal or you can choose from their extensive array of award-winning ales and lagers. Barley Mills is also a proven supporter of their community. Owners and proprietors, Larry Lund, Harley Hatfield and Kevin Hatfield, contribute to such charities and events as Ironman, Boys & Girls Club, youth hockey and breast-cancer survivors. Barley Mills strives to be a leader in the industry by providing quality products and outstanding service to their patrons. Barley Mills Brew Pub and Sports Bistro is the perfect place to gather with friends, have an intimate dinner for two, or relax with a pint on your own. 2460 Skaha Lake Road, Penticton BC (250) 493 - 8000 www.barleymilspub.com

The Bunkhouse Bar & Grill

76 years ago, workers at the Keloka Orchard in Kelowna would have been surprised to see someone "playing through" the apple trees toting a golf bag. Today however, this is a typical sight from the windows of The Bunkhouse Bar & Grill, located on the grounds of Orchard Greens Golf Club. The Bunkhouse Bar & Grill began life in 1929 when it was created by Patterson and Black, to be used as a truck shed and horse barn for the orchard. Over the years the horses and trucks were moved

out and remodeling began to make the building suitable as living quarters for the workers. In the early 1990s the Turton family, a father-daughter team, gave the Patterson and Black building another makeover, turning it into the Bunkhouse Bar & Grill. This charming family restaurant is open throughout the year and has a menu sure to please the entire family. A friendly, pub-style charm permeates the non-smoking dining room and an outdoor dining area provides a charming view. Either area lends itself to the "home away from home" feeling that keeps folks coming back. The Turtons pride themselves on exceptional service and generous portions of delectable home-style meals. Entrees include: New York Steak, Seafood, nightly specials and an incredible home style hamburger. The finishing touch for your meal is fresh apple pie made from apples gathered in the surrounding orchards. When you are finished with your meal you might enjoy a walk through the working orchard or perhaps you'd prefer a leisurely round of golf on the Turtons' nine-hole course. 2777 Klo Road, Kelowna BC (250) 868 - 3844 www.orchardgreens.com

Campo Marina Café and Restaurant

Campo Marina Café and Restaurant serves up the wonderful cuisine of Southern Europe in a warm and comfortable atmosphere in Osoyoos. This local favourite was opened in 1994 by Michael and Gemma Oran, who primarily focus on providing fresh, quality foods with fantastic presentation and exemplary service. They have succeeded magnificently in their aspirations and, once you enter Campo Marina Cafe and Restaurant, you'll immediately sense you are in for a truly satisfying experience. Savour the aromas and flavors of Italian and other Mediterranean-influenced dishes while you relish the relaxed ambiance supported by the friendly, well-trained staff of this elegant eatery. Chef Ryan Toop, who has been important to the success and reputation of Campo Marina Café and Restaurant, prepares delicious meals using only the freshest and highest quality ingredients. Specialties include crisp salads served with savory dressings, pasta covered in rich, flavorful sauces; fresh seafood dishes, expertly prepared, bread made from scratch daily and a choice selection of local and international wines. Michael and

Gemma have created an oasis fit for royalty. Once you've visited this delightful Treasure, you'll want to return. Come see for yourself why this charming restaurant is the best place for your next Southern European dining experience.

5907 Main Street, Osoyoos BC

(250) 495 - 7650

Salty's Beachhouse & Black Pearl Lounge

The purpose of Rob Wylie's life has been met. Rob is the owner of the Salty's Beachhouse and Black Pearl Lounge and the restaurant exemplifies excellence. That's excellence in service and in the carefully prepared selections. The staff is top notch, with attention to detail and meeting the customers' needs as their top concerns. The restaurant was established in 1988 and offers delicious dining with a unique twist. The menu features entrees from around the world in a beautiful Okanagan setting, which are designed to stir favorite romantic memories from special travels. Although this is sumptuous dining at its best, the staff at Salty's Beachhouse really wants patrons to enjoy themselves. Salty's menu includes Rob's "10 Commandments of Traveling and How to Really Enjoy Yourself," and you won't want to miss Salty's Sea Rag, a newspaper that features menu choices and changes. It also compares the changes and shifts the world will make to a recipe, as well as to a person's life. Salty's Beachhouse and Black Pearl Lounge has the best selection of rum in the Okanagan. If you are in the Penticton area, don't miss the renowned dining and service at Salty's. 1000 Lakeshore Drive, Penticton BC (250) 493 - 5001 www.saltysbeachouse.com

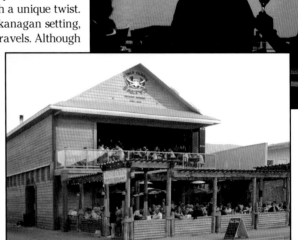

Sir Winston's Pub & Liquor Store

How can you go wrong visiting an establishment dedicated to wowing both regular and new clientele? Owners James Minshull, Tammy L'Heureuz and Jeff Exner want to hear customers are impressed, satisfied and eager to come back to Sir Winston's Pub and Liquor Store each and every day! They are proud of their staff and attribute their success to the winning combination of great staff and awesome customers. Named for Sir Winston Churchill, the Pub sports WWII photos, newsclippings and memorabilia. Sir Winston's offers great food in beautiful surroundings. Known for delicious food, Sir Winston's will tantalize your taste buds with incredibly good chicken Souvlaki, BBQ pork sandwiches and ribs, beer-battered fish and crispy chips. If you want something that isn't on their menu, tell them and they'll do their best to bring it to you. Their martinis are wonderful and regulars come back again and again for the incredible Bellinis and mudslides. Having satisfied your hunger, you might want to hang out at the pool table, in the dart area or just relax on the patio. The liquor store is the newest addition and offers the same great style and service. However you decide to participate, you are sure to have a good time at Sir Winstons Pub & Liquor Store.
2705 32nd Street, Vernon BC (250) 549 - 3485

Di Vino's Ristorante Italiano

There's nothing more exquisite than the incredible taste of a perfectly prepared meal on the tongue. But wait, maybe the sound of Duncan Newton serenading you with Italian Opera while he expertly prepares each special entrée in the kitchen will add to your experience. The luscious scents of chicken, veal and seafood co-mingle with the contented sounds of satisfied patrons at Di Vino's Ristorante Italiano in Northern Okanagan, voted Best Restaurant 2004 by *Okanagan Life magazine*. Duncan and his wife Georgina have a right to take pride in the excellence of their appetizers, home-made pastas and delectable desserts. After all, Di Vino's Ristorante Italiano has earned the prestige of being named THE 5 star restaurant in Vernon, and that's worth singing about.

3224 30th Avenue, Vernon BC
(250) 549 - DINE (3463)
www.dininginvernon.com

Granny Bogner's Restaurant

Enjoy fabulous continental cuisine created by Chef/ Owner, Peter Hebel, in a stunning 1915 Tudor home that's surrounded by lush, well-tended gardens. Visit an era long past while luxuriating in the warm hospitality and superb service you'll find at Granny Bogner's Restaurant in Penticton, British Columbia. Hebel is a European-trained chef who honed his culinary skills in hotels and cruise ships around the world before taking over Granny Bogner's. The restaurant has been voted best restaurant in the Okanagan Valley several times by the readers of *Okanagan Life magazine*. Peter's primary focus is to exceed the expectations of the status quo, and those of industry standards, by providing the best quality foods and extending impeccable service to his customers. Patrons of Granny Bogner's will delight in the warm and captivating charm that exudes from the dining room and sitting room. Relax and absorb the beauty and elegance that is created, in part, by the working stone fireplaces, stone and hardwood floors and delightful period pieces. Open for dinner only, Peter specializes in Continental and German cuisine and utilizes fresh West Coast fish and seafood along with locally grown produce and Canadian crafted cheeses. A full menu provides delicious appetizers, soups and salads. Favourite entrees include slow roasted rack of lamb, veal oscar and Granny's beef rouladen served with spaetzle and red cabbage. Dessert items include such decadent offerings as crème caramel and merlot poached pears on French vanilla ice cream with Belgian chocolate. Come experience fine dining in a classical setting at Granny Bogner's Restaurant.

302 Eckhardt Avenue, Penticton BC
(250) 493 - 2711
www.grannybogners.com

The Phoenix Steakhouse

Like the legendary phoenix, your tastebuds will feel reborn after your first tantalizing bite at The Phoenix Steakhouse. Intent on bringing a measure of sophisticated elegance to the realm of the steakhouse, the Phoenix rises proudly, enfolding you in a casual fine dining atmosphere. Warm wood, leather seating and soft lighting invite you to relax and enjoy your choice of spirits and appetizers. Succulent steak and seafood are not the only fare offered. A neatly balanced variety of entrees, including vegetarian dishes, is served there. The vegetarians in your party will be welcomed and catered to just as much the steak lovers. This jewel of a steakhouse is located in a beautifully renovated historic building that's a must-see during your next visit.

3117 30th Avenue, Vernon BC
(250) 260 - 1189 www.thephoenixsteakhouse.com

Martini's on Martin

In August of 2004 something exciting happened in downtown Penticton. That something was the opening of Nick Tsoycalas' Martini's on Martin, a sophisticated tapas & billiards lounge located on Martin Street. Nick, an innovator and originator of the Okanagan Valley's nightlife, was tired of the same old venues. Therefore he created a place where mature patrons could enjoy an intimate and classically-styled nightspot. Martini's on Martin offers visitors a casual, yet elegant place to relax the mind and stimulate the taste buds. Here is the perfect place to enjoy a fantastic meal with friends, or have a working lunch with colleges, while enjoying the jazzy-rhythm and blues feel of this spectacular club. At Martini's they understand their guests want variety and as accommodating hosts they offer an extensive array of beverage options along with terrific meals. At the wine bar you will find an exceptional collection of wines, 90% of which are local. If wine is not to your taste, indulge in one of the many domestic Cobra beers or microbrewery selections. Of course there are the martinis; with over 120 different types of liquor in stock the combinations are limitless. Tapas, the hors d'oeuvres served with cocktails in the Spanish tradition, are a featured item at Martini's. A choice assortment of excellent tapas is available including veal uvetsi, tzatziki with pita, prawns pesto and their global mussel bar. Entrées include artisan thin-crust pizzas, Madras chicken curry, roasted vegetable pastry and delicious burgers and sandwiches. So, on your next visit to Penticton make time for Martini's on Martin.

260 Martin Street, Penticton BC
(250) 490 - 0304 www.martinisonmartin.com

Rose's Waterfront Pub & Coyote's Waterfront Bar & Grill

"Cold beer coolers and Ciders to go Until 11:00pm" That is just the beginning at Rose's Waterfront Pub & Coyote's Waterfront Bar & Grill. Rose Sexsmith's mission statement reads like that of a hospitality center "Every guest coming to Rose's and Coyote's will feel welcome, will enjoy a friendly, clean, happy and delicious experience so they will look forward to their next visit." Service-driven Rose expresses her passion for community service and enriching others lives through her business. The variety in the menu exemplifies Rose's dedication to diversity and unconditional welcome. Along with a wide variety of fabulous local and imported beers, the menu includes just about anything you might crave. Fantastic and popular with the regulars are a wide selection of tapas or you can feast on wraps, awesome sandwiches, burgers, pizzas, salads and delectable desserts. A full menu is also available. Rose's and Coyote's isn't just about food. Sunday night Jam Sessions at Rose's Waterfront Pub are well known by all types of music lovers and musicians. The house band, The Young'uns has been entertaining at Rose's for over six years. Having been visited by some big name musicians, it has been decreed that you just never know who will stop by to jam on Sunday night. If you still want more music, Thursday night is rock night with a different band each week. Several bands from Okanagan Valley play all your favourite tunes. Hear them play blues, classic rock and the latest off the charts.

Hunker down for a challenging game of pool or relax on the heated patio. No matter what you decide to do, Rose guarantees that you'll have a good time!

Rose's Waterfront Pub: 1352 Water Street, Kelowna BC (250) 860 - 1141 www.rosespub.com
Coyote's Waterfront Bar & Grill: (250) 860 - 1266

The Village Cheese Company

Are you looking for a good time? The Village Cheese Company is known for its good time atmosphere and its famous, award-winning Canadian Farmstead artisan cheese. Farmstead quality starts with handpicked cows bred for milk quality. Everyday special care is taken milking cows and transporting the top-grade milk from the family farm to the cheese factory. Artisan production means doing things by hand and paying attention to details. It is a labor of love created by cheese makers who have great expertise. Visit the store and sample a scrumptious warm slice of Okanagan apple pie and a wedge of delectable cheddar cheese… go for cheese and stay for lunch! Enjoy chicken pot pie, shepard's pie, Spanokopita, soups, sandwiches and yummy desserts from their lunch menu. While you're eating you can listen to ragtime music on their authentic nickelodeon. Top off your visit with old fashioned homemade style ice cream. Fresh cheese curds are their specialty; people drive for miles for those babies. Choose a gift from their selection of local jams and spreads. Dwight and Linda Johnson, owners and operators, invite you to sample some of their cheese blends, wine cheeses and the smoked flavours that are exclusive to the Village Cheese Company. 3475 Smith Drive, Armstrong BC (888) 633 - 8899

Old Bauerhaus Restaurant

Nestled in the mountains near Kimberley is the Old Bauerhaus Restaurant. Originally an old farmhouse in Germany, with a family of 10 living inside, the home was imported from Munich and was established here in 1989. There are 350 years of history to be discovered within these walls, just ask your server for the photos of the building as it stood in Germany. As a proud supporter of the slow food movement their goal is to provide fresh, local and organic ingredients whenever possible. The menu is shaped to what is available regionally. Each entree is made especially for you and menu items are prepared when you order them. The Old Bauerhaus Restaurant is closed Tuesdays and Wednesdays so please plan ahead and call in for reservations.

280 Norton Avenue,
Kimberley BC (250) 427 - 5133

Chef Bernard's Inn & Restaurant

Chef Bernard, wife Julie and daughter Nicole came to Kimberley in 1989. They stopped to have coffee and never left. Thank goodness for that because Chef Bernard's Inn & Restaurant has become quite the legend in these parts. Serving up fantastic food, Chef Bernard's provides the best experience for travelers looking for great food, fresh to your table and some say the best coffee ever! Chef Bernard has experience as a master chef with Hilton Hotels and the King of Tonga in London, England. Using his abounding talent and personality to spice things up, he has created an international menu that gives you the feeling of a free trip around the world. This Chef's motto is "Life's too short to eat fast food." In addition to writing his own cookbooks, Chef Bernard is avid about cigars, sporting some of the best available right here. Chef Bernard's is a 5-star Award Winning Restaurant. Chef Bernard's Inn & Restaurant also offers three guest apartments with hot tub, air conditioning and VCR/DVD/TV, above the restaurant at affordable rates. 170 Spokane Street, Kimberley BC (250) 427 - 4820

Max & Irma's Kitchen

Every other Monday is ethnic food night at Max and Irma's Kitchen, a Kootenay restaurant owned and operated by Steve Kirby and frequented by little Kate. The authenticity of dishes is carefully researched for ethnic night, featuring exotic tastes of other countries and offering a culinary adventure in the process. All of the meals at Max and Irma's are created from fresh local ingredients. A wood-fire oven provides the catalyst for some innovative dining ideas, and a spectacular thin crust pizza. Bread is baked fresh every day, and fish is selected each day, as well. A wood-oven grilled steak and prawns with blue cheese butter is only one of the masterpieces created in the oven, and it's well on its way to becoming a legend. Steve Kirby trained at the Southern Alberta Institute of Technology, cooked for Smuggler's Inn Steak House and L'Eva's in Calgary. Remember, while you wait for your selection to cook in the fire-wood grill there is also a large selection of superb appetizers to choose from. The pizzeria features thin crust small pizzas topped with spinach, tomatoes, asiago and cracked black pepper. To top it all off, they provide a merciless selection of fantastically rich desserts. Weekends provide live entertainment from local talent and the incredible food will keep you coming back. For a taste of something special, try Max & Irma's Kitchen, you will love it.
515A Kootenay Street, Nelson BC (250) 352 - 2332 www.maxandirmaskitchen.com

Moon Dance Café

Cranbrook exists because the railroad company's tracks went through the area, but in this beautiful setting near the Kimberly Alpine Ski Resort, visitors can be grateful for the railroad. Rick and Wendy Lewis operate the Moon Dance Café in Cranbrook, one of Cranbrook's original soup and sandwich destinations. Just ask anyone, the Moon Dance Café enjoys a loyal following among locals and return visitors alike. Their long-term relationships with regular travelers and residents have made this a comfortable place where favourite dishes are well-known and often sell-out daily. The café provides

gluten-free muffins, cookies, soups and cakes, in addition to the rest of their fare. They also cater to the business clientele, with room to stretch out, and the only Internet access available in the downtown core. The Moon Dance makes all of their own sandwiches with local bakery bread and offers all of the fixings for that custom deli sandwich. They offer specialty coffees, teas and fruit smoothies. Moon Dance catering services will host business lunches, weddings, reunions, parties and will even do your Christmas baking for you. Weekly features with a hearty local following are: Tuesday quiche, Thursday sushi, and the Friday seafood chowder. The café serves breakfast and lunch. A tip to the newcomer, "squares" are popular items that are hard to keep in stock. If you see one, buy it! Homemade soups, salads and sandwiches are freshly made, every day. The regional flavor extends to the décor where local East Kootenays artisans' works grace the walls. Visit Moon Dance Cafe any weekday and you'll return time and again.
#5-12th Avenue South, Cranbrook BC
(250) 489 - 5434

The Outer Clove

For over four thousand years garlic has been held in high esteem for cooking, medicinal and protection purposes. While we no longer need to wear garlic garlands to ward off evil, we do still revere it as a healthy and tasty, staple of a good diet. The Outer Clove, in Nelson, offers patrons an eclectic array of appetizers, salads, sandwiches and dinner entrées. Owner Katri Skogster is a native descendant of Finland and has used Finnish-inspired, garlic-honouring artwork throughout this warm-toned, earthy restaurant. Sit back and relax while Katri's friendly and helpful staff serves up a wonderful selection of quality natural foods. Begin your garlic-laden culinary adventure with one or two of their Stellar Starters, like the inner & outer cloves - whole heads of roasted garlic, a wedge of double-cream brie and seasonal fruit served with crusty French bread or the garli-mari rings, tender deep-fried squid with a side of lemon aioli. Moving on to the next course takes you to the heights of garlic-nirvana with such offerings as the roasted garlic manicotti. At press time Katri and her team are working on a new menu that guarantees first rate garlic cooking. Their small kitchen also produces notable specials, all paying homage to the pungent herb. Whether you're a vegetarian or a dyed-in-the-wool meat eater you will find something absolutely perfect for your taste buds at The Outer Clove. The restaurant also serves desserts, usually, but not always, without garlic in them. They are open six days per week and have both a dine-in and a take-out menu. Come get your daily dose of wholesome and delicious garlic at The Outer Clove. You will be so glad you did. 536 Stanley Street, Nelson BC (250) 354 - 1667 www.outerclove.com

Village Bistro

Invigorate your senses! Fresh herbs and ingredients bring out the flavour as well as the scent of great food. There is no mass production done at the Village Bistro as their chefs make food using the slow movement method. Featuring French and Italian cuisine, real French sauces are made to order, an extensive wine list and "The Free Ride Chef" the Village Bistro is definitely a place that you will want to visit again and again. With a combination of diverse and characteristic settings, Co-Owners Renee and Erica strive to maintain the quality and consistency of each edible production. Maintaining the atmosphere and providing you with a memorable experience are essential to the staff at Village Bistro. Customers are always the key element here and it shows. From the moment you walk in the door, you'll know you're in for a great experience. They even offer T-shirts proudly sporting "The Free Ride Chef" so you can remember your visit here for years to come. 349 Spokane Street, Kimberley BC (250) 427 - 2830

Riverrock Pub & Restaurant

Loyal customers know that Riverrock Pub & Restaurant is the best steakhouse in town. It is truly a Quesnel treasure. Overlooking the city, the restaurant is beautiful, bright and spacious and boasts an impressive rock fireplace. The heated patio is a favourite spot for taking in the extraordinary views of mountains and rivers. Indoors, the atmosphere is warm, comfortable and family friendly; a relaxing place to wind down after a busy day. The Lidders, husband and wife, have been in business since 1997. They are justly proud of the friendly and professional staff that provides wonderful food and expert service. Their goal is to make all guests feel welcome and to accommodate their dining wishes. The menu is wide-ranging from pub fare, such as burgers and steaks, to East Indian specialties. For an enjoyable meal with attentive service in lovely surroundings, you'll find Riverrock Pub & Restaurant has it all.
290 Hoy Street, Quesnel BC (250) 991 - 0100

JJ's Pub & Restaurant

Jody and Brian Payne have created a pub that is more than the sum of its great food, style and service; it's a home away from home for the many regular customers. In fact the locals call JJ's their happy place and the centre of excellence. The restaurant is bright and spacious with a family-style atmosphere where everyone is welcome. The menu is mouthwatering and the food is plentiful. Stir-fries and the steak sandwiches and quesadillas are among the favourites. The pub is a sports lover's paradise, especially hockey fans. JJ's supports local hockey and also brings the best of the sport to the big screen. You can linger in the bar or relax on the beautiful patios. There is a great array of the best brews and cocktails, and you can enjoy appetizers such as delicious nachos or JJ's famous cream cheese crab dip. This is the perfect place for travellers to get to know the real Prince George. Drop in, meet the regulars, and enjoy the food and fun at JJ's Pub & Restaurant. 1970 Ospika Boulevard S, Prince George BC
(250) 562 - 0001

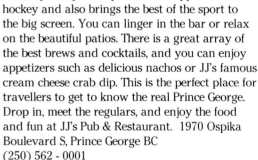

244

Oliver Street Bar & Grill

Entertainment mixed with good food and beverages in a warm and comfortable atmosphere make the Oliver Street Bar & Grill a popular Williams Lake attraction. Oliver Street is especially known for its steaks, prime rib and Sunday Breakfast Buffets. On weekends, it features live entertainment, games and promotions. Impersonators and vintage Canadian rock bands such as Trooper and April Wine have performed there. Oliver Street staff strives to provide great customer service for a rollicking night out. The appetizers are satisfyingly diverse and include two combination plates. A variety of crispy salads, tasty wraps, perennially popular pastas, meat, seafood and stir fry selections fill the menu. Oliver Street Bar & Grill also makes delicious burgers, including buffalo and vegetarian burgers. For dessert you'll find several choices of cheese cake and a mysterious Chef's Special Creation. Visit for the food, stay for the show!

23 Oliver Street, Williams Lake BC

(250) 392 - 5911

The Laughing Loon

Williams Lake is home to The Laughing Loon, an enterprise that has it all. Sandi and Dave Jacobson have managed to create an oasis for every type of traveler. It is a popular stop for locals, too. At The Loon, some of your group can enjoy drinks while the other half shops downstairs in the treasure-filled gift shop, and for those who love the out-of-doors, the garden patio is covered with a spectacular array of flowers. It's a fantastic place to enjoy the fine Cariboo summer. This is possibly the only place a diner can eat fine food and in the next moment, grab some beverages to take home or share with friends while shopping for that special gift. Michael Jacobson manages the restaurant, and Sandi manages the gift shop. She features British Columbian designers, such as artisan Sid Dickens, the company Art in Motion, the Canadian shoe line Robeez, and Cocktails at 5 from Burnaby, Vancouver. The shop carries party, picnic and patio accessories, collectibles, fine nightware, quilts, wine items, clocks, and a host of other delights. The liquor store is part of the gift shop, with a full selection of cold beer, wines and spirits. For non-locals, Sandi will ship gift items. Once you've been to The Laughing Loon, you'll want to come back for more. 1730 South Broadway, Williams Lake BC (250) 398 - 5666

The Keg Steakhouse

Located in the heart of Prince George, The Keg Steakhouse offers a distinctive and beautiful atmosphere. Historic photographs of Prince George's old railway days line the walls. The furnishings are in rich, dark wood with captain's chairs at the tables and intimate seating in the cozy booths. The fare is equally fine. Slow-roasted prime rib, specially aged and seasoned steaks, and fresh local seafood are specialties of the house and each dish is prepared to your specifications. The expert and friendly staff are all long-time employees who provide first-class service to make each and every diner feel welcome. The bar is a destination in itself, fun and energetic, and a great place for casual drinks and dinner. For nearly 30 years, The Keg Steakhouse has demonstrated an unwavering commitment to quality, comfort and value. For your next business meeting, for cocktails with friends or to mark a special occasion, The Keg Steakhouse is the perfect choice.

582 George Street, Prince George BC (250) 563 - 1768

Ric's Grill Steak, Seafood & Chop House

From the opening of the first Ric's Grill in Prince George in 1998, a steadily delivered vision of superior dining experience has been realized by expertly serving the highest quality foods in a beautiful setting at a reasonable price. Starting with Ric's Grill Steak, Seafood & Chop House, these award-winning restaurants haven't lost sight of the passionate craft of cooking, the art of hospitality or the importance of honesty. They serve hand-selected aged Sterling Silver beef. This beef for the discriminating palate originates from cattle fed in prime cattle areas of Western Canada. Each steak comes with its own guarantee of tender, juicy, flavourful perfection. In addition to their unsurpassed steaks, Ric's serves outstanding seafood and pastas. The menu will tempt and intrigue you with mouthwatering options. Ric's customers return to experience the Grill's formula of product, service, setting and value. In *Okanagan Life magazine's* Reader's Choice awards, Ric's Grill Steak, Seafood & Chop House received awards for Best of the Best, Best New Restaurant, Best Steak, Best Seafood and Best "Appies." Just to tempt you a bit, how about some homemade ginger cake topped with hot toffee sauce? For those who appreciate a great meal Ric's Grill Steak, Seafood, & Chop House is a destination in and of itself.

547 George Street, Prince George BC (250) 614 - 9096 www.ricsgrill.com

Cimo's Mediterranean Grill

You might think from Wayne Kitchen's name that he was destined to own and operate a restaurant, but you might not guess that he would be the executive chef, sous chef and pastry chef as well. Wayne bases his philosophy on Virginia Woolf's statement that "One cannot think well, love well, sleep well, if one has not dined well." Wayne considers it his mission to make sure that every customer at the Cimo's Mediterranean Grill has an enjoyable time and leaves satisfied. He has an unbounded enthusiasm for cooking and he especially loves to prepare seafood. In some parts of British Columbia, restaurants that specialize in seafood are quite common, but in the mountains around Prince George they're not so easy to find. In addition to seafood, Wayne offers an extensive array of fresh pastas, prepared daily and cooked to order. Everything there is made fresh, from the sauces to the pleasingly decadent desserts. The atmosphere at Cimo's Mediterranean Grill is accommodating and stylish. From the food to the elegant décor to the friendly service, Cimo's is the hot spot for lunch and dinner. Wayne guarantees you will absolutely love your visit to Cimo's Mediterranean Grill.

601 Victoria Street, Prince George BC (250) 564 - 7975

Kizmet Cafe

Tammy Fitzsimmons and her staff designed Kizmet Café to provide delicious, healthful food in a happy, relaxing environment that encourages harmony of body and soul. Specializing in fresh, homemade vegetarian cuisine, the menu runs the gamut from salads, chicken wraps, and sandwiches to quiche, cabbage and lasagna rolls. The coffee deserves special mention; it's made with Kona beans imported from Hawaii. Either as a dessert or as a snack, fresh cheesecake and an espresso or latte are sure to satisfy. Kizmet (meaning fate and destiny) is a lovely place to meet friends and make new ones. The décor is beautiful and the music, from jazz to Latin rhythms, is both soothing and enlivening. Tammy and the "Kizmet Chicks" invite you to experience the good karma, great service, excellent food and fantastic atmosphere of Kizmet Café.
#101-100 S. Tabor Boulevard, Prince George BC
(250) 561 - 9117

Beautiful British Columbia Mountains

Wineries

Blue Grouse Estate Winery

In choosing the land for their vineyard, the Kiltz family respected the wisdom of the resident blue grouse of the Cowichan Valley. The sunny 31-acre parcel is blessed with an all-southern exposure, gravelly clay soil and pure spring water. Once a hobby for Hans Kiltz, wine making became a vocation when the family settled on Vancouver Island in 1989. His wife Evangeline is devoted to hand pruning and training of the vines. Hans, proprietor and winemaker, takes care of the land and the processing of all the hand-harvested grapes, while producing true varietal wines that capture the essence of their vineyards' climate and soil. Their son Richard, an indispensable hand in the vineyard and winery, is a graduate of the Oenology Program at the Landesanstalt für Wein-

und Gartenbau in Würzburg - Veitshöchheim, Germany, where he specialized in the growing and making of wines from cool climate varietals. Richard is also trained as a cooper in Eussenheim, Germany. Since then, Richard has brought back his expertise to the family winery. Richard continues to travel throughout Europe gaining further experience in the world of winemaking. Their daughter, Sandrina, a Sommelier and a graduate in International Business, promotes Blue Grouse wines in Calgary, Alberta. Blue Grouse currently produces eight grape varieties, from the region's staple, Ortega, to their award-winning Pinot Noir and Pinot Gris. It is the only vineyard in Canada that grows the Black Muscat which is made into a rich, intense red wine with crimson colour, intense lychee nut and black currant aromas and an off-dry lasting finish. The shop offers all the family's estate-grown wines, which can also be found in private wine stores and at distinguished restaurants and resorts on Vancouver Island. Go for a tasting and you will surely leave with a fine wine made from 100% estate-grown grapes. 4365 Blue Grouse Road, Duncan BC (250) 743 - 3834 www.bluegrousevineyards.com

Zanatta Winery

Few sights are as lovely as row upon row of grapevines, heavy with lush, colorful fruit, stretching out over soft, fertile earth as far as the eye can see. Add to that nearly perfect view a charming old farmhouse built in 1903 and you have the makings for a day that will delight every one of your senses, and renew and refresh you. Owner Loretta Zanatta is an Italian educated winemaker and she and husband Jim Moody will make sure your visit to Zanatta Winery, the first winery located on Vancouver Island, will be a memorable experience. Zanatta Winery specializes in fresh, fruity champagne style wines, but with over 40 varieties on site you are sure to find something destined to become your favourite! Every offering is produced from grapes grown in their own vineyards. Come for a day of wine tasting, or plan to enjoy an exceptional meal out on the verandah or in the cozy dining room of Vinoteca, the Zanatta Winery's restaurant and wine bar housed in the original farmhouse. Reservations are required at Vinoteca. Make plans for your special day soon!
5039 Marshall Road, Duncan BC
Winery: (250) 748 - 2338 Restaurant: (250) 709 - 2279
www.zanatta.ca

Cherry Point Vineyards

Cherry Point Vineyards began in 1990 when Wayne and Helena Ulrich purchased 34 acres of land near Cowichan Bay. Grapes had never been grown commercially in the area before as the land had previously been used for mink ranching. The Ulrichs planted several different varieties to determine the best fit for the location. The Cherry Point winery was licensed in 1994. With 10 main varieties and eight limited varieties of grapes, the 34-acre vineyard is now the second largest on Vancouver Island. Its Pinot Noir, Pinot Gris, Gewurztraminer and Ortega wines are award winning. In April 2004, the Khowutzun Development Corporation (KDC), the economic development arm of the Cowichan Tribes of British Columbia, acquired Cherry Point Vineyards. Under the management of the KDC, the Vineyards continue to thrive, producing wines like the 2004 Gewurztraminer, which took Best of Category in the 2005 All Canadian Wine Championships. In October 2004, a new 800-square foot wine shop and tasting room was opened to the public. With a cedar wood interior and an entrance reminiscent of a traditional Coast Salish longhouse, the new facility pays homage to the new owners. Cherry Point promises to be a treasure of British Columbia for many years to come.

840 Cherry Point Road, Cobble Hill BC
(250) 743 - 1059 or (866) 395 - 5252
www.cherrypointvineyards.com

Photo by: Melvin Piro

Photo by Neil Gould

251

Domaine de Chaberton Winery & The Bacchus Bistro

Langley is the home of a winery that embodies the finest French traditions in winemaking. When founders Claude and Inge Violet came to Canada in 1981, they brought with them nine generations of history in the art of fine wine making and traditional grape growing techniques. By combining the expertise of Oenology expert and Winemaker Dr. Elias Phiniotis, these age-old traditions, the latest technology and the gentle microclimate of the Fraser Valley, the perfect environment for superior wines has been created. The winery produces cool climate style whites, full-bodied reds and delicious dessert wines. Specialties include Bacchus, Gewurztraminer, Gamay Noir and Ortega Botrytis Affected wines. Visitors are always welcome at the winery. The European style wine boutique offers wine tastings, tours and a fabulous selection of gift baskets and wine accessories. Public winery tours are offered daily, weather permitting and special private group tours can be reserved by appointment. Domaine de Chaberton also offers custom labels for weddings, clubs, corporate gifts and other special events. Domaine de Chaberton's famous restaurant, The Bacchus Bistro, with its relaxing atmosphere and décor, is located overlooking the vineyard.

Executive Chef Frederic Desbiens offers a sumptuous selection of authentic French bistro cuisine that perfectly complements the wines of Domaine de Chaberton. Open for lunch Wednesday through Sunday, and dinner Friday and Saturday evenings, reservations are highly recommended. The Bistro can also be booked for special events. Domaine de Chaberton Estate Winery & The Bacchus Bistro are located just 45 minutes from Vancouver. 1064 - 216th Street, Langley BC Winery: (604) 530 - 1736 or (888) 332 - 9463 Bistro: (604) 530 - 9694 www.domainedechaberton.com

Glenugie Winery

Christina Tayler's grandmother owned a farm in Longside, Scotland in a glen by the river Ugie, whence it took the name Glenugie. Now that name belongs to the winery that Christina and her husband Gary have run for the past three years in the Fraser Valley. The Taylers' Scottish heritage is also represented on the Glenugie label, which features the tartan of the Campbell of Argyll and the family members' clan crests are displayed in the winery's retail store. After 12 years of maintaining a 10-acre vineyard near Penticton, Gary and Christina established the Glenugie vineyard near Langley in 1997. With five acres of Pinot Noir grape plantings, the first harvest came in 2000. Glenugie's grapes are organically grown, fertilized naturally and never exposed to pesticides or herbicides during the growing cycle. Organic grape farming is highly labor-intensive, but when you stop at the tasting room you'll see what a difference it makes. In addition to Pinot Noir, Glenugie offers excellent varietals such as Chardonnay and Gamay Noir. The winery grounds at Glenugie Winery include a picnic area that's perfect for family outings. Enjoy a delightful day with your family as well as a chance to experience great wine.

3033 232nd Street, Langley BC
(604) 539 - 9463 or (866) 233 - 9463
www.glenugiewinery.com

The Fort Wine Company

The Fort Wine Company is a premium fruit winery. The winery is located just minutes from historic Fort Langley in the picturesque Glen Valley, which is a 45-minute drive in the country from downtown Vancouver. Wine tasting is free when you step up to the bar made from 100-year-old Douglas fir in the beautifully rustic and relaxed atmosphere. The charming winery store also offers many gift items and specialty foods for sale, as well as a comprehensive lineup of fine wines. The Fort Wine Company has been receiving a lot of attention by the press. Word is out that their fruit table and fortified

dessert wines are simply fantastic, and that the country hospitality at the winery is exceptional. This winery has been recognized with numerous awards at major wine competitions for the fine quality, innovation and flavour of its pure fruit products. In fact, The Fort Wine Company wines have been competing with grape wines in some competitions and coming out the winners. Cranberry Klondike, a delicious fortified dessert wine, was recently named Best Fortified Wine in Show at the 2005 Northwest Wine Summit, a prestigious wine competition. The full lineup of specialty dessert wines, Iced Apple Wine, Raspberry Portage, Wild West Blackberry Port, Wild Blue Yonder ands Gold Rush have been richly rewarded in competition, and have been highly rated by Anthony Gismondi, a respected wine critic. The Fort Wine Company's lineup of table wines has been equally distinguished with awards. The flagship wines are the Red Cranberry and the very special White Cranberry. The winery also produces other award-winning labels, including Peach Apricot, Strawberry, Blueberry and Green Apple wines. The winery is proud to be a part of the Fraser Valley Wine Tour. Just follow the signs from Highway 1 to some of the best wines that British Columbia has to offer. The winery is open seven days a week for free tasting and free tours of the winery are offered on Sunday afternoons. A picnic area in the winery vineyard is available for public use.

26151 84th Avenue, Fort Langley BC
(604) 857 - 1101 or (866) 921 - WINE (9463)
www.thefortwineco.com

253

Gehringer Brothers Estate Winery

Located in the Okanagan's premier grape region, Gehringer Brothers is nestled in the heart of the well-known Golden Mile area south of Oliver. It is tucked in among five neighboring wineries, overlooking an expanse of vineyard and orchards as far as Osoyoos Lake. Walter Gehringer went to Germany, studying for five years at the world-renowned University of Geisenheim, graduating with an Engineering Degree in Viticulture and Oenology. His brother Gordon also studied in Germany, acquiring a degree from Weinsberg. Walter spent a further five years gaining experience as a winemaker with Andrés in both B.C. and Ontario. The vineyard was purchased in 1981, followed by the building of the winery in 1985 and crafting of the first vintage. The vineyard's southeast

aspect and gentle slopes gives the vines excellent exposure to sunshine, while the elevated location on the bench keeps the vines safely above the fall frost zone of the valley floor. The high mountain slopes behind the vineyards to the west provide evening shade, resulting in a rapid cool off during summer, which in turn prevents grape acid levels from falling. This is what shapes the Gehringer style: a fine balance between ripe, sweet fruit and firm, clean acidity. Today, the winery boasts an impressive line up of 23 wines consisting of the following brands: Gehringer Brothers, Optimum, Minus 9 Icewine, Dry Rock, and Gehringer Signature Icewine. Walter and Gordon are included in a very select group of qualified winemakers that are B.C.- born yet have learned their craft in Europe. They compete amongst the world's best year after year, and their hard work, and dedication to perfection has not gone unnoticed. R.R. #1 site 23 Comp 4, Oliver BC (250) 498 - 3537

254

Desert Hills Estate Winery

Oliver, British Columbia is the reigning wine capitol of Canada and is home to a premier terroir known as the Black Sage Bench. This is where oenophiles from every point of the globe come to find the vivid and diverse vintages for which the region derives its reputation. Amongst these is the popular Desert Hills Estate Winery, owned and operated by Randy Toor. This family-run winery turns out spectacular bottles of Meritage, Gamay, Syrah as well as robust Cabernets and Merlots. Their 2002 vintage of Syrah won four awards, including the silver medal at the 2005 all-Canadian competition. In 2004, at the Okanagan Festival, The Desert Hills was also awarded silver for the 2002 vintage of their popular Meritage. With the help of his brothers, Jessie and Dave Toor, Randy has made this cozy winery the perfect place to go for a great tour and an education in wineries and winemaking. Randy himself is often to be found in the tasting room with visitors, which makes a tour of this winery feel very much like being a guest in someone's home. Randy is a natural entertainer and truly enjoys his guests and his winery. Thus, you'll always find the atmosphere is a warm, welcoming and relaxed one. After a tour of the winery and tasting room be sure to browse the wine shop, which carries their complete collection of wine. A single visit to Desert Hills Estate Winery will prove to you "true pleasure is only a sip away".

Rural Route #1, Site 52 Camp 11, Oliver BC
(250) 498 - 6664
www.deserthill.ca

Hester Creek Estate Winery

Oliver, British Columbia has long been hailed the reigning Wine Capitol of Canada. Hester Creek Winery enjoys prominence in a lush stretch of land known as the Golden Mile. Their 70 acre vineyard boasts some of the oldest vines in the Okanagan Valley. Here, internationally awarded Winemaker and General Manager Eric von Krosigk pampers guests and makes them feel like they are part of a very special family. Eric and his friendly staff provide exceptional and individualized service that will keep you coming back time and time again. Hester Creek produces many award winning wines such as Pinot Blanc, Pinot Gris, Chardonnay Semillon, Cabernet Merlot, Merlot, Late Harvest, Ice Wines and an exclusive Trebbiano dry white, to name a few. The winery hosts a number of events during the year such as the Celebrity Chef dinner and wine education seminar with internationally renowned Chef, John Bishop of Bishop's Vancouver. Vistas from the winery patio allow visitors to take in the views of the vineyard and the valley. The stunning grounds and wine shop are the perfect place to hold those special events. While touring the vineyard or sitting on the patio, you can treat yourself to a fresh baguette, artisan cheese, pate, antipasto and your favourite wine. With advanced reservations Hester Creek also entertains guests with chocolate and wine tastings, catered lunches and educational seminars for your group. The wine shop offers free tasting and a full range of gifts along with deli items for a patio picnic with that favourite bottle of wine under a vine trellised canopy.

The winery is open year round with varied hours dependent on the season so call ahead or visit their website prior to planning your next trip. Road 8, Oliver BC (250) 498 - 4435 www.hestercreek.com

Red Rooster Winery

Beat, pronounced Bey-at, and Prudence Maher have always had a dream of opening a winery. In 1990 that dream was realized in the Naramata Bench when they converted an existing orchard into a vineyard. Since then the Mahers, with the help of Winemaker, Richard Kanazawa and Manager, Walter Myer, have not only started producing award winning wines but have also developed a number of complimentary endeavors. There's the Red Rooster Winery, ageing cellar and tasting room, opened in 2004, which includes a 4000 square foot guest center. The guest center includes a wine shop, gift shop, gallery and covered patio with grounds. The gardens, vineyards and Okanagan Lake offer visitors the perfect spot to enjoy wine and repast. Guests can bring their own picnic food or light fare is available. The Red Rooster features local artists' work in the gallery and in the gift shop, and the artists are often at the winery when their work is being shown. The Bohemian Art Festival in late summer is one example of the many events at the Red Rooster. It features artists, musicians, and performance artists. The Naramata Bench always provides a lovely escape and The Red Rooster should not be missed. 891 Naramata Road, Penticton BC (250) 292 - 2424 www.redroosterwinery.com

Photo courtesy of Tourism BC

Index

100 Mile House
Accommodations 48

108 Mile
Health & Beauty 150

150 Mile House
Candy, Ice Cream, Bakeries & Coffee 87

Abbotsford
Gifts 129
Restaurants 221, 222

Armstrong
Restaurants 239

Barkerville
Gifts 138

Boston Bar
Attractions 69

Burnaby
Museums. 176
Restaurants 201, 212

Cache Creek
Home Décor, Gardens, Flowers & Markets 166

Chilliwack
Restaurants 221, 222, 223

Cobble Hill
Wineries 251

Cowichan Bay
Accommodations 20, 25
Attractions 57
Restaurants 185, 187

Cranbrook
Accommodations 47
Attractions 75
Candy, Ice Cream, Bakeries & Coffee 86
Galleries 113
Health & Beauty 148
Home Décor, Gardens, Flowers & Markets 171
Museums. 177
Restaurants 241

Duncan
Attractions 60
Museums. 174
Restaurants 193
Wineries 250

Fairmont
Attractions 74

Fort Langley
Attractions 66
Candy, Ice Cream, Bakeries & Coffee 81, 82
Galleries 105
Gifts 129, 130
Health & Beauty 144
Home Décor, Gardens, Flowers & Markets 163
Restaurants 218, 220
Wineries 253

Kamloops
Accommodations 41, 42, 43
Attractions 68, 69
Candy, Ice Cream, Bakeries & Coffee 84
Galleries 109
Gifts 132, 133, 134
Health & Beauty 145
Home Décor, Gardens, Flowers & Markets 166, 167
Restaurants 230, 231, 232

Kelowna
Accommodations 45
Attractions 72
Candy, Ice Cream, Bakeries & Coffee 85
Galleries 110
Gifts 137
Health & Beauty 146, 147
Home Décor, Gardens, Flowers & Markets 169
Restaurants 234, 239

Kimberley
Accommodations 46
Attractions 76
Galleries 112
Home Décor, Gardens, Flowers & Markets 171
Restaurants 240, 242

Ladner
Restaurants 222

Ladysmith
Accommodations 23, 26, 29, 30
Attractions 60
Galleries 90, 91
Restaurants 180

Langley
Accommodations 40
Candy, Ice Cream, Bakeries & Coffee 81
Restaurants 218, 219
Wineries 252

Malahat
Accommodations 24

Mission
Restaurants 219, 220

Nanaimo
Accommodations 24, 28
Attractions 52, 54
Gifts 117
Restaurants 180, 183, 184, 186, 188, 189, 190, 191, 192, 193

Nelson
Accommodations 46, 47
Gifts.. 137
Restaurants 241, 242

New Westminster
Accommodations 36, 37
Attractions.. 63
Gifts.. 120
Home Décor, Gardens, Flowers & Markets 158
Restaurants 201, 204

Oliver
Attractions.. 71
Wineries 254, 255, 256

Osoyoos
Accommodations 44
Home Décor, Gardens, Flowers & Markets 170
Restaurants 235

Penticton
Attractions.. 72, 73
Galleries 111
Gifts.. 135, 136
Health & Beauty 148
Home Décor, Gardens, Flowers & Markets 169, 170
Restaurants 234, 236, 237, 238
Wineries 257

Prince George
Accommodations 48
Galleries 113
Gifts.. 139
Health & Beauty 150, 151
Restaurants 244, 245, 246

Quesnel
Accommodations 49
Attractions.. 77
Gifts.. 138
Health & Beauty 151
Restaurants 244

Radium
Accommodations 47

Richmond
Restaurants 204, 213

Rosedale
Home Décor, Gardens, Flowers & Markets 164

Salmon Arm
Accommodations 43

Shawnigan Lake
Accommodations 29

Sooke
Accommodations 22, 31

Sooke Harbor
Galleries 90

Sun Peaks
Galleries 108

Surrey
Gifts.. 130
Health & Beauty 144
Home Décor, Gardens, Flowers & Markets 162
Restaurants 223

Tofino
Accommodations 20, 21, 27, 30
Attractions.. 53, 54, 55, 56, 58, 59
Galleries 92, 105
Gifts.. 116
Health & Beauty 142
Home Décor, Gardens, Flowers & Markets 155
Restaurants 181, 192

Tsawwassen
Candy, Ice Cream, Bakeries & Coffee 82
Galleries 104

Vancouver
Accommodations 34, 35, 36, 37, 38, 39
Attractions.. 62, 64, 65
Candy, Ice Cream, Bakeries & Coffee 80
Galleries 92, 93, 94, 95, 96, 97, 98, 99, 100, 101, 102
Gifts.................................. 120, 121, 122, 123, 124, 125, 126, 127, 128
Health & Beauty 143
Home Décor, Gardens, Flowers & Markets 156, 157, 159, 160, 161
Restaurants 196, 197, 198, 199, 200, 202, 203, 205, 206, 207, 208, 209, 210, 211, 212, 213, 214, 215, 216, 217

Vernon
Accommodations 44, 45
Attractions.. 70
Gifts.. 135, 136
Health & Beauty 146, 147, 148
Home Décor, Gardens, Flowers & Markets 168
Restaurants 236, 237, 238

Victoria
Accommodations 22, 23, 25, 26, 27, 28, 31, 32
Attractions.. 52, 56, 57, 61
Galleries 91
Gifts.. 118
Home Décor, Gardens, Flowers & Markets 154
Museums.. 175
Restaurants 181, 182, 184, 185, 186, 187, 190, 193, 194, 195

Wells
Accommodations 49

Whistler
Attractions.. 67
Galleries 106
Gifts.. 131
Restaurants 224, 225, 226, 227, 228

White Rock
Attractions.. 66
Galleries 104

Williams Lake
Restaurants 245